DISSIDENTS OF THE INTERNATIONAL LEFT

About the author

Andy Heintz is a freelance writer based in the US Midwest. His work has been published in numerous progressive media outlets around the world, including *New Internationalist*, *Foreign Policy in Focus*, *The Wire*, *Common Dreams*, *Tikkun*, *Culture Project* and *New Politics*. He is also studying for a Masters in addictions counselling.

Acknowledgements

I want to thank my supportive and talented wife Sara Jordan-Heintz for giving me the love, support and time to work on this book for four years. Without my wife's love and support, I would never have had the self-esteem or confidence to take on this task.

I also want to thank my parents Tom and Ellie Heintz for being amazing role models and sticking with me during good and bad times. Thanks also go to my spirited and supportive older brother Erik Heintz and my grandma Jo Thoele for being the embodiment of what it means to be an empathetic person. Special thanks to my father-in-law Larry Jordan, a veteran journalist who played an integral role in helping me enlarge pictures, and my mother-in-law Julie for showing by example what it means to be classy and hard working.

I'm grateful to the *New Internationalist*, especially editor Chris Brazier, designer Juha Sorsa and marketing manager Dan Raymond-Baker, for believing in this project and working long hours to help me finish it. I also want to thank: Carrie Campbell for all the hard work she put into translating many of my interviews with leftwing figures from Latin America from Spanish to English and childhood friend Kevin Colston for introducing me to Tina Hwayoon Kim, who translated my interview with Lee Sang Yong. Other people who translated interviews from Spanish to English, or helped me find translators, include Joa LaVille, Jodie Bowden-Fuentes, Alexis Acosta, Felipe Albuquerque, Kimberly Brouhard, Joe Henry, Mayra de Catalan and Luis Roman. In addition, I'm indebted to Marieme Helie Lucas, Bill Weinberg, Maryam Namazie, Noam Chomsky, Gina Vargas, Ana Cofino, Alejandro Velasco, Sarah Eltantawi, Sodfa Daaji and Sonia Correa for helping me get in touch with interviewees.

Some of the interview material in this book originally appeared in:
New Internationalist: Noam Chomsky; Kwame Anthony Appiah; Pervez Hoodbhoy
CounterVortex: Teesta Setelvad; Moon Nay Li
Foreign Policy in Focus: Sokeel Park; Bridget Conley
Workers' Liberty: Meredith Tax
Balkan Witness: Bill Weinberg
New Arab: Robin Yassin-Kassab; Gideon Levy
Muftah: Yassin al-Haj Saleh
Al-Jumhuriya: Yassin al-Haj Saleh
Secularism is a women's issue: Diep Saeeda; Marieme Helie-Lucas; Anissa Helie; Houzan Mahmoud; Hawzhin Azeez; Fatou Sow; Maryam Namazie
Europe Solidaire: Harsh Kapoor; Predrag Kojovic; Janet Biehl.

DISSIDENTS OF THE INTERNATIONAL LEFT

Kwame Anthony Appiah, Noam Chomsky, Glenn Greenwald, Anabel Hernández, Malalai Joya, George Monbiot, Meredith Tax and 70 other leftwing thinkers and activists from around the world.

Their own views, their own words.

INTERVIEWS BY ANDY HEINTZ

New Internationalist

Dissidents of the International Left

First published in 2019 by
New Internationalist Publications Ltd
The Old Music Hall, 106-108 Cowley Road
Oxford OX4 1JE, UK
newint.org

The interview with Amartya Sen was extracted, with the
permission of Mr Sen, from passages in his books *Identity and
Violence* (W W Norton, 2006), *On Ethics & Economics* (Blackwell, 1987)
and *Development As Freedom* (Random House, 1999).

The interview with Mahmood Mamdani was extracted, with
the permission of Mr Mamdani, from his book *Define and Rule:
Native as Political* (Harvard University Press, 2015) and his article
'Settler Colonialism: Then and Now,' *Critical Inquiry 41* (3), 2015.

Editor: Chris Brazier
Design: Juha Sorsa

Printed by T J International Limited, Cornwall, UK
who hold environmental accreditation ISO 14001.

British Library Cataloguing-in-Publication Data
A catalogue record for this book is available from the British Library.

Library of Congress Cataloging-in-Publication Data.
A catalog record for this book is available from the Library of Congress.

ISBN 978-1-78026-499-8
(ISBN ebook 978-1-78026-500-1)

To think and to be fully alive are the same
Hannah Arendt

....

The world is my country, all mankind are my
brethren, and to do good is my religion
Thomas Paine

....

If liberty means anything at all it means to tell
people what they don't want to hear
George Orwell

CONTENTS

Africa

Middle East and Northern Africa

Europe

FOREWORD
by John Feffer

Polish revolutionaries lived by a powerful motto: for our freedom and yours. When Polish nobleman Tadeusz Kosciuszko fought in the American Revolution, he did so on behalf of universalist values: human dignity, equality and, of course, freedom. He was not doing Americans a favor. He saw the struggle of Thomas Jefferson and Thomas Paine as his struggle as well, the struggle of Poles to overthrow their colonial oppressor. He took up arms in the Continental Army as a form of solidarity, and he expected others to similarly fight in the Polish struggle.

This spirit of international solidarity has long animated the Left. It inspired American leftists to fight in the Abraham Lincoln brigade in the Spanish Civil War. It prompted the Left to support national liberation struggles in Vietnam, South Africa, and Nicaragua. It also motivated progressives to work hand in hand with movements for human rights, which sometimes produced some odd bedfellows, for instance in the Communist world or the Middle East.

But American leftists have had to reckon with the policy of the US government as well. It was one thing to support the anti-Marcos struggle in the Philippines or the Mothers of the Plaza de Mayo in Argentina in opposition to official US government policy. But what happened when the US government was also supporting Poland's Solidarity movement? Or, later, when it proposed launching humanitarian interventions against Slobodan Milošević in Serbia to prevent genocide in Kosovo or Muammar Qadafi for the same stated purpose in Libya? The United States has had a terrible foreign-policy record of starting horrible wars, supporting authoritarian regimes, and instigating military coups. Can it ever act in the world for good reasons? Can progressives nowadays ever support a military intervention?

In this invaluable collection of interviews, Andy Heintz talks to critical intellectuals all over the world in an effort to illuminate this critical debate. It was a no-brainer for freedom lovers to side with Poland against the Russian empire or America against the British empire. It didn't require a lot of reflection for leftists to take a stand against Franco or Marcos. Today, however, the geopolitical landscape has become considerably more difficult to navigate. The thinkers and activists who speak through this book are invaluable guides to this new intellectual terrain.

Intervention is not the only issue covered in this book. Activists around the globe are fighting neoliberal economics, corrupt politicians, sexism and homophobia, climate change, and much more. And they are not just oppositionists. They are also trying to articulate a positive agenda that can form a viable politics.

Here, too, this book illuminates many possible paths forward. This is, as Heintz points out, both a collective effort and an international one. We have to work together, and we have to link arms across borders – because so many of the problems we face today are global.

In this way, the discussions in this book can be a model for our future course. It provides an example of the best kind of globalization: globalization from below. Tadeusz Kosciuszko would have approved.

John Feffer is co-director of Foreign Policy In Focus at the Institute for Policy Studies in Washington DC.

INTRODUCTION

I began to write this book when George Monbiot – a man whose writing I had long admired – was kind-hearted enough to grant me an interview, despite not knowing anything about me other than that I was just some random guy with a vague idea about writing a book about the Western Left. It was the beginning of an adventure that took me to places and exposed me to new ideas that I had never before considered.

The original plan was to write a book focused on the divisions that had split the Left in the Western world. When I use the term 'Left', I'm using the word in its broadest sense, to include human rights activists, women's rights activists, feminists, liberals, progressives, anarcho-syndicalists, democratic socialists and adherents of libertarian and democratic socialism.

I had been following the fragmentation of the Left in the West – mostly in Britain and the United States – from my hometown of Marshalltown, Iowa. One issue being vigorously debated that piqued my interest was: is there such a thing as humanitarian intervention? This question was subsequently followed by the question: is military intervention by the United States or some other Western country in another country justified if that intervention could prevent genocide, ethnic cleansing or crimes against humanity?

The split over this issue, which has probably always existed but hadn't been given a chance to surface, was finally revealed when prominent members of the Western Left quarreled over the legitimacy of military interventions by NATO and other coalitions of Western governments in Bosnia, Syria, Kosovo, Somalia, Libya, Syria, Afghanistan and Iraq. While not completely agreeing with either group, it did seem clear that the US mainstream media would react to any invasion in the name of humanitarian intervention in a manner that was laced with selective amnesia, self-righteousness and double standards.

However, the patriotic presuppositions and widespread acceptance of the narrative of American exceptionalism by the press didn't seem like the only factor to consider when asking if military intervention was justified to stop the genocide and crimes against humanity being perpetrated by Serb-backed forces against Bosnian Muslims. After all, the Vietnamese invasion of Cambodia that removed the Khmer Rouge from power and the Indian invasion of East Pakistan (modern Bangladesh) to prevent the genocidal atrocities of the West Pakistani army did objectively prevent further genocide and crimes against humanity, even if the reasons for the invasions were not entirely altruistic. The Vietnamese regime was guilty of human rights abuses in its own country and the government they set up after Pol Pot's abominable regime fell was far from perfect, but it was still a hundred times better than the Khmer Rouge. India, meanwhile, might have intervened because of empathy for the Bengalis being systematically slaughtered, and perhaps because of worries related to the economic burden that came with accepting millions of refugees fleeing East Pakistan. I'm not telling people when or if they should support Western military intervention in certain cases, but I'm suggesting that one's stance on this issue should not solely be based on whether the West's motives are purely altruisitic.

I hope this book will also make it clear that, just because someone is critical of US foreign policy in Iran, Syria, North Korea or Libya, it doesn't mean they are apologists for Bashar al-Assad, Muammar Qadafi, Vladimir Putin or the Iranian regime. One can be against arming the Syrian rebels, while still ideologically siding with the Syrian revolutionaries. In addition, one can oppose harsh sanctions on Iran because of the belief these sanctions will hurt ordinary Iranians, while still voicing support for the pro-reform and pro-democracy movements within that country.

Unfortunately, opposition to unthinking American exceptionalism has led some on the Left to embrace an inverted form of this doctrine that Meredith Tax has labeled 'imperial narcissism'. This group, whom some have labeled the Manichean Left, have accepted the reductive notion that the enemy of my enemy is my friend and have minimized, rationalized or dismissed serious crimes of real and perceived enemies of the United States such as the Iranian regime, Putin's Russia, Assad, or Serbia under Milošević. This ideology is irrational because instead of arriving at an answer after critical thinking where one attempts to be as objective as possible, these leftists – mirroring those whom they correctly criticize of ignoring or rationalizing US crimes – distort and bend the evidence available so it aligns with their ideological predispositions. Occasionally this group will make good points that perhaps elude other elements of the Left with different ideologies, but they will arrive at these conclusions through a way of thinking that is tainted by blind spots – and such blind spots can lead to future rigid and irrational views that turn the oppressed into the oppressors.

The early interviews I conducted with Monbiot, Bill Weinberg, Stephen Zunes, Stephen Shalom and Alex de Waal left much to be desired simply because of my own inexperience, and it is only thanks to their patience that I didn't decide that I was in way over my head right then and there. My interview with Bill Weinberg was interesting, and life-changing. The veteran journalist expressed his displeasure with the American Left and said he was more inspired by feminists from the so-called Muslim world like Houzan Mahmoud, Karima Bennoune, Maryam Namazie and Marieme Helie Lucas. A lightbulb went off in my head that maybe instead of just interviewing members of the Western Left, I should interview left-leaning figures from around the world.

Maryam Namazie was nice enough to grant me an early interview and offered me names of other feminist activists such as Pragna Patel, Inna Shevchenko, Gita Sahgal, Yanar Mohammed and Fatou Sow. I researched these figures, and then I started sending out interview requests via email. To my surprise, they were all kind enough to grant me an interview. These interviews revealed some of my own blind spots, and I began to realize that there are problems other than Western imperialism that should also be confronted if we want to create a better world. I found myself gradually accepting the idea that, instead of focusing on just one problem rooted in injustice, it was necessary to critique, oppose and advocate against all forms of injustice simultaneously.

I made a conscious effort – although I didn't talk to everyone I wanted to – to speak with people in regions of the world that are often depicted – by Western intellectuals who should know better – in ways that are Orientalist, reductionist and patronizing. This affinity for stereotypes can be seen when politicians describe the Balkans or the Middle East as places where groups have been fighting for thousands of years instead of understanding the conflicts in the region in their modern historical, political and cultural contexts. For this reason, I sought out interviews with Syrian intellectuals and journalists (Yassin al-Haj Saleh is one of the most brilliant men I have ever corresponded with), people from countries that were involved in the Balkan wars (Sonja Licht, Lino Veljak, Predrag Kojovic, Stasa Zajovic), and anyone I could talk to who had made contact with defectors from North Korea (Sokeel Park, Daily NK and Jieun Baek).

Lastly, I confess that my interviews with Michael Kazin and Michael Walzer changed my original opinion that patriotism could not be defined in a way that was worthy of support. I have been, and continue to be, a critic of conventional patriotism in the United States. I often perceive it as discouraging critical thinking and promoting tribalism on a national scale. But now I think Kazin and Walzer are correct that the Left in any country must have some personal attachment and relationship to its people, along with a positive, inspiring patriotic message that can be used to promote justice and equality both domestically and overseas. But – and this is a big but – this kind of patriotism would have to be acutely self-critical, intellectually consistent, self-reflective and fused with a spirit of international solidarity to avoid sacrificing important values in the name of pragmatism.

The book's interviews are grouped by region but within each region the interviewees appear in alphabetical order.

Talking to leftwing figures from around the world has taught me that there are such things as universal values despite the rhetoric of religious extremists of all varieties.

At the end of the day there is no First or Third World, there is only one world. The sooner we accept this, the sooner we will have countries and a global system we can all be proud of. I hope the 77 interviews I have conducted via email, Skype and phone with leftwing figures from around the world can play a minor role in bringing the world we wish to live in closer to becoming a reality.

Andy Heintz
November 2018

North America

KWAME ANTHONY APPIAH

 Kwame Anthony Appiah is one of the world's foremost philosophers on ethics, identity, ethnicity and race. Originally from Ghana and Britain, he now lives in the US, where he is Professor of Philosophy and Law at New York University. Among his books are: *In my Father's House*; *The Ethics of Identity*; and *Cosmopolitanism: Ethics in a world of strangers*.

How can cosmopolitanism triumph over rigid worldviews such as Islamic fundamentalism on the stage of global public opinion?

The appeal of malign fundamentalism begins with cultural resentment. It's attractive to people who think their historical Muslim identity has been assaulted and beaten back over the last century or two by something they refer to as the West or Christendom. It's similar to a broader pattern of the anti-imperial resentment that you find in much of the post-colonial world. It is a recognizable state of mind. In the long run, the only way for that to go away to is to make people feel like the identity, civilization or nationality they represent is doing well in a positive way in the world – and for that to happen, the situation has to change in many places. There must be real democracy in Pakistan, there have to be real jobs available in Egypt, and so on. People have to feel confident and positive about their situation.

Is the good Muslim-bad Muslim culture talk misrepresenting the other identities Muslims have?

Everybody has lots of identities: almost no-one is acting on just one of them all the time. It's true that there are small numbers of people in the world who are motivated to do terrible things in the name of Islam, but it doesn't follow that they are acting in the name of Islam – in the same way that if someone blew up a gay bar in the name of Christianity, that wouldn't mean they were acting in a Christian way.

When someone acts in the name of something, it doesn't follow that their act is justified by the religion or ideology they are referring to. Whatever explains the attitude of people who commit terrorist acts, it can't be Islam, because if Islam explained it, there would be a billion people doing the same – and there aren't. So, the fact that someone does something in the name of an identity doesn't mean we can blame everybody in that group.

When people do bad things in the name of the US, we repudiate them and claim that that isn't what America stands for. We don't say 'OK, we [as Americans] accept responsibility for that'. I don't think Muslims should accept responsibility for people who have done terrible things just because they have claimed to have done it in the name of Islam.

Some people who have been vocal about the need for moderate Muslims to speak out against Islamic fundamentalism still defend the Iraq War and supported atrocious regimes in Central America, Southeast Asia and Africa during the Reagan administration. Is there a double standard at work here?

If we are going to ask people to repudiate things, we should be on the same page ourselves: there are a lot of things we might want to repudiate. There are two problems here. One is that there is disagreement in this country about which actions should be repudiated. As an American, I'm happy to repudiate the Iraq War, Guantánamo Bay, and so on. But there are people who think those things are OK.

Many in the US think that the conditions in Guantánamo Bay are fine, and the Iraq War was a mistake strategically, but not morally. A lot of people who think our assassination by drones is unlawful and the wrong way to deal with terrorism – they believe it shows a lack of respect for national sovereignty, and it causes a lot of collateral damage, killing innocent men, women and children. But most Americans are not going to repudiate drone strikes because they don't think they are wrong. And even when

Americans are forced to accept that we did something wrong, we're not very good at repudiating it. We haven't managed to get an American president to apologize for slavery, which ended in the 1860s.

Do you think some of the world's problems derive from an assault on the autonomy of the individual? Could you comment on the attempts to place people into cultural boxes by claiming Asians have Asian values, Africans have African values, Westerners have Western values, etc?

In general, when you have politicized identities, people demand that members of their group agree with certain things they care about. But while some people do have things in common, if you take large categories like Asia, Africa, or the West, there is a huge amount of in-group disagreement. There are people who think Christianity is the truth and people who believe atheism is largely correct. But they are all Westerners, and you can't say Westerners believe in something, say gay marriage, when there are anti-gay movements in America and France.

These large categories tend to be much more heterogeneous within than people recognize. Even if I am Asian, and even if there were such a thing as Asian values, it's not obvious why I should be obliged to go along with them. I could think that maybe there are not many democratic traditions in Asia but I'm an Asian, and a Democrat. I don't decide whether I should back abortion rights by taking a poll of my neighbors and trying to think about what the American view is, I think about the issue itself. It's best to ask what's right, not what's traditional. In the conversations about what's right we have a lot to learn, not just from our neighbors with whom we share an identity, but from everybody.

You have referred to Africa as a European concept. One of your criticisms of the Pan-African movement is that it was race-oriented and that it failed to recognize the multiple identities that all human beings have and the many differences between the societies that were located in the geographic space that

Europe monolithically referred to as Africa. Can you expound on this subject?

Just as most Europeans were not aware of themselves as Europeans until a certain point, most of the population in continental Africa didn't see themselves as part of continental Africa because they were unaware there was such a thing as continental Africa until sometime in the 19th century. They certainly didn't know about what was going on in the rest of continent. They didn't know about the traditions, customs and histories of the other people, in much the same way that Romanians didn't know anything about the history of Denmark. So the term African became an important identity during the slave trade, especially during the 18th century. People discovered that this category was going to be used to determine their treatment. So by some time in the 18th century it became permissible in the Western world to only enslave people who were Africans.

Part of what happened is that Europeans started to think of Africans as one united person – as Negroes who had a sort of shared debt of properties and a shared essence. That idea made its way into African thoughts about politics in the 20th century largely through the thinking of New World Pan-Africanists, like WEB Dubois, who took these 19th-century American racial ideas into their account of how they thought about black identity everywhere. Now there is a debate about when Dubois became less racial in his thinking, but that's just a question about one intellectual. The movement as a whole continued to make these assumptions about the natural uniformity of Africa because they assumed that all black Africans had something deep in common and that was a mistake. The deep thing they had in common was that they had all been victims of European imperialism and racism. ■

PETER BEINART

Peter Beinart writes for *The Atlantic*, a US-based magazine, and is a senior fellow for the New America Foundation. He also writes for the Israeli newspaper *Haaretz*. *The Week* named Beinart columnist of the year in 2004 and he was the editor of *The New Republic* magazine from 2007 to 2009. He has authored three books: *The Crisis of Zionism; The Icarus Syndrome: A history of American hubris* and *The Good Fight: Why liberals – and only liberals – can win the War on Terror and make America great again.*

You are a Zionist who has been highly critical of Israeli foreign policy. Can you explain where you think Zionism has taken a wrong turn, and what needs to happen for the Zionist movement to get back on the right track?

There have always been different species of Zionism. In Israel, everyone enjoyed citizenship and the right to vote until the 1967 Israeli-Arab War. However, because of Israel's victory, it suddenly had millions of people living under military rule. This is the core of what is wrong with Israel and Zionism today.

What are your thoughts on the notion of American exceptionalism and its impact on US foreign policy?

The definition of American exceptionalism has changed over time. There was a time when the term represented the idea that an ordinary person could succeed in America despite his or her class. Today, American exceptionalism is the idea that America has a special mission in the world. This isn't a problem, but the tendency to view America as unequivocally on the side of the angels is dangerous.

Has this view made it hard for the public to understand why many people in the Middle East and Latin America have negative opinions about US foreign policy?

Americans are not well educated about US foreign policy or the history of American foreign policy. The media doesn't cover America's more nefarious actions overseas very well.

You have criticized this idea that the Islamic State is at war with America because of our freedoms. While there is no doubt that ISIS hates what most Americans would consider to be freedom, how important is it for Americans to understand this is not the reason they are launching terrorist attacks on our country?

It's very problematic because this notion that they are attacking us because of our freedoms blinds us to what is really going on. We are trying to maintain influence in the region. It is our military involvement that is leading to these terrorist attacks. They are at war with us, but we are also at war with them.

Did you feel the same way when President George W Bush claimed that al-Qaeda had attacked America on 9/11 because of our freedoms?

People who know more about al-Qaeda never bought that argument. ∎

MICHAEL BERUBE

Michael Berube is a professor of literature and Director of the Institute for the Arts and Humanities at Pennsylvania State University. He is the author of eight books to date, including *Public Access: literary theory and American cultural politics*, *The Left at War* and *Life As We Know It*, the last of which was a *New York Times* Notable Book of the Year.

Why hasn't there been an international progressive socialist movement against neoliberalism and religious fundamentalism?

It's not clear what kind of coherent vision the international Left would flock to. The Occupy Movement in the United States did try to create a movement that opposed growing inequality and neoliberalism, and that flourished for a while; in 2015-16 it made itself felt in Bernie Sanders' insurgent campaign for president. When it comes to deciding whether to organize around freedom or equality, it seems much more plausible and viable for an international Left to organize around equality – because, as I put it in *The Left at War*, organizing around international freedom sounds a bit like organizing around an international system of weights and measures. It's the kind of thing that people care about if they are part of Human Rights Watch, Amnesty International and Doctors Without Borders.

There is a loosely affiliated international Left opposed to neoliberalism and austerity. But you're correct that there is no international movement to combat Islamic fundamentalist groups like ISIS. There isn't a popular groundswell for human rights around the globe. For the international Left, perhaps it seems like too abstract a goal.

How much of Islamic extremism can be attributed to a genuine grassroots movement, and how much can be attributed to US foreign policy?

I think it's a mistake to attribute every form of backlash and blowback to US foreign policy, while on the other hand it's a mistake to pretend that US policy has not had any influence on the contours of resistance movements. Let's take the example of Iran. As vexed as I was by Jimmy Carter's presidency (the registration of a peacetime draft, the saber-rattling over Afghanistan, pulling out of the Olympics), I have some degree of retroactive sympathy for whoever was in the White House in 1979-80 because, between Iran, Nicaragua and Afghanistan, they had no idea what was happening. They interpreted all three of those things in Cold War terms, and with Afghanistan and Nicaragua that made sense. I realized that to a lot of people in the State Department and the CIA the most important thing was that they had lost their listening station in Tehran, which allowed them to monitor Soviet Union communications. They didn't understand that what was happening in Iran couldn't be seen in terms of the Cold War. This was an Islamic fundamentalist republic that wasn't going to have any allegiance to the Soviet Union or the United States. This was going to be truly a third force.

The revolution took the shape it did because of the United States' friendly relations with Shah Pahlavi, all the way back to the CIA-sponsored coup of democratically elected Prime Minister Mohammed Mossadegh. I think there is no denying that. On the other hand, the fact that the revolution turned into this specific type of fundamentalist movement had a lot to do with the internal politics of Islam and the Muslim Brotherhood, which would have happened regardless of the overthrow of Mossadegh. In other words, while the US certainly played a part in stoking the Islamic Revolution in Iran, the revolution didn't have to take that form. To take a parallel example with a very different outcome, you could say the US atomic bombings of Hiroshima and Nagasaki were not appropriate in moral or military terms, but those bombings didn't lead to an anti-Western Japanese fundamentalist movement that spread across the globe.

How should the Left confront claims made by terrorists that their attacks are in retaliation for US invasions in the Middle East, one-sided support for Israel over Palestine and US support for corrupt authoritarian leaders in the Middle East?

I think Osama bin Laden's criticism of US government policies regarding the Israel-Palestinian conflict was purely opportunistic. I am not convinced he cared very much about the fate of the Palestinians; I think he was more focused on the dream of restoring the Caliphate. Nevertheless, the basis for the complaint is real. The occupation has gone on for nearly 50 years. The mistake is thinking that anyone who makes these critiques of US imperialism does so in the name of democracy or socialism; Islamic fundamentalists make these in the name of something far worse. The terrorists who complain about US imperialism don't have the same goals as you or me. We have to separate a legitimate critique of US policy from an illegitimate and violent terrorist response. ∎

NOAM CHOMSKY

Noam Chomsky is a renowned linguist and arguably the most famous dissident intellectual in the United States. Chomsky has written an abundance of books deeply critical of US foreign and domestic policy, including *Manufacturing Dissent, Deterring Democracy* and *American Power and the New Mandarins*. Chomsky is frequently interviewed by mainstream and alternative media outlets the world over.

What do you see as the consequences of Trump's climate-change denial for future generations? Does effectively combating climate change require international co-operation between nation-states, grassroots projects or a little of both?

It's not just Trump. It's the entire Republican leadership. It is an astonishing fact that the most powerful state in human history is standing alone in the world in not just refusing to deal with this truly existential crisis but is in fact dedicated to escalating the race to disaster. And it's no less shocking that all this passes with little comment. Effective actions require mobilization and serious commitment at every level, from international co-operation to individual choices.

What are your thoughts on Trump's rhetoric towards North Korea? What do you think would be a wise foreign policy to adopt towards North Korea?

On 27 April 2018, the two Koreas signed a historic declaration in which they 'affirmed the principle of determining the destiny of the Korean nation on their own accord'. And for the first time they presented a detailed program as to how to proceed and have been taking preliminary steps. The declaration was virtually a plea to outsiders (meaning the US) not to interfere with their efforts. To Trump's credit, he has not undermined these efforts – and has been bitterly condemned across the spectrum for his sensible stand.

What do you think US foreign policy should be towards Syria? And what do you think of Syrian dissidents who feel like much of the American Left has misinterpreted the origins as well as the complexity of the civil war in that country?

No-one has put forth a meaningful proposal, including Syrian dissidents – among them very admirable people who certainly merit support in any constructive way. Constructive. That is, a way that would mitigate the terrible crimes of the regime and the jihadi elements that quickly took over much of the opposition ,rather than exacerbating the disaster that Syria has been suffering. Proposals are easy. Responsible proposals are not.

By now it seems that the murderous Assad regime has pretty much won the war, and might turn on the Kurdish areas that have carried out admirable developments while also defending their territories from the vicious forces on every side. The US should do whatever is possible to protect the Kurds instead of keeping to past policies of regular betrayal.

Why are the war in Iraq and the war in Indochina described by so many liberals and progressives as strategic blunders instead of as outright war crimes?

The same is true generally. Commentary on the Vietnam War ranges from 'noble cause' to 'blundering efforts to do good' that became too costly to us – Anthony Lewis, at the dissident extreme. And it generalizes far beyond the US. Why? It's close to tautology. If one doesn't accept that framework, one is pretty much excluded from the category of 'respectabililty'.

What do you make of the criticism you received from liberals for comparing the consequences of the missile attack on the al-Shifa pharmaceutical plant in Sudan to the terrorist attacks on 9/11?

I wrote that the scale of casualties was probably comparable, which, as it turned out, may have understated the impact on a poor African country, unable to compensate for the effect of destroying its main source of pharmaceuticals. The consequences were radically different. Sudan didn't launch a 'global war on terror'. As for the criticism, I have also received criticism from Soviet apologists for accurately describing the crimes of the State they defend. Not quite an accurate analogy: such behavior is much more shameful in free countries where there are no penalties for telling the truth about ourselves.

You rarely use the term genocide in your commentary on foreign conflicts, including in your comments and articles on Bosnia, East Timor and El Salvador. Do you shy away from using this word because you believe it has been politicized?

I think that, if we use the term, we should restrict it to what I regard as its original intended use. Take El Salvador, with some 70,000 killed, overwhelmingly by forces armed and trained by the US. To call that 'genocide' stretches the term far beyond its intended use.

Do you think the estimate of 8,100 Muslim men and boys murdered in Srebrenica given by the International Commission for Missing Persons is correct, or do you think there are alternative estimates out there that are more reliable?

I've never had any position on the number of people killed, and simply take the standard estimates as plausible. I'm perfectly willing to leave the appealing task of intensive inquiry into the crimes of others (which we can do little or nothing about) to the great mass of intellectuals and would rather devote finite time to the vastly more significant topic of trying to learn something about our own crimes, which we can do something about. And even in these far more significant endeavors, I haven't paid much attention to trying to assess the exact numbers.

Did any of the critiques raised by Diana Johnstone in her book *Fool's Crusade* make you doubt the overall theme of mass

rapes, mass executions and torture provided by refugees about the Serb-run concentration camps in Omarska, Keraterm and Trnpologe?

Johnstone discussed the way fragments of evidence were radically distorted and given extraordinary publicity as proof of horrendous crimes of enemies. That is the kind of work that is constantly done by intelligence services, human rights organizations and researchers who have concern for the victims and seek to unearth the truth. No valid questions have been raised, to my knowledge, about her discussion, which, as a matter of logic, has no bearing on the veracity of the refugee reports about the camps, including of course those she did not investigate.

Some critics interpreted your comments about *Living Marxism* (*LM*) as implying that the picture filmed by ITN television crews and featured on the front page of *Time* magazine of an emaciated man named Fikret Alic behind a barbed-wire fence was staged. Do you believe Doctor Merdzanic's accounts of the nature of the camp, specifically that, while some people could come and go, others were prevented from leaving by armed guards?

Then 'some critics' should be more careful. There were reports that the photograph was misinterpreted, not staged – notably a cautious and judicious account, which I cited, by Phillip Knightley, one of the most highly respected analysts of photojournalism. Knowing nothing about Dr Merdzanic, I have no reason to question his account, or to comment on it. But it has no bearing on the *LM* affair and the shameful way a tiny journal was put out of business by a huge corporation that exploited Britain's scandalous libel laws – also condemned by Knightley.

You have criticized Samantha Power's widely acclaimed book about genocide. What is your main criticism of the book and why do you think it was so highly regarded by the mainstream media?

I didn't actually criticize the book but rather its reception across virtually the entire spectrum of intellectual opinion. If someone wants to write a book about the crimes of enemies and how we should react to them more forcefully (without explaining how in any credible form), that's fine, but it is pretty much more of the norm, of no particular interest. True, it was a little different in this case, and more welcome to liberal opinion, because the condemnations of the crimes of others were framed as a criticism of the West, and hence seem courageous and adversarial instead of merely conforming to the doctrinal norm.

What is of no slight interest is the enthusiastic reaction to a book that keeps scrupulously to crimes of enemies, ignoring crimes for which we are responsible, crimes that not only are sometimes comparable or even more severe than those on which attention is focused here but that are dramatically more significant for us in moral significance for a simple and obvious reason: we can do something about them, in many cases by simply terminating them.

Take one example, a particularly striking one. The book was written in the 1990s, during the final phase of what is arguably the most extreme slaughter relative to population since World War Two, by 1999 reaching new paroxysms of horror: the US-backed Indonesian invasion of East Timor. Power does not entirely ignore it. In passing, she criticizes the US for 'looking away' from the crime. In fact, Washington looked right there, intensely, from the first moment, providing crucial arms and diplomatic support and continuing to do so until the last moment in September 1999, even welcoming the mass murderer in charge (Suharto) as 'our kind of guy' (1995). Power's predecessor as UN Ambassador, Daniel Patrick Moynihan, took special pride in his memoirs for having rendered the UN 'utterly ineffective' in reacting to the invasion and crimes (which he recognized), following State Department directives. So matters continued, with ample support from other Western powers as well, right into the huge new atrocities of September 1999, until finally, under substantial international and domestic pressure, Clinton quietly informed the Indonesian generals that the game was over and they pulled out, permitting a peace-keeping force to enter – something the US could have done at any time. And to magnify the obscenity, that is now hailed as humanitarian intervention.

It may be comforting to become immersed in the other fellow's crimes, joining in the general anguish, winning accolades and prizes. And serious investigation of these matters can be a valuable contribution. But it is immensely more significant – on moral grounds, in terms of human consequences – to unearth the truth about our own actions, to bring crimes to an end, and to internalize the lessons that will inhibit them in the future. ∎

JUAN COLE

 Juan Cole is Richard P Mitchell Collegiate Professor of History at the University of Michigan. He has tried to place the relationship between the West and the Muslim world in a historical context, not least via the website he founded, *Informed Comment*. He is a regular guest on PBS's *Lehrer News Hour* and is a regular columnist for *Truthdig* and *The Nation*. He is the author of *The New Arabs, Engaging the Muslim World* and *Napoleon's Egypt*.

Could you talk about the differences in the way the press covers Saudi Arabia compared to Iran?

The coverage of the Middle East in the American mass media is shameful and really hews very closely to the government line. Negative adjectives are used for regimes like that of Iran that are at odds with the United States, whereas positive adjectives are used for a regime like Saudi Arabia. Saudi Arabia is a major abuser of human rights and an absolute monarchy. It's engaged in a brutal aerial bombing campaign in Yemen that clearly involves war crimes. Without expressing any support for Iran or its policies, I would say the press certainly doesn't treat the two countries fairly or in a dispassionate way.

Can you discuss the CIA's role in the 1953 coup in Iran?

The US media and public complain about the negative statements made by Iranian leaders toward the United States today. But those leaders were involved in a revolutionary struggle in the 1960s and 1970s against a dictator, the Shah of Iran, who was imposed on the Iranian people by a CIA coup. So, if you understand that history, while you would hope for more maturity on the part of the Iranian leadership, you can certainly have a better idea of why there are strong resentments towards US policy in Tehran.

Do you think the word terrorism has been politicized?

The words 'terrorism' and 'terrorists' are frankly without any meaning any more. In the Federal Code back in the 1990s there was a definition of terrorism which I thought was maybe useful for social scientists: 'The use of violence by non-state actors against civilians for the purpose of political gain.' In other words, violence being directed against civilians. So, you have a small group of people whom nobody elected who exercise violence against the civilian population to get what they want put in place: that's terrorism. That was a pretty good definition but it's not generally the one being deployed by politicians or the press when they talk about terrorism. And, yes, the US has supported a large number of such groups. The Contras in Nicaragua in the 1980s are an example. There isn't any doubt that, where there was a government in Nicaragua the US didn't like, its intelligence security apparatus had no compunctions about supporting violent insurgencies against that government. This included groups that were engaging in what the US Federal Code would have defined as terrorism.

I think the other side of the coin is that the US uses the term terrorist for groups that are often anti-occupation and national liberation movements. The Algerians who fought the French in the late 1950s and early 1960s certainly did employ terrorism, but they were more than just a terrorist group, and they prevailed against the French and became a country in 1962. But from the Western point of view the National Liberation Front was a terrorist organization. The inability to see anti-occupation or national liberation groups as having a legitimate political orientation is a blind spot in the West.

Do you think the nations with permanent membership of the United Nations Security Council have too much influence?

The Security Council has a lot of problems. One of its problems is that it's not powerful enough and it can only really call for countries to do things; and if they don't want to do these things there's nothing the Security Council can do about it. It's also internally divided so it's rare that all five permanent members can agree on some policy. Since they all have a veto, in most instances the Security Council is irrelevant. I think that's unfortunate and that the veto ought to be abolished. The permanent members of the Security Council have undue power because they don't reflect the geopolitical realities of our temporary world. It's crazy that Brazil and India are not permanent members of the Security Council. And if you're going to put in India, you might as well put in Pakistan as well. I could think of at least three major powers that should be added as permanent members, and their absence has made the organization very unbalanced.

Can you talk about how the veto has been used by members of the UN Security Council to prevent action against genocidal regimes?

It certainly prevented intervention to stop Milošević's actions in the former Yugoslav Republic because of the Russian veto. Syria is another example. The Bashar al-Assad regime in Syria is genocidal, and the world hasn't been able to do anything about it because of the Russian and Chinese veto. ■

BRIDGET CONLEY

 Bridget Conley is research director at the World Peace Foundation (WPF). She specializes in mass atrocities, genocide, museums and memorialization. Before she joined the WPF she served as research director for the US Holocaust Memorial Museum's Committee on Conscience for 10 years, where she helped establish the Museum's program on contemporary genocide.

What are some policies that have helped prevent potential genocides in the past?

In most cases, there is a tradeoff between using influence to condemn and isolate a regime or other actors that might be willing to use violence against civilians, and actively engaging such regimes to resolve the core political crisis that drove them to pursue such policies. It must be made clear that atrocities are not an outcome that can be tolerated, but this is balanced with an approach that does not push a regime or other actors further into a corner where they feel like they have nothing left to lose. It's that tradeoff that is very difficult to manage, and it's rarely managed well. The people who are strong advocates for intervention will always be more in favor of cracking down on regimes, while there will always be another side that is willing to appease beyond the last moment. Wisdom often falls within the nuanced area in between, and rarely receives accolades from either side.

Do you believe that kind of nuance is often missing in public discussions in the media about how to stop genocide or mass atrocities?

Media discussions are rarely that helpful. The media tends to tilt towards paying attention to the more extreme positions: it's either we're against atrocities (which we all should be), or we are to accept them as a political reality. This isn't necessary. You can be really critical of a regime while still engaging with it and working on ways to increase protections for civilians. This is what diplomats often try to do. But the discussions in the public realm seem to focus on two clear-cut opposing positions: you're either for this or for that.

Do you think the public's perception of the definition of genocide varies from the actual definition of genocide that was established in the 1948 Genocide Convention?

I think there is a wide variance between the public perception and the actual definition that was established at the Convention. In my opinion, the quirks of the Genocide Convention render it particularly difficult and possibly unhelpful to understanding campaigns of violence against civilians. I think there are better articulations of genocide. 'Mass atrocities' has been the more relevant term in many situations.

Are there times when crimes against humanity that don't fit the exact definition of genocide are even worse than some previous examples that do fit the definition of genocide?

I once had a young student who, when I was giving a presentation on genocide, asked: 'What about the slave trade? Wasn't that genocide?' I don't think it was genocide, but I think 400 years of institutionalized dehumanization has its own exigencies. I think people have a responsibility to understand harms, rather than ranking harms. I think ranking harms is a very distasteful endeavor. For me, the challenge is to understand the harm being done to people and to work against this harm in whatever form it appears. That's what social justice should be about, not about ranking harms.

Do you think it would be smart to add class and political organization to the number of victim groups (ethnic, racial, religious and national are the current groups listed in the international definition of genocide) listed when it relates to genocide?

No, and it's not because I view class-based or politically motivated killings as less harmful than ethnic, racial, religious or national group-related killings; it's because I think trying to correct the Genocide Convention is less of a fruitful path than trying to use other terms that we already have, like crimes against humanity. This already provides a legal path for the type of prevention and protection that might be necessary in some cases.

What is your opinion of the UN's Responsibility to Protect (R2P) doctrine? Is this a good idea?

I think that the core concepts and ideas of the Responsibility to Protect are deeply valuable and I think we have seen them play out as coalitions have been built around the idea. My caveat is that I do think it's dangerous to create a policy spectrum that includes an authorization for war within a protection mandate. Military intervention should be held out of R2P as a separate way to engage in a conflict. I just don't think it should live in the same house as prevention and a non-coercive response.

Do you think providing protections to the citizens of Benghazi would have been a better policy than helping to overthrow Muammar Qadafi's regime in Libya?

I remember the time when Qadafi's forces were slowly moving eastwards towards Benghazi and there were legitimate and strong fears that something terrifying would happen if they took it. There were some other towns that Qadafi's forces had taken where massacres had not taken place, but the leadership in those towns had already fled, so Benghazi was seen as kind of the last stand for the resistance fighters. I do think there is logic to seeing Benghazi as a place where there was a strong imperative to provide protection for civilians. However, regime change is a very radical step.

You don't have to be an apologist for Qadafi to say regime change wasn't the right policy. Changing how a State functions is exceptionally difficult, and finding a new leader is a key part of that process. Often the new leader will repeat the old patterns of the leadership they have just overthrown. Political relationships are more complex than one person and if there is no structure to hold in place a different type of relationship then you get what happened to Libya after Qadafi was overthrown. The situation was very chaotic and highly lethal.

You seem to stress the importance of seeing conflicts on a country-by-country basis as opposed to seeing Sudan as another Rwanda, or Syria as another Iraq?

There are obviously lessons to be learned from the past and mechanisms that can be put in place – like smart, focused sanctions on regimes involved in mass atrocities. How these mechanisms and tools can be deployed should always be in relation to a really deep understanding of the nature of risk, and the nature of the political community you want to impact. ■

GLENN GREENWALD

 Glenn Greenwald is an investigative reporter and co-founder of the adversarial news media organization The Intercept. He won the Park Center IF Stone Award for Independent Journalism in 2008. Among his books are: *No Place to Hide, With Liberty and Justice for Some* and *How Would a Patriot Act?*

Do you think Americans can simultaneously oppose the Russian meddling in the 2016 presidential elections, while also becoming more educated about the US government's history of overthrowing foreign governments in ways that were much more consequential for the citizens in those countries?

I think for a long time Americans haven't cared at all about the fact that their government has been interfering in severe and aggressive ways in the internal affairs of other countries. Now that Americans have discovered their distaste for this type of intervention – because it was done to them and not by them – I think it is a good opportunity to force them to confront what they have been overlooking, ignoring or favoring.

Is one of your worries about the Trump-Russia investigation that the lionizing of current or former members of the CIA, FBI and NSA in the media because of their anti-Trump positions will make it harder to criticize these agencies in the post-Trump era?

I think this has been happening. There is a perception, probably an accurate one, that parts of these agencies are devoted to undermining the Trump presidency and have been from the very beginning. In this era when people are convinced Trump is this singular evil, anyone who is seen as opposing Trump or doing something to undermine his presidency is viewed favorably.

Among the main factions being viewed this way are the security state agencies that you just described, even though they have been involved in some of the worst evils in American history.

For readers who are not aware of some of the most notorious episodes in these agencies' histories, could you discuss some the most egregious actions of the CIA, FBI and NSA?

The CIA has been overthrowing governments for the past seven decades because of their perception that those governments were not serving US interests. They have used violence and all types of deception to destabilize countries and overthrow countries throughout Latin America and Asia. Even in Europe, the CIA is involved in a number of countries, including Russia.

In the post-9/11 era, the FBI has been focusing in all kinds of disproportionate ways on American Muslims: infiltrating their mosques, monitoring them and surveilling them. They helped round them up after 9/11 and kept them imprisoned for months with no trial or charges of any kind.

The NSA has been engaged in all kinds of mass surveillance, including domestic surveillance that the courts have ruled to be unconstitutional. This is just a small portion of the evils committed by the institutions in the last several decades.

The conventional argument for the clandestine nature of these agencies is that they must exist because they exist in every other country. How can these institutions be democratically accountable?

There was a pretty significant movement to reform some of these agencies in the mid-1970s after the Church Committee discovered abuses by the CIA and the FBI that were carried out with no accountability. Some of these abuses were carried out without even Congress being aware of them. The movement sought to impose oversight and transparency requirements on the agencies. However, even some of the modest reforms these agencies were forced to implement were killed during the Reagan administration or after 9/11 in the name of terrorism.

These are really sprawling agencies. Even the people who

direct them admit they often have no idea what they are doing, they are just too big to monitor and keep track of. There is almost no transparency. Most of what we have learned about them has come from whistleblowers and leakers like Chelsea Manning and Edward Snowden.

Since you have a finite amount of time in your day, how do you go about deciding whether to write about your criticisms of the mainstream media's coverage of the Trump-Russia investigation, or the Trump administration's attacks on democratic institutions?

I try to use my platform to maximize the impact of the reporting I'm doing. So, if there are things that I want to say that a lot of people are already saying, then all I would be doing was joining a chorus or an echo chamber. I don't take up my time or my readers' time writing about those sorts of things because they don't seem particularly fruitful to me. I tend to try to use my platform to write about or say things that nobody else is really paying attention to.

What are your thoughts on the relationship between Trump and Putin? Are you as confused as a lot of people about what the state of US-Russian relations is today?

Trump ran on a platform explicitly saying that he thought the US and Russia should have a better relationship, in part because they have large nuclear stockpiles pointing at each other's cities, and in part because they have a lot of common interests in the world. President Obama actually viewed Russia the same way. He worked a lot with Russia to get the Iran deal done and on fighting terrorism in the Middle East.

There is a lot of ideological affinity between Trump and Putin. They both tend to be pretty nationalistic and conservative. They view the world through a fairly similar ideological prism, so I don't think it's surprising that they have a good personal working relationship. Trump tends to admire people he perceives as strong, and he perceives Putin as strong – probably stronger than he really is – and he likes him for that reason.

However, at the same time there is a huge, powerful, national security apparatus in the United States and in Russia that Dwight Eisenhower warned Americans about, and any sophisticated observer of Washington and Moscow understands this. The political classes and the military classes of Russia and the US have hated each other for many decades and they still hate each other. I think there is a lot of animosity between Russia and the US that is still visible, and Trump's policies are not necessarily because of Trump's own personal views – they may even be despite his own views. There is this divergence between Trump's statements on the one hand, and his policies on the other.

What would you like to see revealed to the public after Robert Mueller completes his report on the Trump-Russia investigation?

I would like to see as much as possible revealed without endangering the lives of people. Obviously, if the Americans have intelligence sources inside the Kremlin, those should be protected. If there are specific ways that the US has been eavesdropping on the Russians or otherwise monitoring their communications, those should be legitimately concealed as well. But, in general, I think we should see as much evidence as can be disclosed to demonstrate that Robert Mueller's allegations are accurate and not just something that we are taking on faith. ∎

MICHAEL KAZIN

Michael Kazin is co-editor of *Dissent* magazine and an expert on social and political movements in the United States. He contributes to newspapers, periodicals and websites such as the *New York Times, Washington Post, Politico, The Nation, American Prospect* and *The New Republic*. Kazin's book *American Dreamers: How the Left changed a nation* was named the best book of 2011 by *The Progressive, The New Republic* and *Newsweek/ Daily Beast*.

Can there be a patriotism that doesn't confine empathy to one's borders and regards the lives of people in other countries as of no less importance than American lives?

I think most people in the world have a group feeling. Sometimes it's an ethnic group, tribe, religion or nation. I think that can be turned to positive ends or very negative ones. I think it's important for people on the Left to be connected to people in their own country. We're not going to change the world all at once. That's not how change happens. It would be nice if there was a worldwide Left that could be active in the same places, but I think it's human to care more about the people you know who speak the same language as you.

The problem occurs when you see your people as superior to other people, as opposed to you being more comfortable with them. I think it's politically necessary for the Left in different countries to be able to rally their people in shared solidarity. Again, patriotism can be positive or negative. One of the things that happened in the 19th century is that a sense of nationalism got connected to liberalism or radicalism. The French Revolution is the best example of that. Although I'm someone who believes internationalism is absolutely necessary, I think there needs to be a balance struck between national feeling and international solidarity.

Do you think American exceptionalism has become its own secular religion, in the same way that Soviet communism and other forms of authoritarian socialism were in the past?

I think there has always been a degree of American exceptionalism. If you go back to the 18th century, Thomas Paine was talking about how he wanted America to be an asylum for mankind. So I think this is not something recent. American political rhetoric has always been exceptional, especially rhetoric by white people.

The best-selling book by Ta-Nehisi Coates talks about how white Americans have a dream, black Americans have a nightmare. I don't think American exceptionalism is so much a stated ideology as it is something people can cloak themselves in to make themselves feel better. One of the few things that has united Americans – though I'm not sure if it unites Americans any more – is that this country stands for ideals and that is not true in many countries. In France it's true, but it's not true in many countries. I co-edited the book *Americanism: new perspectives on the history of an ideal* with my good friend Joseph A McCartin and I discussed this in the introduction. I think this ideal is very powerful and it has bound Americana together. I think it has made it hard for socialists to make substantial inroads with the public because in some ways Americanism substitutes for socialism as an egalitarian ideology that people can turn into a reality. In a sense, it's a secular religion, but it's not enforced in the same way Marxism-Leninism is enforced. It's more of a mood and an impulse.

My main concern about American exceptionalism is that events which undercut this premise, such as the genocide of the Native Americans, the slavery of African Americans or the war in Vietnam, will be rationalized or not mentioned. Do you agree?

I think that's true, but at the same time American exceptionalism does give people on the Left something to strive for. America has these great ideals like equality, democracy, equal opportunity and treating people fairly, so how come we are betraying them by doing what we're doing? Whereas in some other countries where the binding glue of nationalism is more ethnic, regional or religious, you don't have those ideals to harken back to. The Left in places like Russia, Germany and India have to come up with ideals that are perceived by many as anti-Russian, anti-German or anti-Indian. For example, the Hindutva movement and its idea of Hindu supremacy is prevalent in India after the election of Narendra Modi to prime minister.

Americanism can be a resource for the Left if it's used the right way. If you just condemn it, then you are trying to channel support for a country you are perceived as hating. There is no example in history of the Left being able to transform a country where most of the non-Left in that country perceive the Left to view the country as something they don't like or don't trust.

Why is there that perception? Why can't people on the Left simultaneously say most US military interventions have been wrongheaded, but that they still love their country and want to see it live up to the ideals espoused in the Declaration of Independence?

I think that sort of patriotism has worked. I think that when the Left has made gains in this country it has done so in part because it was able to embrace those American ideals. As long as most Americans are patriotic and want the country to do well, the Left will have to do so as well.

People like me in the New Left of the mid-1960s condemned America and spelled America with three Ks. It's certainly true that more people were willing to carry Vietcong flags than American flags during the Vietnam War, which I think is a shame. I think we should have carried American flags and said 'we're better Americans than you because we are upholding the values of America by opposing an immoral war.'

There is a great speech by former president of the Students for a Democratic Society Carl Oglesby during an anti-war march in 1965 where he said 'the Vietcong are fighting a revolution against a foreign power, much as the United States was against the British.'

Obviously, there are differences; one was led by communists and one was led partly by slaveholders, but they were both anti-colonial in nature. He asked: 'Why does a country based on one colonial struggle kill people in a war based on another colonial struggle against us?' I think it was a very effective speech and I think it was a mistake for people to get away from that, as people did during the late 1960s. This helped doom the New Left and bring on a new conservative era. ■

MICHAEL LERNER

 Rabbi Michael Lerner created *Tikkun* as the Jewish, liberal and progressive alternative to the Jewish conservative magazine *Commentary*. He founded the Tikkun Community in 2002 – an interfaith organization dedicated to nonviolence, peace, justice, generosity and caring. The organization changed its name to the Network of Spiritual Progressives in 2004 to show that the interfaith organization was not just for Jews. He is the author of *The Left Hand of God, The Socialism of Fools: anti-semitism on the Left* and *Revolutionary Love*.

Do you think the American Left hasn't been proactive enough in seeking out members of the religious Left who share the same positions as them on most issues?

I think it's a tragic error of liberal and progressive forces to not have made much greater efforts to integrate in their activities, their thinking and their organizations people who are either religious or spiritually inclined. The truth is, all polls show that the vast majority of Americans go to church at least once a month. The liberal and progressive forces talk about a democratic transformation of society, but they are unwilling to reach out to many potential supporters who are either religious or spiritual, except by reaching out in a way that conveys a disdain or demeaning view of people who believe in religion or spirituality.

I did book tours and speeches around the country for my book *The Left Hand of God: taking our country back from the religious right* and I heard thousands of people tell me how they were trying to be part of a liberal-progressive movement but they ran into what is best described as a deep religio-phobia and antagonism to people who are religious. Liberals and progressives would like these people to be there when it comes to voting for our candidates and demonstrating on the streets. But the culture and assumptions in liberal and progressive circles reflect a deep prejudice that goes something like this: 'Yes, we want you in our movements, but we think you religious and spiritual people, especially you religious people who believe in God, are at a lower level of intellectual or psychological development than us.'

There are plenty of religious and spiritual people who have accepted that about the Left, but they nevertheless agree with the Left on the issues, so they don't let this secular elitist attitude drive them away. They end up making the following choice: 'If I'm going to be part of a liberal and progressive movement then I have to leave my religious or spiritual apparatus at the door.' This means the Left doesn't get the benefit of the wisdom that religious or spiritual progressives could bring.

What do you think has changed in the US that has caused a schism between secular and religious progressives? At one time many of the most progressive movements against slavery, child labor and unsafe tenement buildings came out of the church...

The American Left and the liberal forces tend to be very narrow in their focus. They look at one specific issue, instead of coming up with a coherent worldview that helps people see the interconnected nature of our problems and need for a fundamental transformation. We do that in our Network for Spiritual Progressives and through *Tikkun*. We are trying to get people in the social progressive world to reopen themselves to a coherent worldview.

The best articulator of that worldview, apart from the people who are connected with our Network of Spiritual Progressives, is Pope Francis. The Pope today is the most significant progressive thinker in terms of his impact and outreach to a huge following of people and, in time, if he isn't killed or he doesn't die or get forced to resign by unrepentant conservative forces in the Catholic world, he could have a huge impact in transforming the Catholic Church into being more connected with liberal and progressive movements. That's just what infuriates the conservatives, who have always sought a more repressive, hierarchical and patriarchal perspective.

Can atheists and agnostics recognize these same human needs without being part of any organized religion?

I don't think that it's necessary to fit into a traditional religion to have an awareness of spiritual consciousness. To be spiritual means to look at the world from outside of the categories that the empiricists have developed. The empiricists developed a worldview that said: 'That which is real is that which can be verified through our data or be measured. And that which cannot be measured or subject to empirical verification to our data is not really real.'

This worldview has become the dominant worldview in global capitalism. It's shared by many people on the Left, Right and Center. This is the dominant religion of the contemporary world. It's a religion because it has no foundation based on its own criteria; because it cannot be verified through data or be measured. But everybody believes it, so it's considered common sense. When you're in a religion, the pervasive religious belief is just obvious, so you accept it instead of asking yourself what the basis of that belief is. The people I call spiritual are those who reject the empiricist worldview and say, 'no, there are other ways of knowing that are not subject to empirical verification or measurement'.

Do you think international leftists should be pushing for capitalism with a friendly face or for something different that we haven't discovered yet?

I'm not for capitalism with a friendly face. I'm working for a different society, a society based on love and generosity. Such a society would have to have elements of economic justice and democratic control of the economy that were the intent of socialism (though unfortunately often implemented in a bureaucratic way that rarely gave ordinary people the power it had promised). So I'm calling my vision Revolutionary Love. That society would seek 'a New Bottom Line' so that every institution and social practice – corporations, economic policies, laws, government policies, health and education – would be judged to be efficient, rational or productive to the extent that these institutions and the social practices they fostered maximized our capacities to be loving and caring, kind and generous, ethical and environmentally sensitive and responsible. We need to support each other to be capable of responding to human beings as embodiments of the sacred and capable of responding to the world with awe, wonder and radical amazement.

This is what the Network of Spiritual Progressives is all about: to change the consciousness of America and foster a spirit of generosity and create 'The Caring Society' – caring for each other and caring for the earth. Despite the political power of the most selfish elements in our society, most people yearn for a different kind of world, and in my book *Revolutionary Love* I expand on these ideas. ■

SARA MERSHA

 Sara Mersha is the director of grantmaking and advocacy at Grassroots International. She was born in Ethiopia but has spent most of her life in the US. Grassroots International is a non-profit organization that works all over the world to help small farmers and other small producers, indigenous peoples and women, win resource rights to land, water and food.

Do you think Grassroots International's emphasis on resource rights requires reimagining democracy as a continually evolving process as opposed to a system where people just cast their vote in a ballot box every few years?

At its core, resource rights is about guaranteeing the human rights to land, water and food sovereignty as well as climate justice. To ensure these rights, it's important for people to be able to exercise a deep level of democracy. For example, food sovereignty was defined at the Nyeleni Forum on Food Sovereignty as 'the right of peoples to healthy and culturally appropriate food produced through ecologically sound and sustainable methods, and their right to define their own food and agriculture systems'.

This requires respect for local processes, for community members to come together and discuss these issues so that they can decide together how they want their food systems to be set up – what kind of food is produced, who produces it, and how it is produced in a way that is healthy for people and the planet. Similarly, with rights to land, and with climate justice.

In February 2016, we came back from visiting our partners in Mexico – most of which are indigenous communities in Oaxaca and Chiapas who have a long practice of deep democracy. Each community or village has a general assembly where community members come together to make decisions. They name people to represent them as members of the communal authority, and those members see their role as serving their broader communities and implementing the decisions made by the general assembly. More and more indigenous communities throughout Mexico are using the power they have through their local assemblies and decision-making processes to create communal statutes to protect their natural resources (such as land, water, and food systems) from extractive industries such as mining companies.

In the US, there are other examples of communities passing resolutions at the local level to ensure food sovereignty (such as a number of local resolutions in Maine about the right to produce and sell food at a local level) and protection of natural resources (such as resolutions to prevent fracking or other forms of extraction, through resolutions on the Rights of Nature).

Why do you think NGOs have not been more eager to get input from grassroots organizations in the countries they are trying to help?

There are vast differences in the types of NGOs that operate at the international level. Unfortunately, the top-down model that has been used by large-scale institutions like the World Bank is often replicated among some large international NGOs and foundations. Our model at Grassroots International is about solidarity with social movements that are at the forefront of working toward the kinds of changes the planet needs. For that reason, it is important to us that we have close relationships with groups in each country where we work, and that they let us know what the priority areas are that they would like us to fund. We also have a reciprocal relationship based on mutual trust and transparency, so that they can also share their feedback with us about our work as a whole, including advice for our advocacy and education work in the US.

Many NGOs rely on commercials featuring starving children to get donations. Do you think this has a negative effect?

Grassroots International's work is focused on solidarity, not charity. Our partners are powerful agents of change, and we strive to communicate about their work with others in a way that educates others about the amazing work they do, and about our responsibility, honor and opportunity to work to address the structural issues that are the root causes of the conditions that peasants and Indigenous peoples face throughout the world.

Depicting people in the Global South or impoverished communities as destitute and in need of help feeds into the North-as-savior myth that drives many international development models. This model ignores both the root causes of poverty and hardship (like corporate deregulation, unjust trade policies and a long history of economic and political piracy, capitalism, white supremacy, patriarchy, colonialism, neoliberalism, etc) and the power and resilience of local communities to develop and implement vibrant alternatives.

Why do you think access to water, food and land are often not cited as basic human rights, and do you see this changing any time soon?

While some may associate human rights more with civil and political rights, we have witnessed over the past decade a marked increase in the recognition of land, water and food (and other economic, social and cultural rights) as human rights. That said, rights to land, water and food are still too often overlooked because those rights stand in the way of increased commodification of natural resources for the profit of industries and private investors. Likewise, the loss of the commons (including water systems) is a necessary step to feed the neoliberal model. In such a system, a river's utility is measured in its ability to generate power via a dam to energize mining operations or industrial agricultural projects, regardless of the human and environmental damage such schemes cause.

Many critics of globalization have been lumped into the so-called anti-globalization movement. Is your organization's advocacy of globalization from below an attempt to counter that negative term?

Grassroots' partner La Vía Campesina is one of the social movements that has promoted the idea of what movements can and need to globalize – their slogan is 'Globalize the Struggle, Globalize Hope!' The importance of linkages between social movements across geographies and across sectors is also key to our philosophy and theory of change.

What would trade agreements look like if grassroots organizations in the Global South had the same influence over the terms of the agreements as corporations and pharmaceutical companies?

I think the short answer is that if grassroots organizations in the Global South had their way, there would be no free-trade agreements at all! Some of our partners and allies work towards the goal of fair trade – based on the principles of the solidarity economy. ■

JEFFREY SACHS

 Jeffrey Sachs is the director of the Earth Institute and was special advisor to former United Nations Secretary General Ban Ki-moon on the Millennium Development Goals, having held the same position under Kofi Annan. He is also director of the UN Sustainable Development Solutions Network, co-founder and chief strategist of Millennium Promise Alliance, and director of the Millennium Villages Project. He is the author of *The End of Poverty, Common Wealth: Economics for a crowded planet, The Price of Civilization* and *To Move the World: JFK's quest for peace.*

What do you think is the solution to the Syrian crisis?
The US has pursued a regime-change strategy in the Middle East and other parts of the world during the entire Cold War and post-Cold War period and it's reached an end because it's now in a disastrous stage of sharply negative returns. Both the Syria and Libya debacles that followed the Afghanistan and Iraq disasters have left us in a situation of war, massive terrorist blowback, and a massive displacement of people.

We need an approach that is not based on US-led regime change. The United States should have never been in the business of toppling Assad, a decision that was made by President Obama and Secretary of State Hillary Clinton without public debate or Congressional backing. Whatever one thinks about Assad, it wasn't an appropriate foreign policy of the United States to team up with Saudi Arabia, Turkey and other Gulf States to bring down this regime. The UN Security Council should always have a role in trying to frame international support for regional solutions. This would mean finding common ground with Russia and China, as well as with American allies like France and Britain. There needs to be a co-operative approach to encourage a different Middle East reality.

We also need active diplomatic solutions where Iran, Syria, Turkey, Saudi Arabia and Egypt play a role to help broker a reasonable path forward for Syria and the region more generally. This means not letting this Shi'a-Sunni proxy war (i.e. the virulent anti-Iranian positions of the US and its allies) spin even further out of control.

The second aspect of global diplomacy is to remember that this region is experiencing an ecological and developmental crisis. There are many crucial steps to take in the Middle East concerning water, energy transformation, education and job creation. These are the truly important issues for the region. There is an urgent and positive sustainable-development agenda that is extremely significant in the Middle East and must be part of any realistic, core long-term approach. Moving from a US strategy of perpetual war to a regional strategy of peace, and moving from a strategy of US-led regime change to a strategy of regional sustainable development, is the only sound and sensible approach. If anyone thinks we are on a sound course right now, they don't have their eyes open.

Do you think it would be problematic to arm the secular Syrian rebel groups?

I think arming any faction in the region now as a first-line approach makes no sense. We need to know what we are trying to do. What are the goals, what is realistic? There is no military solution to the Syrian and Middle East problems and there never was. And we have not properly discussed or agreed on a diplomatic solution globally.

Do you think these negotiations will have to involve all the external and internal sources involved in the Syrian conflict to prevent the arms flow into the country?

Syria is a classic proxy war: lots of different interests are being fought in Syria. This isn't working to anyone's advantage, least of all the Syrians, of course. The proxy war is a disastrous negative sum game being played out right now. The United States views Syria in Cold War terms vis-à-vis Russia; the Saudis view it as part of their war against Iran, as does Israel. There are enough political conflicts inside Syria to last for quite a while, unless directly tamped down in the interests of peace. The Turkish engagement in Syria has also been very complex because it's been both based on the Turkish role in the Sunni world and Turkish-Arab relations, but it's also deeply implicated in Turkish-Kurdish issues.

The Syrian war is a proxy war with arms pouring in from all sides because everybody is placing their bets and defending their positions. The way out of a proxy war is to have an approach that brings the interested parties together and out of the illusion that they can win on the battlefield. This proxy war has also led to terrorism and bloodshed that is out of the control of any of the countries involved to a large extent. I don't think the ISIS phenomenon is in any of the countries' agendas and interests in terms of creating it, but I do think there is a shared interest in stopping it because it has carried out a campaign of mass murder across a very large area. There are strong interests of Russia, the United States, Iran, Saudi Arabia and Turkey that are reflected in war, but should be a basis for a peaceful resolution.

What needs to happen on both sides to develop better relations between the United States and Russia?
I think a Cold War and unipolar mentality is at the core of US foreign policy. So, at the end of the Cold War, rather than saying now we can build a world based on international law and multi-polarity, we know there were strong neoconservative views inside the United States that thought now we can build a world based on unipolar US leadership. That was a powerful and profoundly misguided vision that played on many deep strands of US exceptionalism. I think this vision has been a major fuel for US-fought wars since 1991. It's also been one of the main reasons for stoking a new, albeit lesser, Cold War with Russia, which I think is also very dangerous. The idea that everything

that has happened is because Putin is a tyrant is an absurdity; it's for people who don't follow the storyline. The storyline is that the US has also made a lot of provocations towards Russia in the post-Cold War era.

Do you think Russia and the United States can come to a strategic and morally acceptable agreement about how to deal with the situations in Syria and Ukraine, where both countries have pursued foreign policies distinctly different from one another?

Yes, I do. I think there are a lot of common interests, but there is no winner-take-all outcome possible. I don't think the US idea that we were going to defeat Russia's ally in the region was a proper starting point in Syria. I also don't believe encouraging Ukraine to join NATO was a proper idea. I think the US just pushed too far. We should have been much more reticent, and we should have understood Russia's economic, geopolitical and security viewpoints. If we had done so, we wouldn't be in the current situation. But we have a hardline neoconservative vision of the world that is entrenched in US foreign policy, and it's an incorrect and dangerous vision.

Is there another way for developing economies to prosper than the sweatshop-driven model, so workers can play a bigger role and have greater input in their societies?

I would say that the best overall framework we have is the sustainable-development framework that countries agreed on at the United Nations. One of the core pillars of the framework is that economic development should be combined with social inclusion and environmental sustainability. I think this kind of development approach is possible. It means each country aims for a mixed economy where private-sector production, trade and investment is combined with a very active state that is guaranteeing quality education, quality healthcare, access to infrastructure and protection of the national environment.

Countries must hold themselves accountable from the national to the local level, not just for GDP growth, but for economic fairness, social inclusion and environmental sustainability as well. This is closest to the social democratic approach of northern Europe and Costa Rica. This model is feasible because it respects the land tenure and community rights of *campesinos*, and it ensures that large companies can't use bilateral investment treaties to grab land and destroy the environment. It has some very inclusive features to it, but it is still a market economy in a mixed system. It totally rejects the idea of privatizing core human services and human needs, like health and education, both of which I think need to be publicly guaranteed and publicly provided.

In this sustainable-development approach, basic needs should be met early on: access to healthcare, education, water, sanitation and basic infrastructure. I don't know of any other way to ensure human needs and an advance in living standards. I think the development work will require a couple of generations ahead of us because a generation of young people needs to grow up with better education, better skills, better nutrition and better health situations. We need to have new entrepreneurs and companies to develop; and all of that takes time.

How important is it for governments not to let the hidden environmental costs of extraction and other polluting industries be left off the books or passed on to the public?

Environmental sustainability is not merely an option; it's a matter of survival for vast numbers of people and places around the world. The current global production systems, especially those based on high-carbon energy, are creating devastating costs. Some of these costs are short-term in the form of massive pollution that could be put to an end in future years, but the longer-term and persistent climate costs will be even larger than that. It's not possible to deny human-induced climate change without denying all of the science we know about how Earth's systems function. We are beyond debate on this issue, and that's why sustainable development needs to be a central organizing principle for our time, not an option to be debated. We are not there politically in the US because one party [the

Republican Party] is so profoundly corrupted by big oil it won't breathe the truth, and the other party is half-corrupted, so it won't implement the truth with any vigor.

How vital is gender equality to creating a global sustainable economy?

Gender equality is vital for sustainable development; hence its inclusion as Sustainable Development Goal Five. The benefits of gender equality are first and foremost moral – with girls and women representing half the population, of course they should be entitled to the full social, economic, and political rights enjoyed by males. But the society-wide benefits of gender equality are also enormous and very practical: healthy, educated, empowered young women raise healthy, educated and skilled children who grow up to have better lives and higher wellbeing. By helping girls to achieve their full potential – through nutrition, healthcare and especially access to quality education – the intergenerational propagation of poverty can be defeated. ∎

GEORGE SCIALABBA

 George Scialabba is a regular contributor to the *Washington Post, Village Voice, Dissent, Boston Globe* and *The Nation*. Among his books are: *The Modern Predicament, What Are Intellectuals Good For?* and *Slouching Toward Utopia*.

How much of Islamic terrorism can be attributed to US foreign policy and how much of it was a spontaneous, grassroots movement?

Even if I were less ignorant of the various jihadist movements, I would hesitate to guess at the balance among their motivations, any more than I would do so in the case of, say, the Tea Party. I'm sure there are a variety of causes in play: religious sectarianism and cultural self-assertion; resentment of domestic corruption, repression and underdevelopment as well as foreign exploitation and violent intervention. But whatever the proportions, Americans should interest ourselves primarily in the causes of jihadism for which we may have some responsibility and which we may have some ability to affect.

Public statements by al-Qaeda (reprinted in Michael Scheuer's *Imperial Hubris*) have said emphatically that their primary goals in attacking the US were to protest and revenge the killing of Muslims by Western military interventions and to end interference by the West (through military bases and weapons sales) in Muslim countries. In response to the many Westerners who have claimed that al-Qaeda's attack was motivated by hatred of the freedom and openness of Western democracies, bin Laden asked: 'Why then did we not attack Sweden?'

If many American Southerners still, 150 years later, deeply resent the defeat inflicted by Union armies in an excellent cause

– ending slavery – we shouldn't be surprised that Muslims still resent the much more recent humiliations inflicted on them by the West for the sake of controlling their energy resources.

Do you think American exceptionalism itself has become a secular religion that requires its own subtle forms of blind faith and absolutism?

The nationalist, as George Orwell once remarked, has an uncanny ability to see the atrocities committed by other nations and not to see those committed by his own. In other words, there is nothing exceptional about American exceptionalism. Every state portrays its motives as disinterested and generous, and insider intellectuals in every society are happy to parrot the State's propaganda. The American propaganda system is unusually effective (see Edward Herman and Noam Chomsky's *Manufacturing Consent* for a detailed description). But in every society, those intellectuals, editors, scholars et al who toe the official line are rewarded with power and influence. Still, the US is a relatively free society, so we can find the truth – if we can tear ourselves away from television and social media.

When do you think humanitarian intervention has been warranted in the past (Bosnia, Rwanda, Kosovo)? What are your thoughts on R2P ('responsibility to protect')?

International law certainly recognizes a responsibility to protect. It belongs to the UN Security Council, when appealed to by a State or population under attack. Of course, the United Nations is now largely non-functional in this respect, because the superpowers have never fulfilled their obligations under the UN Charter. But, rather than give individual great powers the authority to intervene militarily, as at least some versions of the R2P doctrine envision, it would be preferable to address honestly the defects of the UN and try to repair them. The populations of the great powers must force their governments to obey international law, which those governments will never do otherwise.

How should progressives approach the freedom-of-speech issues that are being put to the test by Islamic terrorist attacks against speech they don't find acceptable?

I think the traditional distinction between speech and action – action may be regulated, speech not – is by and large adequate. In general, the best remedy for falsehood is truth, the best remedy for wounding speech is healing speech, the best remedy for hateful speech is loving speech. Libelous speech is not protected, but the definition should be narrow, as in the US, not broad, as in the UK. The right to insult people and ridicule their beliefs is essential in a free society. It may, of course, be foolish or even immoral, but it shouldn't be illegal.

How should progressives approach the Israeli-Palestinian conflict? Some commentators claim that if Hamas had the same technological sophistication as Israel, they would try to annihilate the country. Do you think these claims have any credence?

As the poet WH Auden observed: 'Those to whom evil is done/ Do evil in return.' I wouldn't be surprised if many members of Hamas harbored murderous resentments. They have been badly treated for generations by Israel, with the support of the US. But those violent impulses must not be indulged, and Americans must not encourage or excuse them. Large-scale nonviolent resistance is not only the most moral strategy, it is also the most effective one. The best thing Americans can do for all concerned is to force our government to be serious, for the first time, about pressuring Israel to make a comprehensive peace – full return of the West Bank, an end to the strangulation of Gaza, reparations for dispossessed Palestinians, equal rights for Arab citizens of Israel – while it still has unquestioned military superiority.

In the United States, there was some talk by liberal commentators about Dick Cheney being jailed for promoting torture, yet very little mention was made about charging George W Bush for war crimes for invading Iraq. What, if anything, does this say about the mainstream press?

I think it reveals one tenet of the conventional wisdom: individual Americans can sometimes do bad things – after slavery and Vietnam, this would be a little awkward to deny – but as a state, the US is law-abiding.

What role should the US play in combating ISIS?

I think the US should acknowledge and apologize for past crimes against Muslims and then show the world's billion Muslims a shining example of enlightened secular democracy and prosperity. Of course, the US should also participate in any discussions and actions taken by the United Nations Security Council in response to actions by ISIS.

What role, if any, should the US play in Syria?

Again, I think adherence to international law, particularly regarding the paramount role of the Security Council as arbiter of humanitarian military intervention, would be a good first step. Beyond that, of course I hope for the emergence of a unified, non-sectarian democratic regime without Assad.

In the mainstream press, events like the overthrow of democratic leaders in Guatemala, Iran, and Chile have been covered, yet the majority of commentators still write in a way that portrays the US as a country with a long history of fighting for freedom and human rights. How can they report on these events, yet remain unmoved in their beliefs about our country?

How can they, indeed? Actually, some don't, but if they try to share their newfound beliefs about our country with their readers/viewers, their editors/producers ask if they're feeling all right, or if they need to take some time off. And if they insist that, no, they've actually come to see the world in a radically different way, they're eventually shown the door.

What you would like to see changed about the international Left?

I'd like to see it around a hundred times bigger. ∎

STEPHEN R SHALOM

 Stephen R Shalom is director of the Gandhian Forum for Peace and Justice and is on the editorial board of *New Politics*. He is the author *of The United States and the Philippines: A study of neocolonialism, Imperial Alibis: Rationalizing US intervention after the Cold War*; and *Which Side Are You On?*

What are your thoughts about the sharp disagreements within the American Left about what US foreign policy should have been during the Syrian civil war?

I thought that basic leftist principles call for a concern and solidarity with democratic and progressive forces anywhere in the world. People in Syria are living under a vicious dictatorship and, during the enthusiasm of the Arab Spring, Syrians came out in the street looking to democratize their society. The first point for a leftist should have been sympathy with protesters because we believe in progressive change, democracy, ending dictatorships and ending the situation for people who are depressed and suffering. Unfortunately, there was a tendency of many sectors of the Left to look at Syria and say, 'well, because Assad is an enemy of the US government, and since we don't like the US government, the enemy of our enemy is our friend.' Therefore, anyone trying to overthrow the Syrian regime is involved in the terrible practice of regime change.

If you're a leftist, regime change should be one of your most important goals, because unless a country is run by a progressive socialist democratic regime, of course you should want it replaced. That doesn't mean I'm calling for the United States to replace the Syrian government, but for many leftists the mere fact that Assad was portrayed as anti-US was enough for people to side with him and to oppose all efforts at challenging his dictatorial rule.

What do you think US government foreign policy should have been in Syria?

The US government's largest intervention in Syria, contrary to the popular myth that it was seeking regime change, was to make sure the rebels didn't get the one weapon they needed in their uprising against Assad: anti-aircraft weaponry. We know the CIA was very carefully monitoring what kinds of weapons were coming in, and explicitly excluded anti-aircraft weapons. Had the United States stopped blocking those weapons from getting to the rebels, there was a chance the uprising would have won in the early days before the more secular democratic forces were overwhelmed by the jihadist groups who already had access to weapons.

Did this behavior remind you of the reaction of some leftists to the Green Revolution in Iran?

The Green Movement in 2009 was protesting a questionable election and the people who came out and protested in the street were reflecting progressive leftist values. But some on the Left said that because the regime in power was opposed to the US government they felt we should oppose the Green Movement and dismiss everything going on in Iran as a CIA plot and as an illegitimate attempt at regime change.

Given the finite amount of time we have each day, how much time do you think should be spent criticizing other leftists, and how much time should be allocated to opposing the Trump administration?

The problems in the Left are long-term because the Left isn't in power. The Left doesn't actually help or harm people, except at the margins right now. Trump hurts people tremendously every day, so I spend much more time opposing the Trump administration's policies than on intra-Left concerns. I do focus on trying to rid the Left of its bad tendencies as a future contribution to producing a Left that can be worthy of our respect and commitment.

Do you find it difficult in today's political discourse to articulate a viewpoint that doesn't embrace mainstream American exceptionalism, Trumpian nationalism or the Manichean Left's anti-imperial absolutism?

One of the reasons I'm happy to be working for *New Politics* is I think it tries and generally manages to express a view that has none of the defects of those three belief systems. You mentioned the Trump view and the Stalinist Left view, but there is also a problem with the liberal view. I'm encouraged when Alexandria Ocasio-Cortez can challenge the centrist democrats because I don't think Americans should embrace any of those positions.

Do you think some leftist critics of US foreign policy in Syria and Russia have been unfairly accused of being pro-Putin or pro-Assad?

There are certainly cases of people being accused of things that aren't warranted. But there also are leftists who deserve harsh criticism. There is a group called the White Helmets that goes and digs out buildings that have been bombed by the Assad and Russian air forces in Syria, and there are some on the Left who note that they have received funding from various Western forces and that therefore they are legitimate targets. So, when the White Helmets are bombed, you have some analysts saying, 'this is great, and this is what they deserve because they are supporting terrorists'. The people who are saying this are justifying war crimes. Saying it's justified to target the White Helmets, who are unarmed first responders, is just grotesque. It's been a basic principle of humanitarian law that you don't shoot medics.

A pro-German medic during World War Two may have had rotten views but it was still a war crime to intentionally target medics. The people taking the view that killing medics is acceptable are basically echoing the Assadist view that everyone against him is a terrorist and he has a right to massacre anyone. There are things about US foreign policy in eastern Europe that should be strongly condemned. The United States told Gorbachev in the late 1980s that if Germany was reunited, NATO would not be moved further east. But NATO has moved further east and this is a provocative move, and people who have criticized the expansion of NATO shouldn't be denounced as Putin puppets. On the other hand, people who insist there is no problem with what Russia is doing in eastern Ukraine or Crimea are adopting the 'enemy of my enemy is my friend' approach. When you look at Soviet leaders, at least the people they were trying to put the thumb on the scale for were people on the Left of their respective societies. So, if Soviet money went to any parties in western Europe, they were likely to be communist parties. But today, Putin's money goes to rightwing forces in Europe.

Do you think leftists are neglecting to pressure the Trump administration to lobby Russia for mutual reduction of nuclear weaponry?

I think some people in the Democratic Party have gotten so enthusiastic about Trump's political vulnerability in terms of his positions on Putin that they have overlooked that it has always been a progressive position that the nuclear arms race is a) very dangerous, b) very wasteful, and c) something that we should be trying to reverse.

Trump acts randomly based on his own ego, so it's hard to see a consistent foreign policy. If there is a consistent foreign policy position on an issue, it's a John Bolton intention, which is not good in any case. But it is good to reduce tensions on the Korean peninsula, even though one step in reducing the tensions involved Trump because he wanted to make himself look like he had been a great negotiator. Although Trump did it for narcissistic reasons, I think his decision to stop the annual joint US-South Korean exercises was correct because they are not helpful. The South Koreans want to see an end to the Korean War, the North Koreans wants to see an end to the Korean War, and progressives have always been saying that one way to reduce tensions on the Korean peninsula is to end this state of war. Let's see if we can do things that could build mutual confidence and, in turn, lead to a less militarized situation. I supported this position before Trump was elected, and I still support it. But I also believe there was nothing in the Trump platform to suggest he will lead us to a more peaceful world. Trump has increased military spending, pulled out of the Iran nuclear deal, making war with Iran much more likely, and aligned himself with the Far Right forces in Israel. These are not the policies of a peace candidate.

Could you talk about the consequences Trump's decision to pull out of the nuclear deal and apply sanctions on Iran will have for the pro-democracy and pro-reform movements in that country?

Those folks have always said, don't impose sanctions because they make things worse for us. They rationalize repression. Trump's decisions will strengthen the most reactionary forces in Iranian society and will make the democratic space in Iran that much smaller. ■

MEREDITH TAX

 Meredith Tax has been a prominent feminist voice and political activist since the late 1960s. She was the founding chair of the International PEN's Women Writers' Committee and the founding president of Women's World, a global free-speech network that opposes gender-based censorship. Among her books are *The Rising of the Women* and *Double Bind: the Muslim Right and The Anglo-American Left*.

You have written about the Rojava Revolution [a *de facto* autonomous region calling itself the Democratic Federation of Northern Syria]. How do supporters of the Rojava Revolution strike the right balance between being supportive of the people there, while remaining objective about reports of alleged human rights violations happening in that area?

There are good reasons to defend the people of Rojava. First, they fought ISIS more effectively than anybody else on the ground. Second, they are trying to do interesting things politically, particularly in terms of women. To me, they are a great source of new ideas and a possible magnet for progressives in the region and the rest of world as well. They are providing a type of political experimentation that we very much need because we don't have a lot of liberated areas in the world where this scale of political experimentation can be attempted.

We have to recognize Rojava is a work in progress: they are going to get some things wrong and we are going to disagree with them on certain points. I'm not interested in criticizing how anyone does stuff when they are in an existential fight for life against ISIS. You can voice criticisms, but the question is: how can you do this in a way that is productive?

The Rojava self-administration has been very open about letting human rights groups into its areas for inspections and not sending them with minders like dictators do. However, it's been very hard to get into these areas so it's very hard to assess what's going on except from the volunteers who go into these areas and then come out. I would say it's probable that some human rights violations have been committed, but they are not systemic. They would be particular to a person or a small brigade in most cases. The cantons are new and the people who are fighting are peasants, many of whom are just beginning to be educated; and violations always happen during war.

When human rights violations are committed, the self-administration tries to find the perpetrators and they put them on trial if they think they have done something wrong and this is all done in public. They have admitted to recruiting under-age fighters in the past, but they say this practice has stopped. They definitely practice conscription, but they also do not send people to the front lines who don't volunteer. People who are conscripted are used as domestic police or border guards. As far as I can tell, they are trying to address human rights violations. This is what is being said by the people I know who have served with them.

The main accusation that has been leveled by the Turkish state and Syrian opposition groups against the YPG/YPJ [the Kurdish 'People's Protection Units'] is ethnic cleansing. This is the accusation that was pushed by Amnesty International. There was a United Nations report that completely exonerated the Kurds of this charge. The report assesses all parties involved in the Syrian civil war. It accuses many of the groups of horrible abuses, such as using chemical weapons, bombing civilians, starvation tactics, summary executions, etc. The worst thing it says about the YPG/YPJ is that they have been accused of recruiting child soldiers (people under 18), detention under harsh conditions of a 17-year-old who was accused of working for ISIS, and confiscation of computers and cellphones in areas that were liberated from ISIS. I suspect they confiscated computers and cellphones to gather intelligence from them, not for personal use. If that's the worst that you could say about a party in this civil war, it's not that bad.

How should the Left respond to Far Right nationalist and religious movements around the world?

I don't think they have responded very well at all. I don't think they have a clue. The US Left, which is the part of the Left that I know most about, needs to understand what's going on in the world. There is a tendency now to view everything through the prism of domestic policy, and to only talk about fighting back against Donald Trump over domestic issues. While I think the domestic stuff is central, it can't be considered in isolation from global factors.

We live in a period of globalization. We live in a period when essentially fascist or proto-fascist forces, from Trump to rightwing forces in France and Germany and Holland and Russia, are coming together and coalescing as an international movement as they did in the 1930s. I think that is what we're seeing today. The people who are attracted to this movement in America certainly have their roots in White Supremacy, but that is true in Europe and other places as well. Unless you can see the global component of this and how these groups are supporting each other, you are going to be up a tree.

What are your thoughts about rightwing groups' claims that leftists are trying to suppress free speech on college campuses?

I think it's important to oppose giving a platform to people who are really Nazis and fascists and Klan people. However, if a Harvard idiot sociologist writes bad things about black people, he should be answered by arguments, not by closing him down. The whole tendency to try to shut down discussion is very bad for the Left. I think we need to distinguish between people who are just idiots or have a rightwing agenda, and fascists who are advocating the murder of certain groups and hate crimes. I'm not a free-speech absolutist because I think we do have to identify people who are encouraging hate crimes and try to prevent their word from spreading. I'm talking about people who literally say, 'go out and kill Muslims'.

Some commentators have said that identity politics has hurt the American Left. What are your thoughts on this topic?

I think it's important to think about the politics of identity in a complex way. Everybody has multiple identities. That's what intersectionality is all about. For example, I'm a Jew, I'm a leftist, I'm a feminist, I'm old. The problem isn't that people bring their identities into politics, it is when they have no politics other than their personal identity. That subjective approach leaves out people and it fragments movements. This is the kind of stuff that goes on at college campuses, according to some of the students I talk to. Identity politics can be very reductionist. For instance, the people who stress class politics often underestimate race; and in the US a lot of issues come down to race. And they also tend to leave out the oppression of women. I think such mechanical materialism has to be countered by a more holistic analysis that would attract people to a better way of doing politics.

Do you think that the commentators who claim democrats have to choose between supporting marginalized groups and promoting a class-based form of politics are offering a false choice?

Absolutely. You have to do both. You can't frame the working class solely in terms of white people. The working class is multi-racial and multi-ethnic. It holds a lot of immigrants, including ones that are undocumented. If you want class politics, you have to look at all that. You also have to deal with the contradictions within the working class. For example, the conflicting positions on the environment between some of the skilled workers and construction workers who supported the Keystone Pipeline and everybody else who wants their children to be able to breathe and survive. I also don't think we can leave climate change out of this topic. Climate change has to underpin everything that we do. We need to build a vast coalition that insists the planet isn't completely destroyed. ∎

MICHAEL WALZER

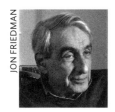

JON FRIEDMAN

Michael Walzer is one of the US's most prominent intellectuals and has co-edited the leftist magazine *Dissent* for several decades. He is the author of many books, including *Just and Unjust Wars* and *What it Means to be an American*.

What would you change about the international Left today?

Leftism is primarily a domestic politics. It has always been primarily a domestic politics. On domestic politics, we are pretty good. We favor greater equality, we favor welfare, we favor education, we favor State action on behalf of minorities, etc etc... Socialism at home is easy for the Left.

Internationally the Left has a very bad record. We have supported and apologized for tyrants and dictators and terrorists. We have failed to acknowledge the realities of the world we live in. Many European leftists opposed rearmament against the Nazis all through the 1930s. Appeasement was a policy of the English Right with a lot of support on the Left. We don't have a great record.

So, I want an international Left that is alert to the realities of the world and honest in confronting them. Let me use the example of the Iran nuclear agreement right now. The Iran deal [concluded by the Obama administration] is, I think, a good deal but people on the Left are supporting it who know absolutely nothing about it, who aren't interested in learning anything about it and who would support it even if everything the Republicans say about it were true... everything. That's an irresponsible Left, and there are too many leftists of that sort. One international Left organization that I belong to but won't name here circulated its statement in support of the Iran deal a month before the deal was signed, and a month before they knew any of the details of the deal. That is irresponsible. People on the Left have a great deal of difficulty imagining themselves in power and responsible for the wellbeing of their fellow citizens.

I want a responsible international Left with active, engaged citizens who are capable of recognizing the dangers of Nazism in the 1930s, the dangers of Stalinism in the 1930s and 1940s and the dangers of Islamism today. I want the international Left to criticize their government, but to also be aware of the dangerous world we live in. So, there is my soul exposed. I really hate those leftists who don't think about the wellbeing of the people they claim to be acting on behalf of.

The narrative that all US wars are fought for our freedoms is widespread in American culture. What will it take to foster a culture where Americans can look at their history and say, 'OK a couple of these wars were to protect our freedom, but most of them were not'?

We thought we were achieving that in the 1960s with the anti-war movement. We thought we were persuading Americans to look at an American war and say, 'no, it's wrong'. Obviously, we didn't do that. I was very engaged with the anti-war movement. In Cambridge, Massachusetts, we organized a group called the Cambridge Neighborhood Committee on Vietnam, which did SDS [Students for a Democratic Society]-type community organizing against the war. We forced a resolution on the ballot saying the city of Cambridge was opposed to the Vietnam War, and we got 40 per cent of the vote. We carried Harvard Square, but we lost all the ethnic and working-class neighborhoods in Cambridge.

A sociology graduate student did a study of the vote and found that the higher the value of your house, the higher the rent you paid, the more likely you were to vote against the Vietnam War. We were losing the working class, and one reason was that we marched around with Vietcong flags, we spelled America with a K, and their kids were fighting over there and our kids weren't. We were right to be against the war, but we opposed it in a way that alienated the very people we should have been trying to convince.

Do you think a better strategy could have convinced the working class to look more closely at American interventions?

You have to try to devise a strategy that evokes their patriotism against American crimes and I think that can be done. I think we could have done a much better job in the 1960s.

Does it worry you that the US military is the one group that is considered above scrutiny for a lot of people in this country?

You know, I wrote a book called *Just and Unjust Wars* that was adopted as a required West Point text by a group of Vietnam veterans who had been so shaken by the war that they wanted the cadets at West Point to read my book, which included a critique of the war. Because they are using my book, I sometimes lecture there, and I can tell you the officer corps of the United States Army is much more critical of US foreign policy than most Americans are.

They are critical of some of our wars. They are unhappy about the way we fight some of our wars because too many civilians are being killed. They hate the business of military contractors fighting alongside our soldiers. In Iraq we had as many military contractors as soldiers and the contractors were not subject to normal military discipline or justice. The military contractors killed people without any possibility of punishment.

I was once driven up to West Point by an Army colonel who said he had canceled his subscription to *The New Republic* because they had supported the Iraq War. The professional soldiers, because they have some sense of the honor of the military, are often critical about what politicians do with the army. They are committed to civilian control of the army, so they don't challenge the government, which I suppose is a good thing, but they are often critical of what politicians do.

Do you think there is a need to discern the difference between physical bravery and moral bravery when it comes to how

American citizens view the US soldier?

Most soldiers in most wars are kids and they have been told by their teachers and preachers and political leaders that the war they are going to be fighting in is just – and then they go, and they fight. It's the grown-ups who have a responsibility to oppose the war. You can't expect an 18-year-old kid in Vietnam to oppose the war. That was our responsibility.

Do you think progressives who supported the war in Afghanistan in the name of self-defense would also have to support Guatemalans, Nicaraguans and Cubans if they had used self-defense as a rationale for bombing American military installations because of US war crimes and US-backed terrorism in their respective countries?

Had the Vietnamese been able to manage an attack against American military installations here at home, that certainly would have been justified. It wouldn't have been terrorism, it would have been war. We were at war and when you go to war you have to accept your own vulnerability to attack. And after the Cuban invasion that we sponsored in the Bay of Pigs, I guess a Cuban response directed at the places where we were training Cuban insurgents would certainly have been justified.

You have talked a lot about progressive solidarity. How should progressives try to establish solidarity with progressive forces in other countries like the Rojava Kurds, the Organization of Women's Freedom in Iraq or the Local Coordination Committee in Syria?

You have to think first at the level of the Left and then what we want governments to do. At the level of the Left we should be providing ideological support; we should be providing political and moral support; we should be raising money for these groups to help fund them; if there was an international Left capable of this, we might be organizing an international brigade in some of these cases. Right now, the international brigades come from the Islamists, not the Left. Maybe Doctors Without Borders and Amnesty International are the contemporary international brigades for the Left. At least they defend life against people who are tyrants and terrorists who take life. That's what the Left should be about: to give whatever support it can give.

There has been a lot of talk about Islamophobia in the press. How should progressives approach freedom-of-speech issues that are being put to the test by Islamic terrorist attacks? How do we discern Islamophobia from legitimate critiques of Islam, which, like any religion, should not be above criticism?

Well, you just said it. We oppose nativists in France or Germany or the United States who hate immigrants. The know-nothings of the 1840s and 1850s hated Catholics and now we have similar kinds of campaigns against Muslims and we have to oppose those types of campaigns. At the same time, we have to be ready to criticize Islamic fanatics. I think it's no different from looking back to the 11th century and criticizing Christian Crusaders while acknowledging that Christianity isn't necessarily a crusading religion.

The jihadist interpretation of Islam is one possible interpretation of Islam, just as the Crusader interpretation of Christianity was one possible interpretation of Christianity. But there are other and better interpretations of both religions and those are the ones we should be supporting. ∎

BILL WEINBERG

Bill Weinberg is the editor of *CounterVortex* and contributing editor for *Native Americas,* for which he has won three awards from the Native American Journalists Association. He is the author of *Homage to the Chiapas: the new indigenous struggles in Mexico* and *War on Land: ecology and politics in Central America.*

What do you make of Noam Chomsky's critique of humanitarian intervention?

In terms of US intervention and the notion that 'our' hands are not clean because 'we' committed all these terrible war crimes in Iraq and 'we' backed the Turkish government when they were killing the Kurds and 'we' backed the Indonesian government when they were committing genocide in East Timor... Well, yes, all that is true. The insight behind this critique is that we have to understand there isn't any such thing as humanitarian intervention; I agree with Chomsky on that. The word 'humanitarian' is referring to motives and I don't believe there is any such thing as pure motives in the realm of statecraft, and especially in the realm of geopolitics. Any intervention the US takes, whatever propaganda or even self-delusion is employed, ultimately is going to be about protecting US strategic interests. Which ultimately means the interests of the US ruling class. To me, that's axiomatic; it goes without saying.

It isn't merely incidental that the US backed genocide in East Timor and then it was shedding all these crocodile tears about genocide in Kosovo and Bosnia. The 'but' is that, for starters, you have these idiots who go to the next level and flip reality on its head and say that in situations like Bosnia, Kosovo, Rwanda, Darfur or Syria there isn't any genocide or ethnic cleansing and the perpetrators are actually the victims and the victims are the aggressors. This is just repugnant bullshit.

But there is still another problem here, and that's making it all about US motives. This isn't the only question we should be grappling with. When the Kosovar Albanians say 'Look, we're under attack from the Serbs, our villages are being burnt down, we're being forced to flee up to the mountains, somebody help us,' I don't think they have to be immediately concerned about the motives of those who are coming to help them. They can be forgiven for having bigger concerns than that.

During the Kosovo intervention, there was the critique that the US was supporting Turkish atrocities against the Kurds at the same time they were bombing Serbia to supposedly protect the Kosovar Albanians.

But if your village has been burned down and you have been forced into a refugee camp across the border, what difference does it make to you that there are Kurds in Turkey that are in a similar situation? How does that lessen your plight? The Kosovars overwhelmingly approved of the NATO intervention, while some notable anti-Milošević Serbian opposition forces did not.

I supported the nonviolent civil resistance in Kosovo led by Ibrahim Rugova. The world would not recognize their movement. People in the United States displayed no interest in knowing this movement existed except for a few lonely voices like me and my friends in the War Resisters League (and Albanian-Americans, of course). This civil resistance came under unrelenting pressure, and that's when the hotheads prevailed and said, 'Fuck this nonviolence shit, we're going to form a guerrilla army'. Ibrahim Rugova's movement was sidelined and the KLA [Kosovo Liberation Army] sort of stole the show and they become part of this big imperial game where the Germans were backing them, and the Russians were backing the Serbs, and the whole thing got really, really, ugly really fast, and it ended with NATO intervention. I see this as a lesson in the criticality of solidarity. If the Left is going to oppose US military adventures, it has got to get serious about solidarity.

You've written movingly about the Rojava Kurds in northern Syria. Do you think we should arm the Syrian Kurds and the Iraqi Kurds? My worry is that if ISIS defeats them, they will have more weapons.

The obvious answer to that criticism is: if they aren't armed, their defeat is going to be more likely, isn't it? Look at the analogy of the Spanish Civil War. No-one on the Left was saying that we couldn't arm the Spanish Republic because if they lost the guns might fall into the hands of Fascists. Conservatives in the West were saying 'hands off Spain, it's not our fight', and were assailed for this by the Left! People on the Left were protesting that the Spanish Republic had been betrayed by the world.

And despite all the conspiracy theories, the US is still doing nothing against [Syrian dictator Bashar al-] Assad. All their efforts are directed against ISIS and al-Nusra. They aren't going after Assad at all.

What is the best way to support progressive elements like the Kurds in Syria?

Give them a voice, act like they exist! I've got friends who are organizing a book drive so they can send books to the university the Rojava Kurds have established in their territory, and that's great. But what's more important about it is the fact that by doing the book drive here, we are affirming that this social experiment in Syria actually exists and countering the stupid Left bullshit that all of the Syrian rebels are jihadists and therefore we should be backing Assad.

Who do you admire on the Left in America?

It's kind of a desert out there. I like the Marxist-Humanists Kevin Anderson and Peter Hudis. I like my buds in the Rojava Solidarity effort, and the followers of the late anarchist thinker Murray Bookchin. I like Meredith Tax, who I believe first coined the term 'imperial narcissism'. As for David Graeber, I have my criticisms of him, too, but he's supporting the Rojava Kurds and I appreciate that. Many of the voices that most inspire me are not on the American Left but are Left and secularist figures in what is called the 'Muslim world'. I'm talking about genuinely heroic figures such as Iraq's Houzan Mahmoud, Iran's Maryam Namazie and Algeria's Karima Bennoune and Marieme Helie Lucas. These women intransigently oppose Western imperialism and political Islam alike, and speak with the moral authority of those who have placed themselves at risk.

You identify as an anarchist. Can you speak about what anarchism means to you?

Some people call it democracy taken seriously. About 25 years ago, when I was more dogmatic, I would have considered myself an anarchist and a pacifist. So, anarchism to me was not about violence, it was about nonviolence. I wanted to see a nonviolent revolution: people putting themselves in harm's way to stop the war machine; and people dropping out of the system as a form of non-cooperation and eventually building a society based on decentralized co-operatives instead of centralized top-down structures. That's what anarchism meant to me. Now, a generation later, I still consider myself an anarchist, although I feel the need to add the caveat that I'm not a dogmatic one: I'm a pragmatic anarchist.

Most of the forces I'm supporting in Iraq and Syria are not anarchist, although the Rojava Kurds sort of are. They don't call themselves anarchists, but they are influenced by Murray Bookchin and his theory of 'Social Ecology', and they're trying to put in place anarchistic experiments like direct democracy and so on, so they are anarchist-leaning and anarchist-influenced. The Local Coordination Committees that started the Syrian revolution in 2011 are a mix. Some are more consciously leftwing than others – there are anarchists amongst them. But for the most part they are basically pro-democratic, pro-secular – and I will take that, that's good enough for me. In a dystopian context like this, that's damn good, and to continue to advocate that in the face of everything from the regime and the jihadists is heroic. The people I've supported in Iraq for the past 10 years now – the Organization of Women's Freedom in Iraq and the labor unions – they are feminist and Marxist and they are coming out of the

Marxist-Humanist tradition. They are followers of the Worker-Communist Party of Iraq, and the late theorist Hekmat Mansour, who founded its sibling organization, the Worker-Communist Party of Iran. And they are, by the way, very anti-imperialist in their politics. You don't have to pass my anarchist litmus test to get my support.

I no longer can call myself a pacifist. I grappled with it long and hard. The year of 1994 was the turnaround for me. Two things happened that year that cured me of my pacifism: the Zapatista revolution in Chiapas [Mexico] that I went down to and covered and experienced. And at the same time the siege of Sarajevo was going on in Bosnia. And I thought: 'You know it's kind of condescending for me to preach pacifist purity from my privileged position.' No-one was coming to burn down *my* village, so I couldn't deny other people the right to self-defense. I believe in the power of nonviolence, but I don't believe in turning it into an ossified dogma, and I do believe there are situations where getting your hands dirty in armed resistance is forced upon you and your choice is to do that or get exterminated.

Postscript by Bill Weinberg:

Since this interview took place in 2015, things have changed considerably in Syria – mostly for the worse. Thanks to massive Russian military intervention, Assad has reconquered nearly all of the country from the opposition and has arguably escalated the genocide. ISIS has been largely defeated, but through US military intervention, with the Rojava Kurds groomed as a proxy force by the Pentagon. In those areas (principally Idlib) still under the control of the Free Syrian Army (FSA) and other rebels, Turkey has stepped in to protect these opposition forces. Yet Turkey is intransigently opposed to the Rojava Kurds. So this has had the tragic effect of pitting the FSA against the Rojava Kurds.

I hope the Syrians can rebuild Arab-Kurdish solidarity against Assad, ISIS and the imperial powers alike. And I hope that progressives in the West can find some way to play a constructive role – which thus far they have overwhelmingly failed to do. ∎

STEPHEN ZUNES

 Stephen Zunes is professor of politics and international studies at the University of San Francisco. He is senior policy analyst for the Foreign Policy in Focus Project of the Institute for Policy Studies, principal editor of *Nonviolent Social Movements*, an associate editor of *Peace Review* and a contributing editor of *Tikkun*. He is the author of *Tinderbox: US Middle East Policy and the roots of terrorism* and co-author of *Western Sahara: War, nationalism and conflict irresolution*.

Do you think most of the US public is unaware of the darker aspects of their government's foreign-policy history?

Ordinary Americans are amazingly ignorant about international affairs, history, and even basic geography. With the possible exception of Australians – who can't do much harm beyond their borders – we're generally ranked last among the advanced industrialized countries when it comes to knowing and caring about different parts of the world. Our relative geographical isolation is just part of it, however.

I think the atomization you have in US culture plays a role. A lot of the things that have kept communities together have been broken down, so people try to reach for some kind of collective identity and Americanism, or whatever you want to call it, has become kind of a second religion – and people don't like to have their religious beliefs challenged.

To give you one interesting example, during the Lebanese civil war, the CIA – working through Saudi intelligence – tried to assassinate a Shi'a ayatollah by planting a bomb outside his mosque that killed 80 worshippers and bystanders on the road (the ayatollah himself actually escaped harm). It was the biggest car bombing in history at the time, so it was front-page news when it happened and, when it was revealed that the CIA was involved, it gained huge front-page headlines. In addition, Bob Woodward, in his book *Veil*, writes extensively about the CIA role in the car bombing, so it is well documented.

Despite this, when I have subsequently mentioned this in discussions of terrorism on US talk shows, people act like I'm some kind of crazy conspiracy theorist. It's kind of like Thomas Kuhn's book *The Structure of Scientific Revolutions*: if something doesn't fit into the prevailing paradigm, it doesn't exist. I can say Iranian-backed terrorism and finish my sentence, but if I say American-backed terrorism it's like, 'Hey, wait a minute!'

Another factor is that because people identify so much with the United States, they consider criticism of US policy as criticism against themselves, which is why ratings for Fox News – which tends to be uncritical of foreign intervention – go up during wartime. I remember way back during the Gulf War in 1991 when CNN reported that a US missile had gone through the door of an air-raid shelter and incinerated 600 civilians in Baghdad, there were protests against CNN outside of its headquarters – not because the protesters denied that it had happened, but because they thought it was unpatriotic during wartime to report it.

Could you speak about the success of nonviolent movements compared to the success of armed resistances groups in overthrowing dictatorial regimes and bringing democracy to different regions of the world?

There have been several empirical studies that have come out about the success of nonviolent movements. For instance, a study by Erica Chenoweth and Maria J Stephan that is featured in their book *How Civil Resistance Works*. Their original article was in *International Security*, which is the most prominent journal on security. They had their book published by Columbia University Press and it won a whole series of awards, including the 2012 American Political Science Association's Woodrow Wilson Foundation Award and the Grawemeyer Award for

Ideas Improving World Order. Those promoting the power of nonviolent action were once on the fringe, but a lot of the more recent work on nonviolent action comes out of quantitative analysis from very mainstream scholars. Just because something is empirically sound, however, doesn't mean it's going to be adopted as policy. However, this research and others like it do seem to indicate a shift in intellectual thinking.

Do you think there are times when US foreign intervention is justified?

In extreme circumstances like the genocide in Rwanda, I think one can make a case for humanitarian intervention. I think that would have been a case where getting peacekeepers on the ground in a hurry could have made a difference. While some people I respect believe US interventions in Kosovo and Libya were justified, I opposed both of those wars. In the case of Kosovo, I believe smarter diplomacy and preventative measures could have been utilized instead and, in the case of Libya, NATO went well beyond its mandate to protect civilians through enforcing a no-fly zone to effectively becoming the air force for rebel armies overthrowing the government. In both cases, the interventions ended up dramatically escalating the violence. ■

Latin America

MARIA TERESA BLANDON

Maria Teresa Blandon is a Nicaraguan feminist. She is the founder and director of the Central American program 'La Corriente', which works to strengthen women's movements in the region. It does this by conducting research, mobilizing mass campaigns and offering training in sexual and reproductive rights.

What are the main demands of the protesters in Nicaragua?

Since the beginning of the crisis – 18 April 2018 – a broad and heterogeneous movement of opposition to the regime of Daniel Ortega and Rosario Murillo has emerged. The consensus points to: demanding the end of the bloody repression; the search for a negotiated exit from the current government, including the advancement of elections for the beginning of 2019; and the punishment of those responsible for ordering and committing crimes against humanity.

What are the origins of the protests in Nicaragua?

The current crisis has multiple and diverse causes. However, I am interested in highlighting the following:

- The concession granted by the government of Ortega-Murillo to a Chinese millionaire for the supposed construction of an interoceanic canal that would directly affect fertile lands in the hands of the Nicaraguan peasantry.
- High levels of corruption, particularly in relation to the resources granted by Venezuelan co-operation, which were estimated at four million dollars.
- Absolute control of the electoral power, which ensured the successive electoral frauds in the election of municipal governments in 2008 and in the national elections of 2011.

- The monitoring and harassing of all organizations or demands that were independent or critical of the government and its policies.
- Open rejection of civil-society organizations and hostility towards the development co-operation agency that supports them.
- Systematic violation of women's human rights, particularly in the field of sexist violence and sexual and reproductive rights, including the absolute criminalization of abortion since 2007.
- Manipulation of religious narratives and rituals – particularly those of the Catholic Church.
- Monopoly of most media and harassment of journalists and independent media.
- Systematic violation of the rights of indigenous peoples in matters of protecting their territories and respecting their own forms of organization.
- Violation of the human rights of LGBTIQ people.

Can you give examples of human rights violations being carried out by the police and pro-Ortega forces?

The Ortega-Murillo regime organized paramilitary groups that, acting in conjunction with the National Police's anti-riot squad, murdered more than 400 people, according to the latest report of the Nicaraguan Association for Human Rights (ANPDH), and 322 according to the Inter-American Commission on Human Rights. The ANPDH also reports nearly 4,000 people injured, and more than 1,200 people kidnapped and disappeared.

The illegal capture of more than 500 people, humiliating treatment, torture and rape of political prisoners have also been documented by various human rights organizations, such as the Nicaraguan Center for Human Rights.

For thousands of Nicaraguans, participating in marches and other civic and peaceful actions to denounce the violation of rights and demand the departure of the Ortega-Murillo regime comes with a serious risk of being kidnapped, imprisoned, tortured or prosecuted. This is the case for more than 120 citizens currently facing trials lacking the minimum legality, where the judiciary, which is controlled by the regime, is prepared to accept false evidence provided by the police themselves and where the prosecutors are also loyal to the regime.

Has freedom of expression been curtailed by the Ortega government?

During the current crisis, the intimidation, threats and repression against journalists from independent media have been exacerbated and generalized; these have been documented by the Inter-American Press Society.

Angel Gahona, a journalist on the Caribbean coast, was killed by members of the National Police at the beginning of the crisis, when he was covering one of the many citizen mobilizations. To try to cover up the responsibility of the police, the judiciary falsely accused two young people of African descent who had already been convicted, despite evidence presented by the youths' defense which clearly indicated that they were not at the crime scene.

Through these months of crisis, independent media journalists have suffered all kinds of abuses by paramilitaries, police and FSLN mobs loyal to the regime. There are journalists who have been beaten by paramilitaries and police, and whose work teams have been robbed or destroyed. Other journalists are constantly being threatened and are victims of stigmatization campaigns.

What are the ideological divisions among the leftist groups that initially supported the Sandinistas after the overthrow of the Somoza dictatorship?

Since the mid-1990s, the Sandinista National Liberation Front [FSLN, which led the revolution against the Somoza dictatorship in 1979] has suffered successive splits that led to the founding of the Sandinista Renovation Movement (MRS) and later to the Sandinista Renewal Movement (the latter has already disappeared). Both the MRS and the Renewal Movement represented splits in the Sandinista party.

The MRS was expelled in the first case, for demanding a true democratization of the party after the electoral defeat of 1990. In the second case, they left after the FSLN leadership signed a pact with the Liberal Constitutionalist Party (PLC) – a party with Somoza traditions and a long history of corruption.

This pact allowed the main leader of the PLC to evade justice for the documented corruption when he was president in exchange for ensuring the return of Ortega to the presidency.

The MRS, in spite of the permanent campaign of stigmatization that the FSLN has launched against it, including the loss of its legal status as a party, has tirelessly struggled to denounce the violation of rights by the regime, and has also participated actively in what has been called 'civic insurrection'.

Other Left groups exist that are more incarnated in social movements such as the feminist movement and environmental groups. They are also part of this national movement that demands the exit of the Ortega-Murillo regime while also denouncing the structural causes of poverty and the discrimination against women, peasants and indigenous people.

What is the state of the feminist movement in Nicaragua?

The feminist movement has probably managed to sustain itself with greater articulation and visibility than any other social movement for more than a decade, despite the stigmatization that it has been subjected to by the Ortega-Murillo regime, which at some point tried to divide it and make it disappear using various mechanisms of pressure.

This movement has a presence throughout the national territory and has placed on the public agenda the complicity of the regime with sexist violence, its pact with conservative groups to justify the violation of sexual and reproductive rights and its complicity in violating the labor rights of women workers.

This self-convened movement has developed various strategies of influence with women from the countryside and the city, but also with young people. In the current crisis, it's participated in all possible ways and at all levels in the complaint, civic protest, and support for young people who are being persecuted by the regime. ∎

ANA MARIA COFINO

Ana Maria Cofino is a founder of the newspaper *La Cuerda* in Guatemala. She is an anthropologist, intellectual, feminist and activist for women's and indigenous rights, and an advocate for gender equality.

Are local, state and federal officials in Guatemala taking any steps to bring justice to victims of gender-based violence?

The actual government is incapable of building a gender politics. It is misogynistic and fundamentalist, so the few institutions for women that resulted from the Peace Treaties are now in the hands of who knows who. Maybe there are some exceptions, but in general the Guatemalan state is patriarchy-oriented. At local level, at least where I live, it's the social movement that is doing things.

Are local, state and federal officials taking any steps to prosecute the perpetrators of violence towards environmental, territorial and land-based human rights defenders?

Thanks to women's organizations, such as UNAMG and others, some judicial processes, like Sepur Zarco*, have gone through a hard road in search of justice. Some judges, like Yasmin Barrios and Miguel Angel Gálvez, are good. Even the Attorney General, Thelma Aldana, has an interest in femicides. But the whole

---

* During the 36-year-long Guatemalan civil war, indigenous women were systematically raped and enslaved by the military in a small community near the Sepur Zarco outpost. Between 2011 and 2016, 15 women survivors fought for justice at the country's highest court. The groundbreaking case resulted in the conviction of two former military officers for crimes against humanity and granted 18 reparation measures to the women survivors and their community.

system is against women's rights. It is said that Guatemala has a very strong and wise legislation but no application. Impunity levels are close to 90 per cent. Mainstream culture depicts human rights defenders as communists or problem makers – and that influences the perception people have of the issue.

Are any steps being taken at the federal level to address racist beliefs about indigenous communities in Guatemala?

Since the Peace Treaties, several institutions have been built to confront racism but, similar to what happens with women's rights, all these have fallen into the hands of unscrupulous and corrupt people who could not care less about the purposes for which they were created. The media and the official culture are racist and misogynist, at a very profound level.

What do you think are the main reasons for the high levels of economic inequality in your country?

There are historical reasons. The colonial system was mainly based on the exploitation of the indigenous workforce and on the natural resources. The original accumulation of wealth was based on that and the land. That is a structural reason, because all the economy and the process of capital accumulation rests on the shoulders of the work of the majorities. Only a small group is privileged with lands and power. They are the inheritors of ancient privileges and a culture of violence, racism and misogyny. Impunity, as a pillar of the Guatemalan society, is one of the main obstacles for justice in many ways.

What changes need to be made so more people will benefit from the Guatemalan economy?

Lots of changes need to be made in the superstructure (laws, language, culture and education) to transform the ways we think and act. But there also need to be structural changes in the distribution of resources and opportunities. People need to have a decent material basis, fair salaries, access to the means of production, and land.

Another form of social relations needs to be imagined,

designed and built. Injustice and impunity have to be eradicated. That is why people are talking about the *refundación del estado* (refounding of the state), which implies an inclusive form of social, economic and political organization. We feminists insist that a new society or a new form of living needs to eradicate violence and mainly patriarchal forms of relations and install care as a primordial issue: care for people and nature.

What are the origins of the gang violence in Guatemala?

The impoverishment of the population and the culture of violence have been imposed on society as the only way to stop the advance of alternative projects. The good results of this business for the army and other groups like narcos is also a reason for the gangs to exist and function.

Is gang violence in Guatemala linked to the country's brutal civil war?

I would say yes, in many ways, because during the 20th century violence became a way of living, a *modus vivendi*, a way of socializing and surviving. Also the war showed youngsters how to organize and to fight. The repressive politics, applied with US support, affected a big sector of the population. The forceful recruitment made many indigenous and ladino peasants change their beliefs and ways of being.

What do you think is the most productive way to address gang violence in Guatemala?

I think there are many steps to be taken, because it is a very complex problem. But one step would be changing young people's culture or opening other alternatives for them other than just consumerism or guns. Creating good enough conditions for them to practice other type of relations: art, creativeness, togetherness, working for the community and for others, are good steps to build a harmonious ambience. A new politics for education is necessary, especially with regard to talking about sexuality in school, which is forbidden.

Do you think the US government should offer reparations to Guatemala for its role in overthrowing the democratically elected government of Jacob Arbenz in 1954 and backing the side guilty of genocide during Guatemala's civil war?

Yes, of course. They should not only offer material reparations but also refrain from intruding in our political and economic issues. They should stop imposing the neoliberal model of development, which has proven to be damaging for our countries and peoples. ∎

ALDA FACIO

 Alda Facio is a Costa Rican feminist lawyer who founded the Caucus for Gender Justice in the International Criminal Court, becoming its first director. She has spent more than three decades advising governments and civil-society organizations on the implementation of the Convention on the Elimination of Discrimination Against Women (CEDAW). She is the author of *Equity or Equality for Women?*

In one of your articles you wrote about reimagining democracy not just through the electoral process but also in the home. How close do you think Costa Rica has come to reaching the goal where there isn't just democracy at the ballot box, but also in people's households?

I don't think a single country in the world has achieved democracy in the home. There is still so much to be done to understand equality between the sexes/genders – or equality between nations, for that matter. Although the idea that men are the head of the household has been legally abolished in most countries, the practice persists and needs to be challenged using CEDAW's Article 5, which obligates states to eliminate any tradition, practice or mentality based on the idea that one sex is superior. Without this change we cannot attain gender equality.

Is patriarchy and the normalization of violence against women more entrenched in some Latin American countries than others?

It's hard to say. The more undemocratic a country is, the less probable it is to make gains in women's rights compared with a democracy where all issues can be more openly talked about. However, even in countries undergoing very difficult situations, like Guatemala, Honduras, El Salvador and Nicaragua, the feminist movements are strong, and they are very clear on what their needs are. I wouldn't say feminist movements in Costa Rica are stronger than in other countries, or that we have achieved more than movements in other countries, it's just less dangerous to do the work we do in Costa Rica than it is to do the same work in Honduras, for example.

How much progress has Costa Rica made towards creating a sustainable economy that is both economically prosperous and environmentally sustainable?

The government has tried to make some changes to make the country less dependent on fossil fuels, but it hasn't done as much in other industries that are just as dangerous for the environment. For example, pineapple plantations are causing a lot of damage to both the land and the people, but it hasn't been addressed because these plantations serve the interests of US-based multinational corporations (Del Monte Foods, Dole, Chiquita). The plantations are huge, and they don't just exist in Costa Rica, they stretch all the way to Guatemala. It is called the Green Desert: everything dies wherever the plantations are because the companies fumigate too much and chop down all the other trees. When you fly over this area it looks very green, but it's a poisonous green.

Leftwing Latin American leaders such as Rafael Correa, Evo Morales and the late Hugo Chávez have been criticized from sections of the Left for not moving away from the extractivist model of development. What are some alternative strategies leftwing leaders can adopt that would meet the needs of the urban population while not ravaging areas where rural citizens and indigenous groups live?

First of all, the term 'Left' has no meaning in many countries because there are so many different segments of the Left. For instance, in Nicaragua many people are supporting President Daniel Ortega because he says he's leftist, even though he's a regular traditional dictator. There are many alternatives that could be pursued by leftwing leaders and movements. For example, there is no reason to have so many cars. There are too many cars in San José [Costa Rica's capital]. It's become impossible to go anywhere: it takes an hour to get to places when it used to take 15 minutes. From where I live to where my office was, it used to be about a 15-minute drive. Today, that same drive takes two to three hours because of the traffic jams and narrow streets.

What would you like to see change about US free-trade agreements with Latin American countries?

Trade policies could be implemented in a way that conveys an understanding of the necessities of the smaller nations. It's not fair to expect companies and entrepreneurs in a smaller country to be able to compete with companies that have the resources to produce so much more than them.

There is nothing free about free-trade agreements. Free-trade agreements just allow the United States to impose its will on smaller countries like it did on Central Americans with CAFTA (the Central American Free Trade Agreement). Central American countries, which had small and weak economies, were not allowed to protect any of their industries, but had to accept everything that was imported into the country by the United States. For example, CAFTA placed no limit on the number of used cars that are brought into Costa Rica from the United States. This is harming the environment and causing huge traffic jams.

It's very hard to put limits to protect the land if a US corporation wants to start mining. This leaves indigenous populations unprotected. It's ironic that the land that was given to indigenous groups, which was the least agricultural, is full of oil and minerals, so the corporations want to exploit these lands. And because of the free-trade agreements these lands can't really be protected.

The medicines the Costa Rican social-security system used to produce itself can no longer be produced because this is considered unfair competition with foreign pharmaceutical medicines. So, we have to buy these very expensive pharmaceutical medicines from abroad.

Do you worry about the popularity of the evangelical community influencing political decisions about gay marriage and a women's right to choose in Costa Rica?

I think they have too much power. They had more votes than any other party in the first round of the 2018 presidential elections. To have a relative unknown get the highest vote was very surprising, which made us realize we didn't understand the power of the evangelical church in Costa Rica. Evangelicals and the Catholic Church have the same positions on abortion, gay marriage and patriarchal family relations. The fact that they will support each other is very dangerous. ■

LINDA FARTHING

 Linda Farthing is a journalist, editor, director, film/ field producer and researcher based in La Paz, Bolivia, with more than 20 years of experience working in Latin America. She has co-authored three books with Benjamin Kohl: *Impasse in Bolivia, Evo's Bolivia* and *From the Mines to the Streets*.

Can you talk about the policies that Bolivian President Evo Morales has implemented which have successfully grown the middle class and reduced poverty?

The lynchpin of Evo Morales' success is built on the renegotiation of contracts with large multinational gas companies in 2006 that appropriated more of the profits for Bolivia. That money has been largely utilized to expand public infrastructure, which has had a stimulus effect on the rest of the economy. The Morales government also tripled the minimum wage, although there is no way to enforce this law, especially not in the informal economy, which makes up most of the workforce.

Conditional cash transfers, which have been adopted throughout Latin America and encompass programs such as payments to children who remain in school, have contributed to record drops of poverty in Bolivia and throughout the region, the most spectacular being in Brazil under Lula. For people who are very poor, even though the amount of money they receive is small, these welfare programs make a significant difference. The criticisms of this strategy are that it fails to create jobs, which is true. But the long-term plan is that these programs will reduce poverty enough that more children will be able to get an education, which will better equip them with the skills they need to get decent jobs in the future.

Morales' party MAS has co-opted the social movements in Bolivia. How has he accomplished this?

We are all a product of history, no matter what society we live in. The most direct historical link to what is happening in Bolivia today is 1952, when a revolution led by a middle-class party with a great deal of participation from *campesinos* and miners overthrew the mining oligarchy. Pretty soon after, the new government started working to control the campesino unions, for example by buying off union leadership. This was the model that the MAS largely adopted when it came to power in late 2005.

Protests in Bolivia, like elsewhere in the world, come in cycles. The Cochabamba water wars in 2000 over the privatization of the city's water supply started a new cycle that culminated with the election of Morales in late 2005. The MAS party had its origins in social-movement organizations, first in the coca growers' unions facing repression under the US War on Drugs. Once the MAS was in power, many leaders of the social movements moved into government positions, which meant that many of the social movements were weakened.

One of my biggest criticisms of the MAS is that it never really questioned the way politics is done in this country. They took a progressive, pro-indigenous movement and incorporated it into the existing neocolonial political system, which effectively has changed very little since MAS was elected. In some ways, politics as usual has gotten worse because the MAS has become such a hegemonic force after its resounding electoral win in 2014; there is very little viable opposition and certainly not from the Left.

Do you think current anti-Morales protests are misinterpreted by the Bolivian public and the US government because their political and historical context isn't considered?

A lot of what I heard from the people involved in these protests is what seems to me to be an ahistorical view of Bolivia. Many seem to forget how dependent Bolivia has been on extractivism in the past 500 years and that democratic governments have been the exception rather than the rule.

Can you describe the informal economy in Bolivia?

Bolivia has the largest informal economy in Latin America, with 46 per cent of the urban population in 2015 still working as day laborers, often men working in construction, and women selling small quantities of goods on the street. One of the accomplishments of the Morales government is that it has managed to reduce the level of informality – a very precarious and poorly paid form of work that is linked to extreme poverty around the world.

Has land reform been addressed by the Morales government?

To a certain extent, yes. You could argue that the heart of Latin America's challenges lies in the persistence in the concentration of control over the land, and the historical failure to address this issue. The Morales government implemented land reform in 2007, but it did so in a context where Bolivia's Congress was dominated by the right wing. The passage of the law fueled rebellion in the eastern part of the country, which has vast expanses of land controlled by the wealthy and was untouched by the land reform enacted after the 1952 revolution. In an effort to defang this rebellion, the Morales government ended up postponing the law's application. Large landowners quickly came up with strategies to divide their lands legally among family members or associates, so that they could maintain large estates, now mostly dedicated to soy production. Nonetheless, more land is now in the hands of indigenous peasant farmers than since the Spanish invasion, although most of the land that has been distributed was already in government control rather than expropriated from large landowners.

The land reform made a huge difference for many small-holders, even if it was unable to diminish elite power in eastern Bolivia. The implementation of the reform increasingly resulted in a preference for individual over collective land titles, which has its roots in how indigenous peoples used the lands before the Spaniards. However, in the highlands, concepts of holding collectively had less influence than in the lowlands because the 1953 Agrarian Reform granted individual land titles to indigenous peasants freed from the *haciendas* (large estates). Lowland indigenous groups have always tended to view land as forming their collective territory. So, while this new land reform redistributed more land than any effort since 1953, it failed to undertake any radical rethinking about how land ownership should function.

Can you talk about the harassment of some leftwing intellectuals and social movements by the Morales government?

In my view, a lot of my middle-class leftwing friends are playing into the hands of the Right because they have been unable to articulate a progressive, but realistic, leftwing alternative to this government. The Morales government has launched repression in the form of spurious lawsuits brought against its critics. For example, lawsuits were brought against Pablo Solon, who was UN Ambassador to the MAS government until 2011 when he left in protest over the construction of a road through an indigenous territory. Ever since, he has been active in denouncing extractivism in the country, most recently two planned mega-dams that will be destructive to lowland indigenous people and the natural environment. These types of action against critics have had a chilling effect, making people cautious about denouncing government politics.

Bolivia's current experience also parallels a lot of the obstacles to a functioning democracy found throughout Latin America. Just like the rest of the region, the lack of an independent judiciary in Bolivia, one capable of checking the President or Congress, has proven to be an enormous hindrance. This has combined with a general failure of Left governments to prioritize strengthening checks and balances, with the result that power has concentrated at the top, undermining popular participation.

Are there alternatives to the model Morales has adopted to redistribute resources to marginalized groups?

I contend that it's extremely unrealistic to think that any government could overcome 500 years of dependence on extraction in just 13 years. Morales' government argues it must keep expanding extractive projects to provide a higher level of services to pull Bolivia out of poverty. This merges with a traditional Left view that has been embraced by the government and argues that only industrialization which imitates that of northern countries can improve the country's future over the long term.

This means there has not been enough thought and economic analysis put into how to develop alternatives to the extractivist model. The fossil fuel-based economy is not viable over the long term for the survival of the planet. In Bolivia, under the rubric of industrialization, the government is investing huge amounts of money into infrastructure for the fossil-fuel industry that is not likely to be of much use in 60 or 70 years, or even sooner. Sadly, the government is investing in industrialization projects based on political rather than economic criteria, burdening the country with a new round of white-elephant projects that repeat the ones the country has always had. So there are sugar factories in places with insufficient sugar-cane production for the built capacity, or a fertilizer plant that was opened before the infrastructure to move the product to market was in place. ■

ANABEL HERNÁNDEZ

 Anabel Hernández is an award-winning investigative Mexican journalist and author who reports on the drug war in Mexico. She is the author of the book *Narcoland: The Mexican Druglords and their Godfathers,* which linked the Sinaloa Cartel to the Mexican government. She has received death threats and she and her family have been attacked by armed groups. None of these intimidation tactics have made Hernandez stop her fearless reporting.

Could you talk about how the amnesty given to the Sinaloa Cartel when Felipe Calderón's government was in power affected Mexican society?

The protection by the Mexican government of the Sinaloa Cartel has helped this crime organization become the most important drug-trafficking cartel in the world. Similar to Google, the cartel generates billions of dollars per year. Because of all this power, the Sinaloa Cartel is one of the deadliest organizations in Mexico. Its war with other cartels has generated thousands of deaths.

Why did the Mexican government give protection to the Sinaloa Cartel and its leader, Joaquin 'El Chapo' Guzman?

What I heard from people inside the government is that the Mexican government has this naïve idea that it's better to negotiate with one single cartel than six cartels. Now the government has to negotiate with six drug cartels and hundreds of criminal cells. That was the official justification for negotiating with Guzman, but I think the real reason was corruption. I know that many high-level officials in President

Calderon's government received a lot of money from the Cartel to have that protection.

Could you talk about the US Drug Enforcement Agency's relationship with the Sinaloa Cartel?

I received information through documents. These documents came from one criminal case in Chicago against one member of the Sinaloa Cartel. What these documents proved is that the DEA connected with Joaquin 'El Chapo' Guzman in 1998, and since that connection they have had an agreement. The agreement with Guzman and the Sinaloa Cartel was that if Guzman would help the DEA jail all his enemies then he would be given immunity and protection. This happened from 1998 until 2012. The last agreement I saw signed between the DEA and the Sinaloa Cartel was in 2012.

When I asked officials of the DEA why they made this deal, some cited the same reasons as the Mexican government: 'We think these guys are less bad and we think it's better to negotiate with one cartel than all the others.' I asked them what they thought would happen when it gave one cartel a monopoly on drug trafficking in the world. What is their plan? I was never able to get answers to this question.

Can you comment about the human rights violations that members of Mexico's military and police have been accused of in their handling of the 'war on drugs'?

Many of the officials in these institutions are very corrupt. These corrupt officials have no respect for human rights. The federal police have been one of the most corrupt institutions in Mexico for decades. This isn't just because they receive money from the drug cartels; it's because members of the federal police kidnap children, rape women and traffic other kinds of illegal products. The federal police often operate like a cartel. They have been involved in very dramatic cases of human rights violations. Documents prove the federal police were involved in the kidnapping of 43 missing students in Iguala Guerrero. The federal police also were involved in two massacres in Michoacan, and another massacre in Oaxaca where six teachers were murdered, apparently by federal police, to dissolve a protest.

The Mexican army was never very close to society, but President Calderón decided to take them out of the battalions and put them on the streets, where they have committed many human rights violations. The army has been accused of many disappearances and murders in Mexico.

What would be a smarter way to address drug trafficking and drug use in the United States and Mexico than the current 'war on drugs'?

I don't really think the Mexican government, the US government, and the international community have been interested in combating these criminal organizations. The only serious way to address this problem is to confiscate the cartels' money. The problem is money made from trafficking these illegal drugs has penetrated the legal market and it's a very important part of the money that is in the world.

This money isn't just in the pocket of Chapo Guzman; this money is in Wall Street; this money is in the most important offshore accounts; this money is in the most important banks in the world. I think there is a lot of hypocrisy in the international community because they said, 'Yes, let's go destroy the cartels in Mexico', but they really don't want to destroy their businesses in their own countries.

It's true that there is a lot of corruption in Mexico and because of this corruption we have these big drug cartels. But these cartels can move tons of cocaine every day into other countries because corruption also exists in these countries. Also, no-one is really fighting against the market of the consumers of drugs or the laundering of money. These are steps that not only the Mexican government but also the international community has to take to try and break down these cartels that are growing more dangerous. These cartels often don't just traffic drugs, they also traffic people, including children, child pornography and illegal products. The world sees the consequences of the drugs, but they don't want to see the other awful crimes these gangs (that exist in other countries as well) commit in the world.

How do you stop the penetration of drug money into the legal economy?

The Mexican government and Mexican societies aren't able to resolve this problem by themselves because this problem is an international problem. That is the big issue for me. The international community has been very indifferent to this problem and there has been a lot of hypocrisy. They have said 'Mexican people are savage, and they are killing each other', and 'Mexico is a terrible failed state', but the international community doesn't really want to see how they are involved in these murders in Mexico. The international community is taking the money and consuming the drugs that are the results of the bloodshed in Mexico.

The cartels in Mexico are the biggest suppliers of drugs in the world, so we all have the same problem. The international community must decide what the international policy against the drug cartels will be. The United Nations must take a strong position on what is to be done about this problem and they must tackle their own corruption.

How hard is it right now to be a journalist in Mexico because of the pressure exerted by cartels and Mexican institutions?

It's a terrible situation for journalists and human rights defenders in Mexico. This has existed since Felipe Calderón's presidency. Mexico is one of the most dangerous places in the world to be a journalist. Many of the crimes committed against journalists were committed by local or federal government officials. We have stronger journalists today in Mexico. I consider myself to be part of a generation of journalists who have decided to break the silence and work for society. A free press in Mexico is extremely important. People must be given accurate information to be able to make their own decisions. Mexican journalists today are caught in between two fires: on one side is a very corrupt government that doesn't like it when you tell the truth about corruption; and on the other side you have the cartels who want the media silenced. No-one is protecting journalists.

The international community has made efforts to protect journalists, but these efforts have failed because the Mexican government is murdering journalists. It is a very difficult situation. You must have strong convictions that journalism is necessary for society because you could be murdered tomorrow. This is not about Anabel Hernández or any other journalist; this is about society. I'm not fighting for my right to have information, I'm fighting for the right of the people to have accurate information, so they can make their own decisions. I really think that good journalists in the world can change the stories of our countries. ∎

ROSALVA AÍDA HERNÁNDEZ CASTILLO

 Rosalva Aída Hernandez Castillo is an anthropologist and activist who lived for 15 years in the Chiapas region of Mexico. She has worked on indigenous women's initiatives in Chiapas, on the human rights of Guatemalan refugees in Mexico and has done field work with African immigrants in the south of Spain. Her books include *Multiple Injustices, Histories and Stories from Chiapas in Southern Mexico* and *Demanding Justice and Security.*

What is the Mexican government's stance on indigenous autonomy?

We see a double standard on autonomy. There is a national law (Article 2 of the Mexican Constitution) that recognizes indigenous rights to their own legal and political systems. However, the application of this legal recognition finds its limit when indigenous people demand their rights to the management of their natural resources or the control over their territories against mega-projects. In these contexts, there has been a criminalization of indigenous peoples, ignoring the legal framework that recognizes their autonomic rights.

In the case of the Zapatista movement, the government broke the peace accords (signed in 1996 and known as the San Andres Peace Accords) and isolated indigenous Zapatista regions. They also militarized all the communities around the Zapatista regions. After the Zapatista uprising of 1994, the National Zapatista Liberation Army took control over an important area of the southern state of the Chiapas where the communities were supporting their struggle. The Zapatistas decided to build their own education and health systems in this area that is under the control of the indigenous communities.

The regions under their control are called Rebel Zapatista Autonomous Municipalities (known in Spanish as Municipios Autónomos Rebeldes Zapatistas, or by the acronym MAREZ). These communities don't receive any money from the federal government. They are subsistent, growing coffee and other subsistence crops while creating a co-operative economic system. The farmers have their own plots of land where they grow their own crops, but there are also communal lands. It's a very interesting experiment of an autonomous society.

They have rewritten textbooks for school from an anti-colonial perspective, which helped the people recover the knowledge of their elders and learn about the history of colonialism and its impact on indigenous communities. The education system uses local knowledge to build the context of the textbooks. Children learn not only inside the school, but also by growing corn with the farmers, and by learning from the local artisans how to produce textiles. The communities also have their own local justice system. This system is based on the idea of not punishing a person who commits a crime but reintegrating that person into society and understanding the reasons for their behavior. Rather than 'ancestral justices', they are historical products that assimilate the principles and epistemologies of indigenous peoples, but also the principle of the Zapatista revolutionary laws. It's a conciliatory system. What is interesting to me, as a feminist, is that they adhere to conciliatory principles of the indigenous law, and they have made laws that deal with gender justice. For example, they have something called a Women's Revolutionary Law that includes the specific rights of women.

Can you talk about other non-Zapatista regions that are experimenting with autonomous solutions to local problems?

In Guerrero, there is an indigenous justice system that has been very important politically to confront criminal violence and to show an example of autonomic solutions to local problems. In 1998, several indigenous communities in the state of Guerrero came together to form the Regional Community System for Public Security, Justice and Re-education, represented in turn by the Regional Co-ordinator of Community Authorities. This organization, known as CRAC, created a network of support among primarily indigenous communities, but also Afro-Mexicans and rural mestizos, people with different cultural traditions, political genealogies, and languages, who had each developed their own strategies for the resolution of conflicts, and created a common system of self-protection and justice.

The 400 communities that participate in the CRAC use this justice system that is conciliatory and involves re-education of people who have committed crimes. This system, which was previously respected by the State Government, and legally recognized by the State Constitution (Article 701), is now being criminalized. The main reason for this is that the indigenous authorities are confronting organized crime. There are areas where organized crime has corrupted state officials, so the officials are using the laws to criminalize indigenous authorities.

One important example is the Nestora Salgado case. She was the first indigenous woman to be a commander in the CRAC in the village of Olinalá in Guerrero. The villagers had been working as a community police under the legal recognition of Article 2 of the Mexican Constitution, and Article 701 of the State Constitution, that recognize indigenous people's rights to their own legal and political systems. This legal system had been able to solve local problems like stealing cows and chickens, and incidents of domestic violence. But organized crime has been trying to infiltrate and work in indigenous territories through kidnapping young men and women for slave work and using men and women in their prostitution and pornography businesses.

The indigenous authorities have had to confront this new kind of violence. Nestora Salgado discovered a network of child pornography that was entering the community. She and other local authorities caught the criminals – who were foreign to the community – and they brought them before their justice system.

The girls who were kidnapped were rescued. The girls were sent for re-education with other indigenous families outside their communities at the request of their families.

The criminals were taken into an Indigenous Justice House (Casa de Justicia Indígena), where they were doing community work. They were forced to attend a re-education system with the elders of the community. While this happened, the governor of Guerrero told Nestora that CRAC was not allowed to detain these kinds of criminals because this was a federal crime. They told her the criminals must be freed because it wasn't under their jurisdiction. She said no because they were in indigenous territory and had already been judged, and therefore would not be freed. The governor warned of consequences for her if she didn't free the criminals. She refused and a week later the federal army came into the Justice House of this community and freed everyone, while capturing the legal community authorities, including Nestora, and charging them with kidnapping.

Nestora was taken to a high-security prison in Mexico and isolated for two years. There were 11 indigenous authorities from the village that were imprisoned. Nestora was considered a political prisoner by Amnesty International and I was involved in her case. I did an expert witness report for the defense to prove that she was not kidnapping people, she was doing justice through the indigenous justice system. This is just one example of how autonomous districts are being criminalized when they confront local interests. I can't prove that this pornography network was linked to the State Government. But the fact that they wanted to free the criminals and criminalize the indigenous authorities gives you an idea what is behind this criminalization of autonomous regions.

How did the Zapatista movement help promote indigenous feminism in Mexico?

When the Zapatista uprising started in December 1994, the base communities of the movement created the Women's Revolutionary Law. Indigenous groups played a primary role in crafting this law or charter. These women discussed their main problems as women before they created the Women's Revolutionary Charter. This charter makes demands to both the Mexican State and the community authorities. For example, the charter includes the right to participate in government bodies, inherit land, choose who they want to marry (many indigenous communities still support arranged marriages), and the right to have as many kids as they want. Many of these rights were already included in the Mexican Constitution, but they were struggling to change customary laws, so this charter included demands of their own local authorities.

The charter also included a health system that was specific to their local knowledge: It required midwives to be recognized by the Mexican State. It also marked the first time a revolutionary movement in Latin America included the demands of women as a central part of their political agenda. The charter was a powerful symbol for indigenous women throughout Mexico and in other areas of Latin America. This led indigenous women in other communities to start demanding gender rights in their communities. What these women are demanding is not the right to reject their culture: they are saying: 'We want the right to our culture, but at the same time we want to be included on how culture is defined in our communities.' It's an interesting double dialogue because indigenous women are demanding from the State the right to autonomy, self-determination and control over their local resources. But they are also demanding that their indigenous local authorities give them the right to decide how to use natural resources, participate in government bodies and make their own decisions on issues that affect their lives. They are combining communal rights with their own gender rights. And these double rights have been appropriated by indigenous women throughout Mexico who are using the Women's Revolutionary Charter as a tool to demand their own rights as women within their indigenous communities. ∎

THEA RIOFRANCOS

 Thea Riofrancos is assistant professor of political science at Providence College, Rhode Island, US. Her areas of expertise include Ecuador, radical democracy, environmental politics, social movements and protest, and participatory institutions. Her work has been published in *Dissent, NACLA Report on The Americas* and *In These Times.*

Do you think President Lenin Moreno will be able to repair the damage that exists between indigenous groups and the Left in Ecuador because of former president Rafael Correa's embrace of extractivist policies?

I don't think the conflict will abate because the Ecuadorian government relies on oil and mining projects for its revenue. So as long as those extractive projects continue – there are two large-scale mines being developed that overlap with indigenous territory, and the President has announced opening bids for new oil exploration in the southern Amazon – the potential for conflict continues. However, whether that potential for conflict will be actualized depends on the organizational strength of indigenous and environmental movements (their framing, messaging, etc).

Moreno has opened dialogue with the indigenous movement and he is a less polarizing figure than Rafael Correa. Moreno has also rolled back some of the economic regulations implemented by the former president. He has been re-adopting some of the aspects of a more neoliberal approach to the economy. He has privatized and deregulated some sectors and implemented some austerity measures. He is doing this partly because Ecuador is in a budget and debt crisis due to the crash in oil prices. The oil prices are not nearly at the level they were when Correa was president, so a major source of revenue for the Ecuadorian state has shrunk. Moreno justifies his policies as a way to solve these economic difficulties. Austerity and privatization are the neoliberal way to deal with a budget deficit and a debt crisis, but they are not always the best way to deal with these problems. There are other heterodox and Keynesian approaches to dealing with deficits and debt.

How do these mining and oil projects violate indigenous and environmental rights?

These rights exist in the Ecuadorian Constitution and internationally in various international conventions that Ecuador is a party to. In 1998, Ecuador ratified ILO Convention 169, which relates to the rights of indigenous people in a host of areas. One of the key rights this convention is often invoked to support and defend is the right to free prior and informed consultation. What this means is if indigenous peoples' territory and environment will be affected by extractive projects (oil, mining, etc) or other mega-development projects, they must be consulted prior to the development of those projects with full information.

There are also national rights that are even more expansive than the rights in ILO-169. The 2008 Ecuadorian Constitution – one of the most progressive constitutions in the world (which was written under the Correa government) – recognizes the right for indigenous people to be consulted prior to development projects on their territory. In addition, it recognizes the right of any community (indigenous or otherwise) whose environment might be affected by a public-policy decision to receive an environmental consultation.

There is also a chapter in the constitution that is devoted to the rights of nature. It considers nature to be worthy of legal rights – which can be claimed and defended by humans because nature can't walk up to the courts and defend its rights. But the subject is the right of nature to be healthy and to reproduce itself over time. This is another set of rights that can be seen as being violated by extractive projects like mountaintop removal mining.

In the preamble of the Constitution it states that Ecuador should be oriented to *buen vivir* (living well) or, in Kichwa, *sumak kawsay*. This isn't a specific right, but it is part of the framing of the Constitution itself. This means Ecuador should feature an alternative to development geared towards economic growth, and instead should see development as communities and people and nature living well. This overarching framework of the Constitution is something activists refer to when they protest extractive projects.

Why did President Correa continue the extractivist model of development instead of adopting this alternative model that is championed in the preamble of the Constitution?

From an outside perspective, I can see how this looked like a change in Correa's position. I think Correa did become more hardened in his support for extractivism over time, but that hardening happened as a result of the polarization of conflict. Correa started to defend extraction more as his government faced increased opposition from indigenous groups. But Correa never changed his position on extraction because he was never against extraction. There were certain areas of the country where he opposed extraction earlier in his presidency, but he was never that critical or skeptical of extraction more generally. Correa's position on extraction aligned with a long tradition of the Left in Latin America. He believed extraction should be carried out, but the revenue from extraction should not all go to foreign companies. He believed the economic benefits that accrue from the sales of these commodities on the global market should benefit Ecuadorians more than they have historically.

Correa's position was kind of a diluted form of what had been many of the social movements' positions on resource extraction in the 1990s and early 2000s. These groups, which included indigenous and labor movements, were not anti-extraction. They wanted the nationalization of natural resources. They wanted natural resources to be nationally owned instead of privately owned or foreign-owned. They also wanted resources to be democratically administered so they could benefit everyone.

What happened when Correa was elected was not that his position changed, but that social movements changed their positions in response to his pro-extraction policies. They began to embrace a more militant, environmental-rights position that was mainly anti-extraction. There were indigenous groups in the Amazon who militantly opposed oil extraction in their territories prior to Correa's election, but the national and highland indigenous federations embraced the idea of nationalizing natural resources.

Correa's political party started out as a very diverse group of leftwing voices that included indigenous rights advocates and environmental activists. But several of the pro-indigenous rights and environmental activists in his administration left after Correa's party began to embrace a more pro-extraction agenda. Even though his coalition narrowed, there was still a diversity of opinions in his administration later in his presidency. During my field work in Ecuador from 2011 to 2016, I talked to many bureaucrats, including high-ranking bureaucrats, who thought Correa was being too pro-extraction and was too swiftly getting contracts from extraction firms and undermining indigenous rights.

How did Correa rationalize his pro-extraction policies?

Correa justified his policies on leftist grounds. He saw them as a way to fight poverty and bring equitable development to the country. Indigenous communities are certainly among the communities that saw poverty levels decrease. Poverty rates declined, and income equality improved during Correa's presidency. There were other developmental indicators – like health, nutrition, education and sanitation – that also improved while he was president. Those are clear benefits from any perspective, Left or otherwise. But ecosystems, economic and cultural livelihoods were disrupted and threatened by extractive projects approved by the Correa government in places they had previously not existed.

Is there a war of ideas between those pushing for a traditional, Correa-style leftist model of development and those championing a more solidarity-based, sustainable economy?

Under Correa's tenure in office that was certainly an axis of conflict. There was a split within the Left. Some had a vision of development that relied on resource extraction to address unsatisfied social needs: income levels, poverty, inequality and housing. The people who held this view saw the State as a key actor in propelling that type of development.

There is another view that is against resource extraction as the basis for economic and social development. People who hold this view champion a vision that is more localist and sees a more harmonious relationship between people and nature. They offer alternatives to extraction such as local agriculture, ecotourism, and local artisanal and handicraft production. The problem with these solutions is that they may not generate enough revenue or income to support the whole nation. They also don't address the masses of people that live in urban areas. The promoters of these visions are often focusing on local development in rural areas because that is where most of the extraction takes place. It's not clear how the anti-extraction movement's alternative visions will meet the needs of low-income and working-class Ecuadorians living in cities. ■

GILDA MARÍA RIVERA SIERRA

 Gilda María Rivera Sierra is a psychologist and founder of the Centro de Derechos de Mujeres (Women's Rights Center) in Honduras. She has worked for decades on human rights and women's rights issues.

What are the origins of gang violence in Honduras? Is the US foreign policy of the 1980s partially to blame for the gangs that have grown in power in El Salvador, Honduras and Guatemala?

These are multifactorial problems, but historical exclusion, inequalities, lack of opportunities, the plunder and robbery of our resources and goods, injustices, the contexts of violence and militarization in which young people are born and grow: all these are favorable spaces for the reproduction of violence and emergence of gangs. Obviously, the United States has a high responsibility for this problem. It has strengthened militarization in our country. US policies have encouraged transnational companies to settle in our territory and appropriate our resources, which encourages corruption. People become servile commodities to the market and to consumption. Values such as solidarity and respect for difference do not matter: what is important is to promote individualism, consumption, etc.

The US gave arms to the Nicaraguan counter-revolution and promoted the installation of the same in Honduran territory. Honduran territory was occupied militarily in the 1980s by the Nicaraguan counter-revolution, the US Army, paramilitary groups and organized crime, and drug traffickers. And all this happened in the midst of a culture that promotes the use of weapons as the way to resolve conflicts and differences. Sad but real.

Should the US stop providing military assistance to the Honduran government because of the connection between drug traffickers and some police officers and politicians in their country?

Of course, it should have a long time ago. There is a link between senior leaders of the national police, the army and politicians at all levels with organized crime and drug trafficking. They are part of international networks of corruption and drug trafficking.

Why is Honduras a dangerous place for human rights defenders, especially those who are working to protect territory, land or the environment?

Because of the weak institutions that exist in the country, which is managed according to the interests of economic power groups, politicians and the transnationals that achieve concessions of territories, water and mines under dirty contracts, disrespecting Convention 169 of the ILO. The transnationals expel the communities from their territories and obviously the communities resist because if they lose that territory (water, forests, lands), they lose their lives. There are more and more organized communities in the country, defending their goods and land.

Would you describe violence against women in Honduras as femicide?

There is no deep investigation in this regard. The impunity rate in violent deaths of women is higher than 90 per cent. Some of these cases are femicides because they seek to kill and eliminate women because they are women, and because of the hatred that this society has built against women. Other cases do not come to mind due to a lack of research. In other cases, they appear to be accidents that did not seek to eliminate the woman – she was in the line of fire by chance. Investigative mechanisms of justice are needed to investigate, but the authorities are not interested.

What can be done to reduce violence against women in Honduras?

It's only by the will of the State and the authorities in charge. In this country, decision-makers at all levels have no commitment to the human rights of women; they believe that they can decide on our bodies and our lives and in this they are also supported by the churches, both Catholic and evangelical.

We have a legal framework that recognizes violence against women, but it doesn't apply – its spirit is not respected. They consider that there are worse crimes to attend to. In addition, there is the complicity of a society that silences, reproduces and hides the violence that women live with, such as sexual violence and rape, and which turns girls into mothers/girls, but that does not matter. The important thing is the double standard that establishes that any type of abortion is illegal and penalized to respect the supposed life of an embryo.

Could you discuss the conflicts between energy and extractive industries and communities in Honduras?

The main interest of the extractivist industry is to appropriate the water, the forests, the territories to guarantee their extractivist project even though it affects an entire community. The communities line up to defend themselves, to defend what belongs to them, what has been theirs and their ancestors' for hundreds of years, because they know that without it their lives are gone.

What policies must be adopted to reduce poverty and income inequality?

Fair and dignified jobs, state budgets that guarantee access to health rights, education, housing and so on to the population. Distributive policies attached to the recognition of historical inequalities; fiscal policies that invest in the population, fight corruption, change the system of government and eliminate corruption.

How can feminist values lead to a decline in violence in Honduras and help make the country more inclusive?

Feminists are trying. People can support us by promoting programs to strengthen the leadership of women defenders of their territories. ∎

JUSLENE TYRESIAS

 Juslene Tyresias is one of the dynamic leaders of Haiti's Peasant Movement of Papaye (MPP). Founded in 1973, this is one of the largest and oldest peasant organizations in Haiti. It advocates for food sovereignty, improved quality for peasant farmers, climate justice and environmental sustainability.

What does MPP promote as an alternative to export-oriented industrial agriculture, and why is it a better option for rural Haitians?

MPP works with groups that focus on family farming. We work with La Via Campesina at an international level. La Via Campesina supports food sovereignty and family farming as an alternative to industrial agriculture that can save the environment. Family farming promotes healthy and sufficient food production that can feed the world's population.

Could you tell me about your reforestation and agricultural work?

A key axis for the MPP is the protection of the environment. In this respect, we work on training the workers on: soil and water conservation; integrated water management; production and planting of forest and fruit trees; maintenance of nurseries; grafting techniques; production, selection and conservation of seeds; production and application of natural fertilizers and natural insecticides; and transformation of agricultural products. We work on the question of sustainable agriculture.

Could you explain your organization's programs on raising livestock and providing healthcare for all farm workers?

MPP has a small livestock program that includes goats, poultry, fish, pigs and bees. In this program, we train people on the techniques of production, food and maintenance. We work on the promotion of agricultural production co-operatives as well as development and credit co-operatives.

Regarding healthcare, MPP has a health center based on disease prevention and training people in the production of natural medicines based on medicinal plants. We also form groups of midwives to accompany pregnant women in rural areas.

Can you explain why structural-adjustment programs don't meet the needs of rural Haitians?

This is because these programs haven't taken into account the reality and context of rural areas. There is also discrimination between citizens living in rural and urban areas. This is explained by the absence of the decentralized institutions of the State, lack of access to basic services in rural areas: health, nutrition, education, communication, etc.

Do you feel that the Haitian government is open to hearing some of the solutions MPP proposes for the farmers in its country?

The government works in favor of the capitalist system, and also the leaders of the big countries. In this situation the solutions we propose for farmers are not part of the government's program to change the social and economic reality of the Haitian people. ∎

GINA VARGAS

 Gina Vargas is a Peruvan feminist sociologist and co-founder of Centro de la Mujer Peruana Flora Tristan, which was created in 1979 to address the structural causes that restrict women's citizenship and/or affect its exercise. She was one of 1,000 women nominated for the Nobel Peace Prize in 2006. She is the author of *The Women's Movement in Peru* and *Feminist Movements in Latin America: between hope and disenchantment*.

Can you talk about what is being done on the ground to oppose gender-based violence in Peru?

Gender-based violence is a problem in the whole of Latin America. In Peru, there are strong social movements in all the regions opposing gender-based violence. I think male power is being weakened in Peru, but at the same time femicide in the country has increased dramatically.

Why has violence against women increased in Peru?

Women are speaking out more publicly against gender-based violence, and the masculine idea of women as supporting the house and men as the sole breadwinner is diminishing because more women are working, and more women have autonomy over their own lives. I think some men are feeling threatened by this cultural change, which is leading to this rise in violence.

Is there any co-ordination between women's rights groups and indigenous groups in Peru?

We are a plural, multiethnic society in Peru. Indigenous groups mostly live in the countryside, while women's rights groups are mostly based in urban areas. Indigenous groups have been historically treated very badly in Peru, so forming coalitions isn't easy. But these coalitions are very important because indigenous women are organizing themselves in defense of their territory and their rights. The agenda of the feminist movement in Peru has been strongly influenced by the demands of indigenous women.

Is it especially difficult for indigenous women because they are confronting the double problem of defending their indigenous territories while also standing up for their rights as women?

Absolutely. Indigenous women are not only discriminated against because they are women, but also because they are Indian. They have a double struggle. They fight to get society and the feminist movement to recognize racism, but at the same time they struggle to get their rights as women recognized in their own communities. These communities are more concerned with fighting against extractivism and defending their territories, and many do not address women's discrimination. Peru is a racist society, which makes the situation even more difficult for indigenous women. Afro-Peruvian women are also organizing to oppose racism in society and inside the feminist movement. The black feminist movement is expanding the feminist agenda with the fight against racism.

Does it come down to the idea that there shouldn't be a hierarchy of rights?

We must defend collective rights for indigenous communities over their lands, culture and territories. The decisions in indigenous communities are mostly made in a collective way, not an individual way. The collective rights to land and territory are central both for indigenous people and for feminists. The problem is when some of these collective rights go against the rights of women. The dialogue between collective rights and women's rights is a process. It's important to know that there are feminist indigenous movements, and feminist movements for people of African descent not only in Peru, but in all of Latin America and the Spanish Caribbean.

You have talked about the three streams of women – working women, poor women and feminists – in Peru. Do you think this theory still applies?

There many more streams in Peru today: women from the countryside, Afro-Peruvian women, lesbian women, transsexual women. They have all expanded the streams and the agendas of feminisms.

Has the LGBTQ community become involved with feminist movements in Peru?

The gay rights movement began to organize with the support of feminists. Then the lesbian feminist movement began to grow, opening up more feminist agendas. There were lesbian women involved in the gay rights movement that started at about the same time that the feminist movement started to grow in this country. We are very supportive of them organizing themselves.

Later, this movement began to organize more frequently as an LGBTQ movement. There is a very strong movement today for recognition of transsexuals because this isn't accepted by everyone in Peruvian society. It's facing especially strong opposition from both the Catholic and evangelical churches. One priest from an evangelical church who is in Parliament said the Bible condemns homosexuality, especially among women. He said if you see two lesbians kissing, you can kill them.

What changes need to happen to help more people gain a foothold in the Peruvian economy?

We need structural changes in our country. Capitalism is causing the acquisition of people's lands and territories. The capitalist Peruvian economy discriminates against most of the population. There needs to be much more redistribution among the population. Limits need to be put on the profits of transnational corporations. Mining companies and other extractivist corporations can no longer be allowed to go into the Amazon, or to the Andean indigenous territory, or to other indigenous territories, and destroy their natural resources (lakes and lagoons) and their communities. The government must prevent them from engaging in activities that cause so much pollution and damage. They must enact laws that ensure the protection of the environment.

Can you talk about how gender equality will be better for males in the long run?

It would be much more democratic. Men and women will gain from it, and society can change, introducing, for example, the 'Ethic of Care' as a responsibility of governments and societies. Young men in Peru are more interested in feminism – they are supporting our struggles and organizing themselves. They are much more open than the older male generation. Some men are beginning to review how they can change their way of being masculine.

What would you like to see changed about the Left in Peru?

The Left gives too much weight to electoral democracy, and does not pay enough attention to the other dimensions of democracy, such as changes in daily life. There are some new movements, such as Nuevo Perú, that declare themselves as feminist, ecologist, anti-racist and pro-sexual diversity. This party's candidate Veronika Mendoza received 20 per cent of the vote in the last presidential election. ■

ALEJANDRO VELASCO

 Alejandro Velasco is associate professor of modern Latin American history at New York University. He is also executive editor of the North American Congress on Latin America (NACLA). He is the author of *Barrio Rising: Urban popular politics and the making of modern Venezuela*.

Is there a leftwing party in Venezuela that isn't entangled with pro-Maduro and pro-Chávez groups?

There is a group called Marea Socialista. They are against Chavista institutionalization and what President Nicolas Maduro is doing. They don't have support from either party. Alternatives to Chavista and Maduro-style governance get swallowed up in the vortex of polarization.

Are there parts of Hugo Chávez's legacy that should be preserved?

What should be preserved and upheld about Chavismo's legacy is nothing that has been institutionalized. It's the impulse of recognizing and highlighting the needs of sectors of the population that have been largely left out. For instance, the urban land committees helped channel demands for housing, particularly in the urban sector. These committees were most effective when they emerged organically through already-existing mechanisms of community organization that made them legitimate in the eyes of the community. The problem was that these models were systematized and reproduced by the government without recognizing why they were effective in the first place.

Did Chávez's popularity decline over time?

His popularity was around 60 per cent when he died; now it's at about 40 per cent. President Maduro tried to peg his political power to the image of Chávez. But as things started to go sour there has been an unofficial and official attempt to divorce himself from Chávez's legacy. This has been a strategic move to place all the blame happening in Venezuela today on Chávez. The fact remains that people still nostalgically refer to Chávez not just because of material benefits, but because of what he rhetorically inspired.

Do you think Chávez would have accepted losing an election?

That question belies how Chávez could have his cake and eat it too. On the one hand he could accept electoral defeat, but he would use mechanisms that could keep his people in power. For instance, when the opposition won the super mayor position in Caracas, he created a super, super mayor position. This is how Chávez often dealt with losing elections. The only time that Chavismo as a movement outright stole an election was during the Constituent Assembly Vote in July 2017.

So much of Chávez's mystique is related to when he accepted defeat after his coup failed in 1992. This created a great aura of accountability because people said that person is honest, even if they didn't agree with how he wanted to attain power. I think that became a fundamental part of his self-image. In this way he was similar to Fidel Castro. Castro was a master at turning a defeat into a victory. I think Chávez would have recognized his defeat in a presidential election, but he would have found a way to turn that electoral defeat into a political victory

What are your thoughts on the comparisons between Chávez and US President Donald Trump by the US media?

It's a facile comparison. They are making comparisons in terms of style, and not taking into context the content and mission differences. The major difference is the purpose for which you use those bombastic speeches. Trump's efforts are about curtailing popular will. Trump relies on a mobilized minority that he can deploy in effective ways because of the US electoral process. Chávez's purpose was a social-justice dimension that sought to privilege the rights for people who had long been sidelined. If you look at the history of Latin America, most major social gains have come under populist rulers as opposed to during the rule of social democratic governments. These gains included improvements in labor laws, welfare and women's voting rights.

What are the policies being promoted by the conservative opposition in Venezuela?

The center of gravity in the opposition is abroad in the exile community. They have a significant amount of weight to throw around, but they view the domestic conservative opposition as completely inefficient, which is true. If the conservative opposition were to come to power, the exile community would have a lot of influence over its decisions. The exile community has a neoliberal agenda and a 'let's go back to the 1990s' mentality. This would be problematic because it wouldn't be inclusive of communities that were left out of the political process before Chávez.

Does lack of talk about economic rights in the mainstream US media distort the narrative of some of the political struggles happening in Latin American countries, including Venezuela?

There is a myth in the US that social class is a choice and not a policy. There is this idea that if you want to be better off, you just work harder. This is the myth of meritocracy and it goes against the idea of social and economic rights. In Latin America, there is a widespread belief in social and economic rights. People know inequality isn't a function of hard work, it's a result of institutions and laws put into place to help an elite group of people. The tension populists bring to light is how these institutions are a barrier to economic and social rights. They are perceived as being set up to preserve the wealth of the elites, which is the opposite of how they are viewed in the United States.

Is there a bottom-up model such as the Zapatistas in Mexico or the landless movement in Brazil that could provide a better

alternative than Chávez-style populist leaders who have a tendency to consolidate their own power?

I think there is an alternative, but I don't think they can come to power without significant social conflict. Privileged elites are not going to give up their privilege willingly. The question any society has to ask itself is: how do you justify the curtailment of some rights in the pursuit of a more socially just landscape? If a nation's elites are unwilling to cede any of their privilege, it becomes a zero-sum game. ■

South and East Asia

JAVED ANAND

 Javed Anand is a journalist and civil-rights activist whose columns appear regularly in *The Indian Express*. He is currently National Convener for Indian Muslims for Secular Democracy (IMSD), and he co-edited the magazine *Communalism Combat* with his wife Teesta Setalvad. The magazine, which suspended publication in November 2012 for financial reasons, had consistently opposed majoritarian and minority communalism.

Is it hard to oppose Muslim minority communalism in India while also opposing the majoritarian communalism being promoted by the Hindu Right?

There is no doubt that, given the demography of India, Hindu communalism constitutes a real threat. But I fight communalism because of what it stands for, so I oppose communalism irrespective of the religious pretext to the word. Since Hindu communalism feeds on Muslim communalism, and Muslim communalism feeds on Hindu communalism, communalism practiced by both sides must be opposed in a principled manner.

Can you talk about the arrests and reforms in Saudi Arabia, which you addressed in an article for the *Indian Express*?

Saudi Arabia was the only country in the world where women were not allowed to drive until the government reversed their decision. In June 2018 there was a royal decree that women would be allowed to drive. More recently, the Saudi Crown Prince Mohammed bin Salman announced that Saudi Arabia would return to 'moderate Islam' open to 'all religions and all countries'. If Saudi Arabia were to change its foreign policy of the past three decades of supporting extremists and terrorists, that would be a welcome thing.

The talk of Saudi Arabia 'returning' to a moderate Islam raises questions because Saudi Arabia has never embraced a moderate form of Islam. It has always been wedded to a highly intolerant brand of Islam championed by Ibn Abd al-Wahhab in the 18th century. Wahhab provided religious legitimacy to the House of Saud, while the Saudis provided political cover for state power to impose Wahhabism on the country's population. The supposed 'return' to moderate Islam makes no sense because it never existed. It would of course be a most welcome thing were Saudi Arabia to turn, not return, towards a moderate Islam.

Should the triple *talaq* [a form of instant divorce], *halala* [a form of Islamic remarriage] and polygamy be opposed because they are un-Qur'anic, or because they go against some of the principles of secular democracy? Can you do both at the same time?

I believe you can do both. The practice of the triple talaq is inhuman and certainly isn't prescribed in the Qur'an. It is also unconstitutional because the Constitution talks about the right to equality and non-discrimination. The triple talaq is transparently discriminatory. I'm sad to say the five-man [Indian] Supreme Court that deliberated on this matter simply 'set aside' the practice. It's unfortunate the judges didn't talk about the extremely discriminatory manner of the triple talaq. What was apparently happening in India was that men were repeatedly pronouncing the triple talaq and then remarrying their wives. The Qur'an says you can only divorce your wife twice. After this you are prohibited from marrying her again, unless she happens to marry another man, the marriage is consummated and either the second husband happens to die, or there is a divorce in the normal course of things.

In a complete distortion of this Qur'anic provision, halala has become a sort of sex trade in the name of Islam in India, Pakistan and elsewhere in the Muslim world. A divorced woman is subjected to a one-night stand with another man (often the cleric offers his own 'sexual service') following which she is promptly divorced and only thus becoming legitimate (halal) to her former husband. Halala is a shameful practice and completely un-Qur'anic and degrading for women. It is unconstitutional as well.

Indian Muslims for Secular Democracy (IMSD), the organization I represent, believes there should also be a complete ban on polygamy in India. It is unconstitutional, and in the modern context, it is un-Qur'anic as well.

You have written about how female Muslims are no longer allowing male Muslims to claim a monopoly over how the Qur'an should be interpreted. Do you see this as a positive development in India and other countries with large Muslim populations?

This became a hot issue in 2011-12 when a Muslim women's organization gave a petition to the Mumbai High Court to seek equal access to the grave of a very famous Sufi Saint called Haji Ali, which receives tens of thousands of daily visitors. The petition said the women had been allowed equal access to the tomb until 2011-12, when the Haji Ali Dargah Trust decided this went against Islam's teachings. The court ruled that women deserve the same access as men to the inner sanctorum; the trustees appealed to the Supreme Court; and the Supreme Court upheld the High Court's verdict. Many of us feel that the Trust's initial decision to bar women from gaining access to the inner sanctum of the shrine was the result of the influence of growing Wahhabism in India.

Do you think the Qur'an should be viewed as a human-made document that can be challenged?

The Qur'an should be read contextually, in the context of the time and culture in which it emerged. The Qur'an was progressive in many ways compared to the culture that existed at the time. The late Moroccan Islamic scholar Fatima Mernissi argued that, if the Qur'an had not made some compromises with the patriarchal culture that existed at the time, there would have been a civil war. Author Asma Barlas, in her book *Believing Women in Islam:*

Unreading patriarchal interpretations of the Qur'an, argues: 'The Qur'an recognizes men as the locus of power and authority in actually existing patriarchies. However, recognizing the existence of patriarchy, or addressing one, is not the same as advocating it.' It is up to Muslims today to push for an Islam that supports gender equality. ∎

JIEUN BAEK

 Jieun Baek is the author of *North Korea's Hidden Revolution: how the information underground is transforming a closed society.* Her book features interviews with North Korean defectors from all walks of life who highlight how a network of citizens have taken amazing risks by circulating banned materials such as foreign films, clothing, medication, television shows, soap operas, books and encyclopedias into the country. She is a Belford Center Fellow at Harvard Kennedy School of Government.

Do you worry that tensions between the US and North Korean governments might lead to a decrease in coverage of internal dissent in North Korea?

It's always a good concern to have. Nuclear weapons will always top the media cycle. One worry I have is that stories about high-profile North Korean defectors will drown out the stories of ordinary defectors.

Can you talk about the black-market economy in North Korea?

The black market is oversimplified. When people say the black-market economy, they are actually talking about the grey economy. The bulk of this economy started during the famine in the 1990s. Markets sprang up in services as diverse as food, prostitution and used clothing. People became dependent on the money made from the market during this period. These market activities proliferated because of the complete breakdown of the public distribution system. Kim [Jong Un, North Korea's leader] wanted to regulate the markets because he couldn't shut them down. Today, much of the market activity is legalized. There are regulations, taxes and permits in place. But, of course, there is a black market for contraband.

Has bribing state officials to turn a blind eye to illegal market practices become a normal part of the market system in North Korea?

Bribing officials is seen by most people as a business cost. Many officials don't make much money, so it's practical for them to turn a blind eye in exchange for a bribe. This system of bribery permeates all levels of North Korean society. There are some bad sides to the system because there are different levels of corruption. For instance, a high-level form of corruption is when political elites demand money-laundering activities, because money laundering plays a substantial role in North Korea's economy.

Would it be true to say that even a government as oppressive as Kim Jong Un's regime can't squelch the power of human curiosity?

The consumption of foreign information materials has been happening for a long time. The famine represented a time of chaos. Sheer desperation will drive people to do things they normally won't do. There was a complete breakdown of social normality and societal infrastructure. This is when media and media devices started coming through China. This is also when there was a big influx of DVDs and movies from across the border. This has created a greater demand from people for information from outside North Korea. Many North Koreans were moving in and out of China at the time because the border wasn't as strictly controlled back then. China wasn't as powerful as it has become today, but it was still more prosperous than North Korea. These citizens were exposed to another country where people had a higher standard of living than in their own country.

Could you describe the roles of groups involved in smuggling information into North Korea?

Some of these are one- or two-people operations. Some use the media to bring attention to their work, while others work under the radar. Many of them are run by people in South Korea. These are civilian-run initiatives to send information to North Korea to fulfill a demand among its civilians. Both President George W Bush and Barack Obama's administrations have supported information campaigns in North Korea through the State Department's Bureau of Democracy, Human Rights and Labor (DRL). There haven't been many signals that the Trump administration is supporting these information campaigns, although recently the DRL put out a notice of funding opportunities for information access projects in North Korea.

Should the Trump administration use these information campaigns rather than solely focusing on sanctions and military threats?

I'm very much in favor of information campaigns. Sanctions and information campaigns need to be pursued in concert with each other. I support military exercises, sanctions and direct talks with the North Korean regime, but information campaigns are much cheaper, and are valuable in a different way. The sanctions are meant to bring the North Korean regime to the negotiating table on the issue of freezing and rolling back their nuclear program, but information campaigns give people more options to decide for themselves about whether they are supportive of the regime. The financial costs of the information campaign are minimal when compared to other means like direct talks with the North Korean government.

Do the defectors you have spoken with cite different reasons for their opposition to Kim Jong Un's regime?

Yes. When people first defect from North Korea, they don't always know the terminology to use to express their grievances. But once defectors settle in their new countries, they learn the terminology to articulate their displeasure with the regime. Their grievances range from political to economic to social. A high percentage of the women defectors report domestic abuse. There are extraordinary amounts of abuse against women in

North Korea because it's a traditional society where women don't have much of a voice.

Is citizen discontentment with the government growing inside North Korea?

It's difficult to survey people inside the country. However, given the stories I have seen, this seems to be the case. More people know what's happening in the outside world, and this is naturally bringing people to understand that their oppressive circumstances are not necessary. People are becoming more enlightened and more aware of their circumstances – especially in comparison to other people's experiences across the world.

Regime change often doesn't happen until the military and security forces refuse to co-operate with the regime. Do you think there is a chance of this happening in North Korea? Could this sort of non-cooperation spark a flowering of democracy?

We have seen the most unlikely people defect from North Korea. The late Hwang Jang-yop defected from the country in 1997 for political reasons. No-one expected this because he is credited with crafting the North Korean ideology of *juche* or self-reliance. After Hwang sought refuge in a South Korean embassy in Beijing, he expressed disillusionment with North Korean-style communism and said he felt that it had betrayed socialism. Other high-level North Koreans have defected. Thae Yong-ho was North Korea's deputy ambassador to the United Kingdom when he defected to South Korea in 2016. You see border guards defecting. These people were thought to be devout believers in the regime.

Once people match private and public preferences, you see political change. I don't think North Korea is immune to this. We see so many defectors who say they bowed to statues and did other perfunctory duties not because they believed in what they were doing, but for self-preservation. I think we will see more officials defect from the regime. Will enough people defect to create political change? We shall see. ∎

PERVEZ HOODBHOY

 Pervez Hoodbhoy is Pakistan's pre-eminent intellectual. He is one of South Asia's leading nuclear physicists carrying out research into quantum field theory and particle phenomenology. He has been a staunch opponent of Islamism and his many articles and television documentaries have made a lasting impact on debate about education, Islam, and secularism in his country.

Do you think the veiling of women is mostly an autonomous choice made by Muslim women in Pakistan, or is it something they have been forced to do because of pressure from Islamists? What do you think sparked the rise of veiling, which was not at all common earlier in Pakistan's history?

Pressure from Islamists to cover up is a fact in all Muslim countries. The extent varies from culture to culture. It is strongest in Saudi Arabia. Turkey was relaxed about it until Erdoğan took over. As for Pakistan, it was once a non-issue, but the pressure has steadily increased from the 1980s onward as people have become more pious.

Veiling has multiple reasons. Some of my women students have confessed to me that it's peer pressure. Increasing conservatism has led to uncovered faces being regarded as sinful. Once upon a time there was no burqa on campus except for the odd one here or there. But today most women at this university – where I have taught for 45 years – are either in burqa or hijab. I have no way of associating names with these covered-up entities. Exams become a real problem, as do thesis defenses.

What are some of the key elements that drive young Pakistani men to embrace radical Islamic beliefs?

The curriculum, textbooks, teachers and exams all act to create an us-versus-them mentality. And then there's the electronic and print media – all privately owned – which drips with piety and with conspiracy theories that attribute all our ills to external actors. It seizes upon their every fault and then multiplies them by ten. So a mindset is created wherein young people imagine that they, and Islam, are beset with enemies lurking behind every bush. There's no introspection, no explanation for what we did wrong. Ask a student why East Pakistan broke off to become Bangladesh and you'll get the pat answer: it was a Hindu conspiracy. He won't know of the genocide we carried out there in 1971.

Attributing religious extremism to poverty or lack of education was once a popular explanation. But local newspapers have countless stories of young religious killers from affluent middle-class families. Several had studied at Pakistan's best-known public and private institutions.

What do you think are some of the modern-day challenges in Pakistani society?

In a nutshell: a) unbridled population growth; b) terrorism; and, c) slowness of cultural modernization. Population control is the most urgent. Demographers estimate the expected number of Pakistanis in 2030 at a staggering 258 million, which must be compared with 28 million in 1947 as well as the current population of 200 million. This growth is the second highest among major Muslim countries in the world. Even if we miraculously acquire the most perfect of political systems, it looks impossible to provide most Pakistanis with employment, education, food, housing, electricity, water and a clean environment. Short of renting another planet, there is no way that the constraints of fixed land and water can be overcome. This emergency situation demands that population planning must be reinstated and contraceptives be made freely available.

In your view, why is religious extremism so rampant in Pakistan?

I don't think that there is just one single reason. Think of a bomb, a fairly complex object. To make one you need the explosive, oxidizer, trigger, shell, etc. None can do the job alone. The same goes for religious extremism in Pakistan. One ingredient is to be found in the country's genesis. Pakistan was brought into being on the slogan that Muslims simply cannot live alongside Hindus. This wove religion into the national fabric. But, in spite of this, and rampant poverty and illiteracy, Pakistan could have moved in a progressive, secular direction. This appeared to be happening in the first couple of decades after independence, but then other factors kicked in. In the 1980s, all progressive trends were rapidly reversed once Pakistan and the United States created an international jihad consortium for fighting against the Soviet Union. That was a turning point.

What is your position on the US drone strikes in Pakistan? Should these be considered war crimes or are they a better solution than having the Pakistani army invade the tribal regions? Is there an alternative solution that hasn't been tried?

Drones are bad. They are programmed, self-propelled, semi-autonomous killing machines. Some guy sitting in Nevada makes the decision of who shall live and who shall die in some Pakistani or Afghan village. Who do drones actually kill? Sometimes we are sure, as when the Taliban or al-Qaeda celebrates the martyrdom of its commanders. But in the absence of independent information, one cannot say for sure. The Pakistan Army, or the CIA, have relatively better information but they too can only guess the damage and fatalities. Their local spies often have their own axes to grind and tribal scores to settle. So, it's grey stuff.

Having expressed my distaste for drones, I have to admit that drones are effective and the best of bad choices. They have prevented large formations of Taliban fighters from acting in concert. And the relatively precise nature of this technology means that killing of innocents is considerably less than it could otherwise be. Now that Pakistan has finally gone to war against the 'bad' Taliban (relations with the 'good' Taliban are these days slightly less chummy too) it uses fighter aircraft and artillery which devastates entire villages.

Although the Left is marginal in Pakistan, can you talk about some of its achievements in your country's history? What explains its present insignificance on the national scene?

About 30-40 years ago – in other words, before General Zia-ul-Haq took over – the Pakistani Left was relatively strong, or strong relative to today. That Left should be credited with unionizing industrial and railway workers, helping peasants organize against powerful landlords, inspiring Pakistan's minority provinces to demand their rights, and setting standards of writing and journalism. But, even at its peak during the 1970s, the Left could not muster even a fraction of the street power of the Islamic or mainstream parties.

One of the most hated words in Pakistan is 'liberal' because that is seen as un-Islamic. But you can't be leftwing without being liberal. By liberal I mean one who values freedom of expression, personal and political. A liberal says you have the right to dress and wear the clothes of your personal choice. Also, liberals support allowing people to eat and drink as they will, and pray often or never, or choose a religion or not have one at all. In the liberal mind, covering a woman's face or head should be entirely optional. Women can have jobs if they want and should not be forced to stay at home. So, every leftist is a liberal by this definition, but all liberals are not leftists.

Do you think Islamophobia has become a problematic term because of the way it has been used by Islamists? Would anti-Muslim bigotry be a more accurate term to describe the cases of discrimination against Muslims in Western countries like the United States?

I know many Pakistani Muslims who have migrated to the United States and have become normal, decent citizens. They have their circles of American friends and enjoy a healthy relationship with the society they have chosen to become part of. I don't hear them complaining of discrimination or Islamophobia. When there is discrimination – which is surely possible – they can go to court and reasonably expect justice.

Unfortunately, I also know far too many other Pakistanis

who secretly despise Americans – especially blacks and Latinos – and think of them as lascivious, debauched and immoral. Their children, though born and brought up as US citizens, are tutored into separating 'us' from 'them'. So, whenever I hear about incidents such as the Times Square bomber, or the San Bernardino killers, I can immediately understand where that hatred came from.

Unless they start behaving differently, Muslims will wear out the welcome they once had in the West – like the welcome I had as a student in the 1970s. Beyond a shadow of doubt, Muslims in the West have much more liberty and rights than they would have in Saudi Arabia or, for that matter, in any Muslim country. Surely it is high time that those who complain of Islamophobia become more sensitive to the plight of religious minorities in their respective countries of origin. ■

MALALAI JOYA

Malalai Joya is an Afghan human and women's rights activist who began her activism while teaching at a secret school for girls under the Taliban regime. She was elected to the Afghan parliament but expelled in 2007 for criticizing the presence in the government of human rights abusers and warlords. She has faced repeated attempts on her life. She is the author of *Raising my Voice* and *A Woman Among Warlords*.

What was your main reason for opposing the US invasion of Afghanistan?

Western and local media want the US invasion to be portrayed as if they are angels of peace and liberation for our people, but I will never be tired of saying that no nation can donate liberation to another nation. Liberation should be achieved in a country by the people themselves, and our people can fight the medieval Taliban and their jihadi brothers-in-creed as long as they are not supported and armed by their foreign masters who shamelessly try to portray themselves as friends of the Afghan people.

What can progressives in other parts of the world do to help you and other like-minded Afghans in your quest to create an Afghanistan where equal rights for women are accepted by most of the population?

I don't expect anything from Western governments. They advance their own agendas, which ruthlessly sacrifice the Afghan people. Their friends in Afghanistan are mostly those who should be prosecuted for their wrongdoing against my people. But the peace-loving and progressive people of the West are quite different from their governments, in my view. They can pressure their governments to stop supporting the Afghan criminal fundamentalists who are in power today. They can pressure their governments to stop pouring billions of dollars into the hands of those responsible for unforgivable crimes and the destruction of Afghanistan.

How important a role does women's and girls' education have in broadening the influence women have in Afghan society?

As I have always said, the key to Afghan women's freedom is education and knowledge. The only way in which women can achieve their rights is through self-education, unity and struggle. It is the historical responsibility of all progressives and peace-loving people to come forward and support this cause. I feel it is my responsibility to struggle for women's rights.

What would you consider a true democracy in Afghanistan?

A society where men and women are equal and free to work side by side for justice, progress and prosperity. A country where the virus of ignorance, misogyny and intolerance is uprooted. Awareness, unity and an uncompromising struggle is the only option available to achieve this goal. ▪

HARSH KAPOOR

Harsh Kapoor is the founder and editor of sacw.net – South Asia Citizens Web. He is an ardent defender of secular democracy and freedom of speech. He also is a critic of religious fundamentalism and a champion of the right to individual choice and autonomy.

Do you see Indian prime minister Narendra Modi as part of a worldwide trend of countries electing nationalist leaders?

There is an international phenomenon of nationalistic and xenophobic forces that are on the rise in the world. There are some similarities, but also considerable local and national differences that have driven Modi's rise. The big common element is creating perceptions of being anti-elite, anti-cosmopolitan, anti-intellectual and nationalist. The local and national conditions are crucial here, though there are international factors, the most notable being the role of India's influential rightwing diaspora in the UK and the US.

What can the Left do to counter the nationalist appeal of figures like Modi? What mistakes have the Indian Left made that have allowed Modi and his Hindu nationalist party to gain such a foothold in Indian politics?

The long rise of the Far Right in India has had its own reasons and history can't simply be attributed to the failures of the Left. The language of Modi is pretty crude, sharp, brazen, uneducated talk – often intended as a spectacle of shock and awe – and that appeals to an impatient public. He is a new type of authoritarian leader – different from the old conservative elites of the Hindu Right – but he is very much part of the rightwing Hindu nationalist movement, the Rashtriya Swayamsevak Sangh (RSS), which dates to the mid-1920s. The RSS, whose founders saw the Nazi Final Solution against Jews as exemplary and made links with Mussolini to refashion their organizational model along Italian lines, has been banned thrice since India's independence in 1947. Modi was an RSS ground-level activist for more than 20 years and rose from the ranks to become the three-term chief minister of Gujarat state, which saw big pogroms in 2002 that received a huge amount of social support. The RSS believes in majoritarianism and defines Indian identity as essentially rooted in 'Hindu culture'. It believes that all other religious groups must lend allegiance to the dominant Hinduness. This ideology is one of creating border lines and cleavages along religious lines or camps and creating an imagined glorious history of the past of India – dominated by all things Hindu and creating an atmosphere of suspicion towards the minorities and whipping up fear. It is the Indian version of fascism. Its growth has been slow and molecular, but widespread across India.

In the post-1990s liberalization phase, there has been a change in the social composition of the middle classes, with a whole vast new section of laboring people with poor schooling and limited familiarity with the history of the Nehruvian period and the anti-colonial period. The liberalization phase has certainly shifted the social fulcrum to rightwing ideas and neoliberal methods as the route to take. The Nehruvian period has been under attack by Modi and the BJP [the Bharatiya Janata Party that Modi leads]. There has been a mass poisoning of minds – crafting a 'communalized' social common sense. The BJP had an organized communications strategy, and has used technology effectively. For example, upon being denied a visa to travel to the US in 2005, Modi spoke from Gujarat to supporters in Madison Square Garden via satellite-link video. The BJP and the Modi regime have engineered a whole new technical ecosystem in the Indian context way beyond anything attempted by other parties. Modi has over 20 million followers on Twitter, and the BJP uses WhatsApp, Facebook and mobile phones massively for spreading their propaganda. A number of very big media networks (owned by tycoons close to the BJP) have been used to great effect via spreading fake news and targeting liberals. The BJP adopted hologram technology in pre-election rallies prior to the 2014 general elections, creating a new visual register as with religious mythology seen on TV. There is also now a Narendra Modi App available for phones and tablets and people are being encouraged and pushed into using this app with direct messages from the prime minister. This is a whole new technical ecosystem that Indian political formations haven't been used to.

The Left has a long history of being unable to directly mobilize the public to challenge communalism hands on. It has had interminable debates on whether 'communalism' is fascism or authoritarianism (or on the character of the Modi regime). It has an old-fashioned 'Comintern' [Communist International] style take on fascism. It explains it away simply by pointing at connections to capitalist big business interests. The slow sustained work by the RSS through propaganda, social work and thousands of schools has had a considerable mind-shifting influence and cultural appeal on society in India. The RSS has over 50,000 branches in small towns and cities across India that hold daily or weekly meetings.

The broad Left (the parliamentary Communist Parties, the socialists, the Far Left and the unorganized Open Left) doesn't run schools or soup kitchens, do yoga in the parks, do relief work with victims of natural disasters, or put on popular festivals. It has no counter-educational program with laboring, poor classes or the middle class who are all today also divided along chauvinistic, identitarian lines.

What are the main sources of Modi's popularity? How much do his promises of economic populism have to do with it? Has his popularity lessened since his election?

Modi's economic policies and promises have not gotten very far (the unemployment rate has gone up from 3.4 per cent in 2014 to 6.2 per cent in 2018), but the facts don't seem to matter. His entire election campaign show was around corruption, but he hasn't gone after the big guys, among whom some are his own funders. He suddenly ordered a hugely disruptive de-monetization affecting millions and harming the vast informal sector of the economy. He used very clever propaganda saying all the millions standing in queues outside banks to withdraw money are facing hardships like soldiers do on the national borders to protect the security of the nation, saying this sacrifice by the people would cleanse the country. Like a showman, he launched a day of yoga where all state officials were on call to be on yoga mats. Big spectacle – as if that would cleanse the country's health in one shot.

Modi has considerable popularity, though recent polls do show a decline. The four-year tenure of the Modi government has really changed the social atmosphere: vigilante mobs roam freely with impunity (they have active connections with RSS affiliates and the BJP), and a widely shared sense of fear has crept in for the minorities. The rare Far Right activists, politicians or senior police officers who were charged with extrajudicial killings and complicity in the 2002 Gujarat riots have mostly been acquitted of charges since Modi's arrival in power.

Social violence has been growing. India was ranked fourth in the world in 2015 – after Syria, Nigeria and Iraq – for the highest social hostilities involving religion, the *Huffington Post* reported on 14 April 2017. Modi still has a star rating of sorts and manages to reach out through high-velocity media spectacles. The big leader with a wide chest that the world takes note of is sold every day. His anti-intellectualism, jingoism, tall tales of mighty nationalism can be intoxicating when laced with religion or identity. There are no simple explanations of his wide popularity, but he has surely spurred a new cult of a high-visibility leader bigger than his political party. He has visited over 50 countries in his four-year tenure. Footage of his speeches abroad, particularly to the diaspora, are broadcast to 'untraveled' audiences in India with glamorous footage of the countries to great effect. His brash oratory seems to sell; he now officially uses the national public radio network for a monthly talk, unlike any previous prime minister of India. Massive use of social media to scale up Modi's persona continues. In any case, authoritarianism and regimentation are popular in Indian society: Hitler's *Mein Kampf* remains among the most widely sold books.

What kind of pushback are you seeing against Modi's sectarian rhetoric by groups and people determined to uphold India's tradition of secular governance?

A wide range of groups have organized public events and citizens' tribunals to inform the public about these violent sectarian campaigns. One of the most impact-making events was the return of state awards by prominent writers: this got a lot of reading people to sit up and take note. The international media has done a remarkable job of giving visibility to dissenting voices in India. But the Modi government has hardly batted an eyelid: it has struck back by trying to discredit writers and intellectuals who speak up by calling them anti-nationals.

There is wide variety of groups speaking up for justice and freedoms. There have been long drawn-out struggles by students and teachers on specific campuses, by national workers' organizations, small urban non-governmental organizations, some protests by media workers but also by new citizens' campaigns speaking out against mob lynchings and shrinking secular spaces. These groups are able to draw out a section of the middle class and the silent majority to speak on single issues. But the divided opposition political parties have largely been absent or silenced and are not mobilizing actively on the ground other than during elections. They are finally coming together to forge electoral alliances for the upcoming national elections in 2019, where much is at stake. ∎

CHULANI KODIKARA

 Chulani Kodikara is a former senior researcher with the Consultation Task Task Force on Reconciliation Mechanisms in Sri Lanka. She is the author of *Muslim Family Law in Sri Lanka* and co-author of *Women and Governance: Sri Lanka*.

Have the corruption and human rights abuses that occurred during former President Mahinda Rajapaksa's administration stopped or lessened since Maithripala Sirisena was elected president?

Many of the violations that occurred during the Rajapaksa years have stopped. The Rajapaksa regime came to power in 2005 and presided over the military defeat of the Liberation Tigers of Tamil Elam (LTTE) that ended Sri Lanka's civil war in 2009. The war – and the last phase of the war in particular – was characterized by massive human rights violations. In the aftermath of the war, there was a need to account for these violations. At the same time, the end of the war was an opportunity to address the root causes of the war, the long-standing demand for devolution of power by the Tamil community and the grievances of the Tamil and Muslim people in Sri Lanka, who are numerical minorities. However, the government's response to the rights violations was to simply deny such violations and discredit rights activists while taking a very triumphalist attitude towards the war. It also chose to ignore historical discrimination against minority communities, especially the Tamil community. Even though the government inaugurated a 'reconciliation' process, it was reduced to development of the northern and eastern parts of the country, which was affected by the war and where most of the Tamils and Muslims live. Questions of truth, justice and reparations were ignored.

The post-war moment was also marked by a resurgence of Sinhalese Buddhist ethno-nationalism. Resurgences of nationalisms following the end of wars are well-documented in many other contexts. This nationalism also privileged the 'family', with implications for women's rights, and women's autonomy over their bodies. The Rajapaksa government's post-war policies had clear implications for minority rights and women's rights.

The 2015 presidential and parliamentary elections must be seen in this context. Maithripala Sirisena, the current president and the National Unity Government came into power in 2015 on various promises, including good governance, respect for human rights and rule of law, constitutional reform and the inauguration of a transitional justice process to address war-related human rights abuses. Unfortunately, many of these promises remain unfulfilled. While human rights violations are not occurring on the same scale as during the Rajapaksa regime, some violations continue. For instance, the government was completely paralyzed in the face of recent attacks by nationalistic forces against the Muslim community in the two cities of Digana and Ampara.

Are secular forces pushing back against both Sinhalese and Tamil-based nationalism?

Sinhalese nationalism has a long history of rising and falling in popularity. The post-war context featured a steep rise in nationalism. This resurgence took us all by surprise. We found out that there were a lot more people than we thought who identified with Rajapaksa and his policies, as well as his nationalistic rhetoric and ideology. The secular forces who pushed back against that trend were limited to certain civil-society groups, journalists and progressive intellectuals. This has always been the case in Sri Lanka, but I think the number of people who were willing to challenge the government shrank in the aftermath of the civil war. The presidential and parliamentary elections of 2015 were a significant victory for civil-society groups who fought for change, but I do think we have to be careful about how we read those elections. I think perhaps they shouldn't be read as a complete challenge to the Sinhalese Buddhist nationalism of the Rajapaksa regime. The election should be seen more as a challenge to family hegemony and the corruption that was rampant during the Rajapaksa years.

Does Sinhalese nationalism have its roots in anger over the lives lost in the civil war?

It has a much longer history. The roots of Sinhalese nationalism can be traced back to the history of colonialism. The British used a 'divide and rule' policy in Sri Lanka. The Sinhalese majority felt that minority groups, and particularly the Tamils, were unfairly privileged by the colonial administration. Sinhalese nationalism was a response to this perceived privileged treatment. The year of 1956 marked the politicization of Sinhalese nationalism. There was a split in Sri Lanka's United National Party (UNP) and SWRD Bandaranaike emerged as the leader of a new party called the Sri Lankan Freedom Party, with an explicit mandate to address the 'grievances' of the majority community. He mobilized the electorate by privileging the majority and promising to make Sinhalese the only language in the country.

Could you talk about the discrimination the Tamils faced before the Sri Lankan civil war?

The Sri Lankan Constitution had a strong equality clause in 1948, but Indian Tamils who had come to Sri Lanka to work on plantations during the colonial period were immediately disenfranchised after Sri Lanka gained independence from Britain. Sinhalese was named the official language in Sri Lanka in 1956. In the 1970s, the government introduced legislation that restricted Tamils from gaining access to universities. There was also sporadic violence and ethnic riots against the Tamils and Muslims. Events in 1983 marked the militarization of the ethnic conflict in Sri Lanka. Thirteen Sinhalese soldiers were killed by Tamil youth in the North in July 1983. When their bodies came to the capital city, Sinhalese mobs started burning Tamil shops and houses and attacking Tamils. This happened for three days and the government failed to clamp down on the mobs. These attacks left many people homeless and internally displaced, while others fled the country and became refugees. This was also the year the LTTE emerged as an armed group.

Have many of the people guilty of war crimes on both sides of the civil war been held accountable for their human rights abuses?

Almost all of the LTTE leadership was killed during the war. One thing the current government promised after being elected was that they would put in place a transitional justice process. This promise was reiterated in a consensus resolution that was passed in the United Nations Human Rights Council. The resolution (30/1) is wide ranging but in relation to the question of transitional justice, it commits to four mechanisms:

- An Office of Missing Persons to find the whereabouts of the hundreds of thousands who disappeared during the civil war;
- An Office on Reparations to provide material and financial compensation to war-affected populations;
- A Truth Reconciliation Commission; and
- A Hybrid Court.

There has been very little progress on transitional justice since these promises were made. The only resolution the government has fulfilled is the establishment of the Office of Missing Persons.

What do you mean by a 'Hybrid Court'?

It's hybrid in the sense that it will comprise both local and foreign judges. But this has been extremely controversial because 'the soldier' has become an icon for Sinhalese nationalists. This makes it impossible for the government to proceed in investigating and holding the military accountable for war-related crimes. Even the Office of Missing Persons doesn't have judicial powers. It's strictly a truth-seeking mechanism, rather than a mechanism to hold people accountable. However, the response of Sinhalese nationalists even to the Office of Missing Persons has been extremely negative. Today there is some progress being made within local courts in relation to prosecution of military personnel. Yet this remains a contested and controversial issue. President Sirisena has said many times that no soldiers will be prosecuted through a hybrid court. The justice minister and other ministers have repeated this mantra. So those within government are contradicting themselves on this question.

You have written about the stigma and shame that makes many women not report when they are sexually assaulted. Are more men being held accountable for sexual and domestic violence against women?

Impunity for violence against women – whether domestic violence or rape – is an equally serious problem. Sexual violence in detention during the civil war has become hyper-visible in the transitional justice discourse in the post-war context. A number of international NGOs like Human Rights Watch, the International Truth and Justice Project for Sri Lanka, and Freedom from Torture have documented testimonies of hundreds of male and female victim survivors of sexual violence in detention and placed these in the public domain. What is significant about these testimonies is that they have been collected from victim survivors living outside of Sri Lanka. Some of these reports talk about people only being willing to come forward if there is a hybrid court and victim protection, and if they are allowed to give evidence from abroad.

What is alarming from my perspective is that most of these organizations tend to make distinctions between war-related violence and abuse, and what is called 'ordinary sexual violence'. Impunity in the case of violence against women has to be seen in terms of a continuum, which lies from 'home front' to the 'war front'. If you look at rape statistics in Sri Lanka, every year the police record more than 2,000 rape cases, including statutory rape, but only a few convictions. In some years not even one conviction. It makes you wonder what happens to these rape cases as they travel through the criminal-justice system. ∎

MOON NAY LI

 Moon Nay Li is general secretary of the Kachin Women's Association in Thailand, which was founded in 1999 to help women in Myanmar/Burma's Kachin state organize themselves to solve their social and economic problems. The organization has documented human rights violations, sexual violence and land-rights violations committed by the Myanmar military.

Can you talk about the violence being used by the military against ethnic groups in Burma?

There have been no charges against military officials guilty of human rights abuses. We have had two female volunteer teachers who were gang-raped, tortured and murdered in 2015. Our network group – Network for Human Rights Documentation in Burma – is working to promote human rights in Burma and to have a reparation policy for these kind of abuses by the military. The democratic reforms in Burma must be complemented by a change in the way civilians are treated, especially survivors of human rights violations. There have been a lot of human rights violations in the past, particularly in ethnic areas. There has been ongoing fighting between the Burmese and ethnic armed groups in the Kachin state and the northern Shan state. The Burmese government is sending more troops into the Kachin areas. This is why our work is so risky. We had a mobile clinic in Shan state and the Burmese took all its medicine and equipment. So even though the government is talking to the military and the ethnic armed groups about a nationwide ceasefire agreement and more political dialogue, the situation in the Kachin areas is even worse than before. There is rape, arbitrary arrests, torture and killings.

Can you talk about the role mining companies play in Kachin State?

There are a lot of problems in the mining areas of Kachin because the government has already sold off a lot of natural resources to foreign companies and their cronies in the jade mining area. There is a lot of illegal land confiscation, but there is no justice. Most of the land is being confiscated from local farmers. There is gold mining, jade mining and logging in the Kachin State. This is forcing local people to relocate. Most of the perpetrators have money and pay off the local authorities. The people whose land has been confiscated have to find new ways to earn money. Some women and girls enter China to look for jobs and become victims of sex trafficking. We have asked for the international community to stop foreign investment and big development projects in conflict areas until peace has been established. This is one way to put pressure on the military and their business cronies.

There have been reports that the military has been targeting women during their military offensives in ethnic areas. Are these reports accurate?

They use rape as a weapon of war. For example, when there is an offensive in the Kachin area, they rape Kachin women.

What are your thoughts on the war crimes that were committed against the Rohingya?

What is happening to the Rohingya people resembles what is happening to the Kachin people. There are the same patterns of crimes and ethnic cleansing that have happened in other ethnic areas.

There have been media reports of widespread discrimination against the Rohingya because they are seen by many as illegal immigrants from Bangladesh. Are these reports accurate?

There is history of people entering Burma from Bangladesh – most of these people settled in Rakhine state. Mismanagement by the Burmese government has helped create this long-term conflict. In Thailand, a lot of migrant workers enter the country to work, but the government has a process whereby these workers eventually become Thai citizens. In Burma, there is no process for the migrant people. It is not just the Rohingya – a lot of people from China migrate to the Kachin and Shan states. However, even though some migrants lack citizenship, we still must respect their human rights.

What is the most effective tactic that can be used to lessen the power of the Burmese military?

We hope that civilians will be able to change this situation. For example, we believe our civilian movement has the power to change the 2008 Constitution in a way that lessens the power of and ends impunity for the Burmese military. We also want the international community to pressure Burma to change to a Federalist-style constitution [federal democracy].

What is the most important message you would like to send to the international community about the situation in Burma today?

The situation in Burma is very complicated. There is ongoing fighting in Kachin State and the northern Shan State and the number of internally displaced people is increasing. The government and the military are engaged in a divide-and-rule policy. The government is just working with the armed ethnic groups that signed the Nationwide Ceasefire Agreement while ignoring the ethnic groups that didn't sign the agreement because it didn't give full equality to the ethnic states. This has been a big problem in the negotiations between the ethnic groups and the government. The international community is trying to get involved in our peace process, but sometimes they are just fueling more conflict in our area because they are only working with the Burmese government. This is making it hard to reach a peaceful goal. They need to work with armed groups, ethnic groups and civil society. The conflict will continue until we have a federal system in our country.

Has the international community discussed the topic of the Burmese government granting autonomy to ethnic groups like the Kachin State?

They are only talking to the military, Aung San Suu Kyi and the National League for Democracy. Aung Suu Kyi is just pressuring the armed groups to sign the ceasefire agreement. Some of the ethnic groups have signed it, but there is still a lot of conflict between ethnic groups and the military. She is not talking enough about the ethnic issues. She doesn't recognize ethnic movements and ethnic problems. This has caused distrust between the Burman people and ethnic people and has led to more conflict in our society. We feel it is hopeless to depend on the government because according to the 2008 Constitution, they have no power. It's very clear the military still has the power.

What would self-determination look like in the Kachin State?

The Kachin state government should have authority over everything: education, health, judiciary, army, and so on. ■

SOKEEL PARK

 Sokeel Park is the director of research and strategy for Liberty in North Korea (LiNK), an organization that rescues North Korean refugees without cost or conditions and helps them on their journey to South Korea. LiNK also has resettlement programs that help North Korean refugees adjust to life in a new country.

What made you want to join Liberty in North Korea?

North Korea maintains an extreme version of 20th-century authoritarianism and totalitarianism. The first time I met ordinary North Koreans (not North Korean diplomats) was in New York when I was doing a graduation internship at the United Nations headquarters. This is a project of great humanity and historical importance. Over the years I've been able to meet and get to know a lot of people from North Korea as friends. At the end of the day, there is no other project I would rather be working on.

How life-changing has it been for you to work with North Korean refugees?

It's amazing and it's a huge privilege to be able to do this as a full-time job. I've learned so much about life, culture and human psychology. Just working with North Korean people has challenged some of my fundamental assumptions. It's very stimulating and very gratifying as well.

However, sometimes you have to find your own gratification – because, in the bigger picture, North Korea is still North Korea. We're dealing with individual people, but we're also dealing with a historical development. It wouldn't be possible to create a state like North Korea in the 21st century, so when the North Korean government goes, that will be it. Humanity will never see a system that closed or regressive again. People may point to Islamic State as a counterargument, but I think that is a different kind of animal. I think this is one of the biggest problems facing humanity today. It is a difficult issue to work on and there are not many people working on it.

There are reports that more outside sources of information are getting inside North Korea. Has this changed the way North Koreans view their government?

It's very hard to know. This is true even in relatively free countries. Look at how surprised political analysts have been by the rise of Donald Trump in the US, which is the most widely surveyed country in the world. North Korea is the least-surveyed population in the world, so it is very hard to know average political views. I think we have to practice a little bit of intellectual humility and recognize when we don't know certain things.

The best that we can say, based on talking to North Korean refugees, is that there is clearly disenchantment. People are risking their lives to escape from the system and people are discussing issues inside the country. It's not black-and-white disenchantment for people inside North Korea. You might disagree with the government on economic policies, but the nuclear-weapons policy might make sense to you because of ethno-nationalism, and you might buy into this idea that North Korea faces an existential threat from the outside world.

People outside of North Korea have this simplistic view that North Koreans either disagree with everything the North Korean government stands for or they agree with them on everything. But when you are on the inside of any system or political culture, there are many more shades of grey.

Is it a culture shock for North Korean refugees to see how their country is portrayed by the outside world, or is it not surprising given their experiences in North Korea?

The level of interest internationally about North Korea surprises some people. In South Korea, there is a lack of awareness and understanding of North Korea. South Korea and North Korea have become so different by this point that some young South Koreans are not that interested in North Korea. North Korean refugees are sometimes surprised when South Koreans don't know the basics about their country. There are also singular narratives about North Korea that treat the country as a monolithic creature without any nuance. Refugees are often surprised by this characterization as well.

Do you worry about the press focusing too much on the bellicose nature of the North Korean regime and forgetting about the suffering the people in that country are enduring, in terms of starvation or being sentenced to life in brutal concentration camps?

It's absolutely inevitable that there is going to be a lot of focus on North Korea's nuclear-weapons program. They have threatened to use nuclear weapons against the United States. That is a story that has got to be told. That kind of rhetoric is not coming from other countries in the world. But our organization wants to balance out this coverage with a more productive focus on the sources of hope and progress that we are seeing internally in North Korea.

Can you talk about the dynastic nature of the North Korean regime and about the different classes of citizens in the country?

That is one of the reasons that North Korea still exists as it does today. Kim Il-Sung came to power at a very early age, which meant he was in power for about a half a century (1945-94). By the time he died, the only person to take over was his son. The cult of personality had become so important around Kim Il-Sung that the only way to pass it over to someone else was to put that cult of personality along a family line. So, in 1994 the only mechanism that was available was to pass the leadership on to Kim Jong-il, and then to Kim Jong-un after Kim Jong-il died.

This constitutes an important factor, because if you look at the changes in other countries that were formerly communist countries, you get big changes in policies when you have changes in leadership. For instance, after Stalin and Mao died, the next leaders had an opportunity to change things and recognize mistakes that were made because their legitimacy wasn't tied to the former leadership. That opportunity was never available in North Korea.

Why has the military in North Korea allowed the Kim regime to stay in power? What are the incentives for the military to allow this regime to continue?

It's very hard for the military to launch a rebellion because the level of internal security and surveillance is very high. The military leadership also doesn't have a reason to overthrow the system because they have privileged positions in the country.

North and South Korea are also competing states, and there is a fear among the North Korean elite that, if North Korea collapses, South Korea will come and take over everything. So, if you're a North Korean general and you can live out your life as a North Korean general, that would be better for your family than if you instigated a rebellion that brought about the collapse of the North Korean system and the absorption by South Korea. What is a North Korean general going to do in a country that has been reunified by the South Korean government? They might go on trial. They might be lynched. The best outcome would be for them to be able to become a teacher or taxi driver or something like that. They would basically lose all their power networks.

You talk about the military being privileged members of North Korean society. Isn't there also a class-based system in North Korea where certain citizens have much better lives than others?

It's a pretty complex system. Basically, it's a system where citizens are classified according to their supposed political loyalty that goes back to their ancestral loyalty to Kim Il-Sung. The system is used to determine what kinds of jobs you can get or whether you can serve in the military. It controls a lot of things, but this system is not well known in the outside world.

If this discrimination were based on skin color, it would look like apartheid South Africa – maybe even worse than South Africa – and there would be a massive international outcry about it. But this is North Koreans discriminating against North Koreans, so it looks and feels very different, even though, fundamentally, it includes the same amount of human rights violations.

So, if someone's ancestors collaborated with the Japanese or fought for the South Koreans during the Korean War, then that person is being discriminated against today based on the political loyalties of their ancestors?

Yes. At this point, people have to operate outside the system and work in the markets. In some ways the system is still important, but people are increasingly having to rely on business activities outside the system.

What tactics can international groups and/or people use to weaken the North Korean government and strengthen dissident movements inside and outside the country?

The fundamental problem here is that North Korea is the most closed and repressive country in the world. The game is to open it up to the outside world, and there are different ways that you can do that. There are certain things you can do above board with the North Korean government. You can do it with certain forms of economic engagement and you can do it through inviting the North Koreans to learn in the outside world. This is being done, so it is possible.

You can have workshops inside the country with foreigners going in and teaching lessons, or you can do it under the radar by providing information and ideas to the North Korean people that the government cannot stop. You can also work with refugees to accelerate their roles as agents of progress through continuing to send resources and money back to their country. Broadly, these are the type of tactics that are available to the international community. Increasing the force for change inside the country is a very under-utilized strategy. So much of the focus goes to North Korea's nuclear weapons and missile programs. The international community focuses too much on North Korea's strengths and not its weaknesses. ■

DIEP SAEEDA

 Diep Saeeda is the founding director of Pakistan's Institute for Peace and Secular Studies and a tireless peace activist. She advocates for nonviolence; equality under the law for all people regardless of race, religion, ethnicity or gender; secular democracy; a nuclear weapons-free Middle East; and peaceful relations between India and Pakistan.

How big a role did General Muhammad Zia-ul-Haq play in stoking religious fundamentalism in Pakistan?

The long-term impact of Zia-ul-Haq's actions on fueling the rise of religious extremism in the country cannot be overstated. With the introduction of sharia courts, the Hudood Ordinance and Blasphemy Laws, Zia effectively institutionalized bigotry. An irreversible process of discriminatory laws and exclusionary policies was effectually instated.

However, the seeds of what was to become a draconian system of persecution of religious and sectarian minorities were sown by Zia's predecessor, Zulfiqar Ali Bhutto. Bhutto caved in to pressure from religious parties and declared Ahmadis non-Muslim. He was also the one to institute a ban on alcohol consumption.

Perhaps the single most detrimental step in Pakistan's constitutional history was the introduction of the Objectives Resolution. At the stroke of a pen, non-Muslims became second-class citizens. Pakistan's Constitution is rife with dangerous contradictions, where on the one hand all citizens are equal, yet only a Muslim can be elected president of the country. The Objectives Resolution set the stage for the blurring of boundaries between religion and State and nipped in the bud any hopes of establishing a secular society – the like of which the Founding Father [Muhammad Ali Jinnah] had envisioned.

How strong are the progressive groups in Pakistan today?

Progressive groups are pretty close to non-existent in today's Pakistan. The systematic persecution of progressives and liberals during Zia's regime forced many to leave the country for fear of their lives. An endemic anti-progressive narrative propagated by the State took root in the country where progressives were considered anti-state elements and essentially villainized.

The handful of progressives in the country today don't present a united front, and are divided among various different factions, making the whole weaker. Compounding the many divisions is the additional problem of what is perceived as the co-option of the liberal class by the 'non-profit industrial complex'. Non-governmental organization workers in Pakistan are largely viewed with suspicion, even disdain, by the general populace for receiving funding from international organizations for self-aggrandizement.

How have you been able to maintain a commitment to nonviolence despite all the violence that has wracked Pakistan over the past three decades?

My commitment to nonviolence stems from the legacy of historical giants such as Mahatma Mohandas Karamchand Gandhi and Martin Luther King, Jr. They are my sources of inspiration, and I continue to seek guidance from their tradition of nonviolent resistance. It gives me no pride to admit that, in my younger days, I was perhaps beholden to a different worldview. I was enraged by social injustice and inequality and believed in my youthful folly that a bloody revolution was the only way to overthrow a capitalist system. But as I grew older, I became painfully aware that violence only begets more violence. Martin Luther King's saying 'Nonviolence is the way of life for courageous people' and Gandhi's teaching 'Be the change you wish to see in the world' became the edicts I live by.

Since I work with young people, it is critically important that I be steadfast in my adherence to nonviolence. My youthful days are behind me, but I remember being a hot-headed, impassioned youth, and I strive to imbibe young people with the passion and courage to choose the nonviolent path.

How did the funding of the Mujahideen by the US, Saudi Arabia and Pakistan to fight the Soviet Union lead to the further Islamization of your country?

Fascism and violence increased, and Islamization reached its peak during Zia's authoritarian regime. The funding and arming of mujahids sent to fight in Afghanistan actively propagated the us-versus-them narrative that dehumanized non-Muslims and laid the foundations for a militancy problem that the country is still to this day struggling to get under control.

When the Soviet invasion was over and the Mujahideen found that they were no longer serving a purpose, they turned on the State that helped create them. Hillary Clinton on a visit to Pakistan made the following observation: it would be foolish to think that our neighbor's snakes won't harm us. This has been the story of the mujahids in the region: when the Pakistani state equips young warriors to fight in Afghanistan or India, they forget that this monster will soon enough turn its wrath against the State that created it.

What is your position on US drone strikes in Pakistan?

This is a sensitive issue of critical importance. As a nonviolence activist and proponent, I am against the killing of any person. Known terrorists have been targeted in precision drone strikes, a fact that the US government uses as a defense against the criticism of drone attacks. The argument they make is that there was no other way to capture these dangerous criminals. Terrorist groups across the world use women and children as human shields, and innocent women and children die in these attacks, which is of course condemnable. I still believe that if negotiations can work, peace talks should be the preferred path forward.

What is the current state of your efforts to promote peace between Indians and Pakistanis?

We have been working to promote peace and friendly relations between Pakistan and India for many years now. As far back as

1995, we started facilitating people-to-people contact between Indians and Pakistanis, with the belief that misperceived notions about each other can only be dispelled through direct interaction. Where in-person meetings were made impossible because of the visa restrictions in place, we organized teleconferences and Skype conference calls between school and college students across the border. When the political climate allowed it, we organized youth exchange programs. Dialogue between youth – over the internet and in person – changes their perception about the other country in a positive way.

In 2005, there was a Peace March from Delhi to Multan on foot, and one from Bombay to Karachi. A Visa Free and Nuclear Free South Asia convention was hosted in India and one in Pakistan by the Indian and Pakistani Soldiers Initiative for Peace and was attended by former Army generals.

We continue our efforts to promote peace between Pakistan and India, but the Kashmir issue, and the absolutely absurd visa policies of both countries, remain huge barriers in our path. Not only is it extremely difficult to obtain a visa to visit the other country, but there are very real deterrents and barriers in the form of mandatory police reporting, and city-specific travel. No other nation restricts travel to a limited number of cities – a visa generally allows you access to all the different cities, towns and villages within any given country. The fact that we make it so overly cumbersome for the people of India and Pakistan to meet and see each other begs the question: why are our governments so afraid of peace?

In Karima Bennoune's book *Your Fatwa Does Not Apply Here*, she writes about how terrorist attacks committed by the Taliban and other Islamic fundamentalist groups are often wrongly blamed on Jews and Hindus by a portion of the Pakistani population. Is this pattern continuing or are more people starting to come to terms with the problem of Islamic fundamentalism?

That is accurate – in Pakistan, we have a huge problem with conspiracy theories. The Taliban are not considered Pakistani or even Muslim by many. This thinking is predicated on the belief that Muslims do not kill other Muslims. Many believe that this is the work of Blackwater, RAW [India's primary foreign intelligence agency] or Mossad – a US/Israeli/Indian conspiracy. The media has a big role to play in this characterization of extremists, by further encouraging and perpetuating these fallacies.

There is no space to speak freely about religious extremism in Pakistan. Moderates who try to explain that Islam is a religion of peace, and that the extremists are outliers, do not receive prominence in the mainstream media, and in some cases are threatened and forced to leave the country, creating an environment that stifles discussion and discourse and further exacerbates the problem of intolerance.

Do you think true democracy will only come to Pakistan when its government commits itself to secular principles that protect women, minorities and non-believers from those who want to impose their interpretation of Islam on people?

What we see in Pakistan is not a true democracy – the head of state defers to the military on all important issues concerning foreign policy, the military budget and other policy and strategic decisions. Military control of government decisions is, to my mind, intrinsically linked with the problem of lack of protections for minorities, and the reason why we are inching further away from realizing the dream of a secular democracy. The military derives its justification for a large standing army with a huge military budget by keeping the conflict with India alive. The public is sold the narrative that India is an enemy because of religious differences between Hindus and Muslims. The same rationale for discrimination applies to Hindus and other religious minorities living in Pakistan.

When the Pakistani military establishment decides that the elected parliament voted into power by the people of Pakistan is paramount and supreme – that is when we can finally have a truly democratic nation. The educated youth of the country are plugged into the global village via the internet and social media. Soon enough they will learn from the democratic and progressive nations of the world, and recognize that we need separation between religion and the State. That is when women, minorities and people of different sects and ethnicities can enjoy equal protection under the laws. It is of the utmost importance to uphold the democratic ideals of protecting and promoting human rights and civil liberties. Rule of law and freedom of expression are essential for a thriving democracy. The Pakistani establishment will be held accountable for the countless missing journalists and activists from across the country. Dissent and difference of opinion should not only be tolerated but celebrated if Pakistan is to become a true democracy. ■

AMARTYA SEN

Amartya Sen is a Nobel-prize-winning economist and philosopher based at Harvard University in the US. His books have been translated into more than 30 languages, and include *On Ethics and Economics* (1987), *Development as Freedom* (1999) and *Identity and Violence* (2006).

You have written about the link between identity and violence. Would you explain the contradictory impulses of community-based identities?

The well-integrated community in which residents instinctively do absolutely wonderful things for each other with great immediacy and solidarity can be the very same community in which bricks are thrown through the windows of immigrants who move into the region from elsewhere. The adversity of exclusion can be made to go hand in hand with the gifts of inclusion.

What is the antidote to identity-based violence?

It can hardly be sought in trying to suppress or stifle the invoking of identity in general. For one thing, identity can be a source of richness and warmth as well as of violence and terror, and it would make little sense to treat identity as a general evil. Rather, we have to draw on the understanding that the force of a bellicose identity can be challenged by the power of competing identities. These can, of course, include the broad commonality of our shared humanity, but also many other identities we share simultaneously. This leads to other ways of classifying people, which can restrain the exploitation of a specifically aggressive use of one particular categorization.

Can you explain the connection between choice, reason and identity?

If choices do exist and yet it is assumed that they are not there, the use of reasoning may well be replaced by uncritical acceptance of conformist behavior, no matter how rejectable it may be. Typically, such conformism tends to have conservative implications, and works in the direction of shielding old customs and practices from intelligent scrutiny.

Indeed, traditional inequalities, such as unequal treatment of women in sexist societies (and of unfavored racial groups in racist societies) survive by unquestioning acceptance of received beliefs (including the subservient roles of the traditional underdog). Many past practices and assumed identities have crumbled in response to questioning and scrutiny.

Can you explain your criticisms of the 'clash of civilizations' theory?

Perhaps its most basic weakness lies in its use of a particularly ambitious version of the illusion of singularity. To this has to be added a second problem: the crudeness with which the world civilizations are characterized, taking them to be more insular than tends to emerge from empirical analyses of the past and present.

The implicit belief in the overarching power of a singular classification is not just crude as an approach to description and prediction, it is also grossly confrontational in form and implication.

What is your critique of Good Muslim-Bad Muslim talk?

[In] disputing the gross and nasty generalization that members of the Islamic civilization have a belligerent culture, it is common enough to argue that they actually share a culture of peace and good will. But this simply replaces one stereotype with another and, furthermore, it involves accepting an implicit presumption that people who happen to be Muslim by religion would basically be similar in other ways as well. Aside from all the difficulties in defining civilizational categories as disparate and disjunctive units, the arguments on both sides suffer, in this case, from a shared faith in the presumption that seeing people exclusively, or primarily, in terms of religion-based civilizations to which they are taken to belong is a good way of understanding human beings. Civilizational partitioning is a pervasively intrusive phenomenon in social analysis, stifling other – richer – ways of seeing people.

You have been critical of those promoting 'Asian Values' as a substitute for 'Western Values'. How is this connected to your theory about how many post-colonial countries are still obsessed with their former oppressor, whether it be through vigorously pro-West or anti-West policies?

[It] is argued that while Europe may have been the home ground of liberty and individual rights, 'Asian values' cherish discipline and order, and this, it is alleged, is a marvelous priority. It tells the West that it can keep its individual liberties and rights, but Asia will do better with its adherence to orderly conduct and disciplined behavior. The West-obsessed form of this grand 'Asian' claim is hard to miss.

This cultural diagnosis is difficult to sustain. Support for ideas of liberty and public discussion, and what may be called basic human rights, has been articulated no less often in Asia – in India, China, Japan, Korea, Indonesia and in various other countries in East, Southeast, South and West Asia – than in Europe. The point to note here is not just the debatable nature of the 'diagnosis' of 'Asian values' and the fact that it seriously underestimates the range – and reach – of the intellectual heritage of Asia. It is also important, in the context of the present analysis, to see the thoroughly reactive nature of the genesis of this view. The need to differentiate from the West is clearly visible in this postcolonial dialectic, and it is also easy to see the attraction for many Asians of the claim that Asia has something much better than Europe.

Can multiculturalism sometimes be used to promote an anti-choice agenda in the name of preserving cultural diversity?

The simplest way of having cultural diversity may, in some circumstances, be a total continuation of all the pre-existing cultural practices that happen to be present at a point in time (for example, new immigrants may be induced to continue their old, fixed ways and mores, and discouraged – directly or indirectly – from changing their behavior pattern at all). Does this suggest that for the sake of cultural diversity we should support cultural conservatism and ask people to stick to their own cultural background and not try to consider moving to other lifestyles even if they find good reason to do so? The undermining of choice that this would involve would immediately deliver us to an anti-freedom position, which would look for ways and means of blocking the choice of a changed living mode that many people may wish to have.

How can cultural liberty increase cultural diversity?

Cultural diversity may be enhanced if individuals are allowed and encouraged to live as they would value living (instead of being restrained by ongoing tradition). For example, the freedom to pursue ethnically diverse lifestyles in food habits or in music,can make a society more culturally diverse precisely as a result of the exercise of cultural liberty.

Can you discuss your rejection of the idea that pursuing one's own economic self-interest should be the only way to measure if someone is acting rationally?

Why should it be uniquely rational to pursue one's own self-interest to the exclusion of everyone else's? It may not, of course, be at all absurd to claim that maximization of self-interest is not irrational, at least not necessarily so, but to argue that anything other than maximizing self-interest must be irrational seems altogether extraordinary.

The self-interest view of rationality involves *inter alia* a firm rejection of the 'ethics-related' view of motivation. Trying to do one's best to achieve what one would value achieving can be part of rationality, and this can include the promotion of non-self-interested goals which we may value and wish to aim at. ∎

TEESTA SETALVAD

 Teesta Setalvad is secretary of Citizens for Peace and Justice, a non-profit organization formed to seek justice for the victims of the anti-Muslim pogroms in Gujarat in 2002. She and her husband Javed Anand co-founded the magazine *Communalism Combat* in 1993 to oppose both majoritarian and minority communalism. She is the author of *Foot Soldier for the Constitution: A Memoir*.

What has led to the ascent of the Hindu Right in India? Did corruption in the Congress Party help give rise to this movement?

I don't think corruption is the only reason. The single biggest presence in education today is the Hindu Right. They are working to change the mindsets of people. I think a lot of the current success and presence of the Hindu Right in the public sphere is because of their high level of organization. Americans even fund schools run by Rashtriya Swayamsevak Sangh or Vishwa Hindu Parishad that promote Hindu supremacy – and often even hatred against minorities – because they think they are charity schools for tribal children. What they are actually doing is trying to refashion a culture and education that is inherently unequal and anti-constitutional.

What compelled you to make the transition from being a journalist to an activist for the marginalized?

It was the demolition of the 16th-century Babri Mosque [by Hindu fundamentalist activists] in December 1992. The demolition was an overt criminal and symbolic act that was meant to devalidate and delegitimize secular discourse. Javed and I decided to quit our jobs in 1993 and start the magazine *Communalism Combat*. We felt we should use our media expertise not just for commercial and professional media, but also to look at the politics of exclusion. We did this through the media because we are journalists by profession. Communalism is misunderstood as something positive in the West but it is essentially the misuse of religion for political ends. Majoritarian communalism generally moves at the fastest pace and puts a stranglehold on democracy; which has happened under Modi. Our policy has always been to condemn minority communalism equally, while recognizing that majoritarian communalism is a real threat to democracy. India is being governed by proto-fascist forces who openly espouse the overthrow of the democratic, egalitarian, republican order laid down in the Indian Constitution.

Can you talk about the charges the Indian government has leveled against you and your NGOs – the Sabrang Trust and Citizens for Justice and Peace – for allegedly coaching witnesses, violating India's Foreign Contribution Regulation Act, and misusing money meant to go to a museum in memory of the victims of the Gujarat anti-Muslim pogroms?

We have denied these accusations in court point by point, and have made all our accounts public, including reports by renowned auditors of a re-audit after the allegations. Both Javed and I – and the trustees of both trusts – pride ourselves on accountability and transparency. The government still hasn't filed a charge sheet against us. The offense was lodged in January 2014, and we have turned over 21,000 pages of our accounts. The aim was always to vilify us in the public domain and keep the sword of incarceration and threats to personal liberty hanging over our heads. Our biggest disappointment has been in a large section of the Indian media, especially commercial television, which is concerned with parroting the agenda of the regime instead of functioning independently.

Do you feel these accusations are political in nature because you have been critical of Modi's role as chief minister in Gujarat

when the anti-Muslim pogroms took place?

They are very clearly politically motivated. They began when Modi was chief minister of Gujarat and they continued when he became prime minister of the country. First the Gujarat police (directly under him), and thereafter the Ministry of Home Affairs in the Central Government, and the Central Bureau of Investigation (CBI), a federal agency that functions under the prime minister's office, have been trained on us. Even now the threat of more intimidation and threats intensifies every day.

Has there been a culture of impunity for the people involved in the anti-Muslim pogroms?

After the genocide in 2002, Citizens for Justice and Peace was able to take up 68 cases related to the pogroms. We have been able to obtain 172 convictions, and 126 of those have involved life imprisonment. The fact that we asked for life imprisonment instead of the death penalty reflected the success of our discourse with the Muslim communities because this went against the 'eye for an eye, tooth for a tooth' way of thinking that some of the people in the communities wanted. I think it's arguably the first time we have seen these types of convictions after an act of communal violence against a minority community.

How important is secular democracy to protecting women and minority rights in India?

I think the two issues are very, very linked. The whole notion of secularism and equality is critical to the issue of gender rights. We have several important sections in our Constitution that are linked to gender and minority rights. Article 14 deals with right to life, and Article 21 deals with equality before the law. Non-discriminatory provisions are included in Articles 15 and 16, and freedom of expression and the right to association is established in Article 19. Article 25 guarantees freedom of faith and often this section is used to reinforce patriarchal provisions with the majority and among the minorities. The whole gender discourse sometimes gets sidelined when we talk about community rights. We need to understand that the individual rights of women in a community are just as critical as the rights of that community. One major lacuna, however, is that the abolition of caste itself does not figure within the fundamental rights, and only a manifestation of caste exclusion (untouchability) has been outlawed by the Constitution.

What would be an effective way to counter the injection of religion into India's educational institutions?

Teaching social studies and history in a more democratized and pluralistic manner, introducing constitutional values within the school syllabus, and interrogating caste, class and gender inequality. Celebrating differences and allowing the young mind to question stereotypes. Given the proto-fascist tendencies of the government in power, we need to look at generating attractive materials in unconventional ways, such as through mass movements and community programs. We can't wait for the government to do this. ■

MANDIRA SHARMA

 Mandira Sharma is a lawyer and a human rights defender in Nepal. She co-founded Advocacy Forum in 2001, which has campaigned for legal reform and has represented the victims of human rights violations committed by both monarchist forces and Maoist rebels during the 10-year Nepalese civil war (1996-2006). She was given the Human Rights Defender Award by Human Rights Watch in 2006.

Have many high-level officials been charged for the war crimes and human rights abuses that occurred during the Nepalese civil war?

There are a lot of allegations against high-level officials. Members of the security forces and political leaders have been implicated in human rights violations. There are a number of complaints filed by the victims to the police office demanding investigations. There are court orders for the police to initiate investigations, but there are no proper investigations and prosecutions so hardly anyone has been brought to justice. The government and major political parties are saying that cases of human rights abuses committed during the civil war will be addressed through transitional justice mechanisms. There is a proposal to establish a special transitional justice court aimed at prosecuting those recommended by the Truth and Reconciliation Commission (TRC). The law is yet to be enacted and implemented. This continuous delay in putting the required legal and procedural framework in place provides continued impunity to those involved in gross human rights violations.

Is the role of the Truth and Reconciliation Commission proving problematic?

One of the major problems is that the TRC is mandated to mediate between victims and perpetrators in the name of reconciliation. It also allows the Commission to mediate between victims and perpetrators even in the case of rape. This is one of the provisions that has been protested by victims and civil-society organizations. The Supreme Court has found this provision to be problematic. You cannot force victims to mediate with their perpetrators. The concept of reconciliation is very narrowly understood. Another problem with it is the provision of amnesty. The TRC Act allows the TRC commissioners to recommend amnesty for those involved in human rights violations irrespective of the nature of those violations. Victims claim that amnesty should be impermissible to those guilty of gross human rights violations.

There is another provision that involves reparations. The TRC can recommend reparations for victims of human rights violations, but reparations are not recognized as rights that victims can claim. The way the TRC Act defines gross human rights violations is also problematic, so there are a number of sections that were challenged by victims, and most of the provisions that victims challenged were recognized by the Supreme Court and found to be incompatible with the Nepalese Constitution and the country's international obligations. The Act has yet to be amended in line with the Court's order.

What effective strategies could be used to reduce poverty and increase employment for Nepalese citizens?

We need to improve the rule of law, so that people feel secure investing in economic development. There are a number of sectors where Nepal could implement policies that could increase economic opportunities and productivity. For example, modernizing the agriculture sector and getting more people to invest in hydropower. We also need to develop herbal medicines and invest in tourism. All these initiatives could create more jobs, but for these things to happen, you need a stable government and functioning rule of law. We need to address corruption and political patronage in public institutions. Thus far the government has not focused enough on ending corruption, strengthening professionalism in institutions and consistently applying the rule of law.

What form does corruption take in Nepalese politics, and how do you think it should be addressed?

One of the problems has been the lack of independence in public institutions. Most public institutions, including the anti-corruption body that carries out investigations and prosecutions, are under the influence of the political parties. They appoint commissioners to run these government bodies who are lenient to the parties that appointed them. If you do not have any kind of connections to the political parties, you are very unlikely to be appointed to run a public institution. This is the main problem that allows corruption to occur.

The second problem is that those in power are above the law. They can defy court orders and corruption allegations against them are never investigated because the institutions that are supposed to do so are not independent. Another form of corruption is the connections between brokers, investors and politicians. They provide huge commissions to politicians, and politicians accept their proposals. If you don't bribe them or provide them with huge commissions, your proposal will not be accepted. We have not been able to disentangle this nexus between criminality and Nepalese politics.

Can you talk about the work human rights groups such as Advocacy Forum are doing to tackle problems like child marriage and discrimination against women and minorities?

There are organizations working to raise awareness on child marriage, and there are groups like Advocacy Forum that challenge torture, enforced disappearances and arbitrary detentions. We monitor and investigate human rights violations and we bring cases against the perpetrators. It's very hard to challenge those in power when you don't have a system that works independently. There have been a lot of attacks on those who demand accountability for the crimes high-ranking officials commit. These attacks may not be physical, but the system makes it difficult for these kinds of groups to function. There are also new regulations that make work for NGOs more difficult, especially those that are critical of government policies.

I think on certain fronts we have made some progress. For example, the representation of women and other minorities or formerly socially excluded groups in politics is improving. We have also made progress in decreasing maternal mortality rates. In addition, the severity and intensity of illegal detention, and of torture in detention have been reduced. But we are doubtful that these changes will be sustained because there are attempts to regress to previous times.

Are there any groups advocating for the many Nepalese migrant workers who have been exploited when working abroad?

There are organizations that have been started by the Nepalese who return from different countries where they were migrant workers. They have been very active in highlighting the plight of migrant workers. Still, a lot still needs to be done, because migrant workers are not just exploited in foreign countries, but in Nepal as well. Nepal now has a new minister who seems committed to improving the situation. The labor ministry has launched very focused discussions and operations that have exposed the exploitation migrants face in Nepal and foreign countries. The focus now is mostly on Nepal because there are a lot of brokers who illegally exploit immigrants by making promises to them, and then provide them with false information, underpaying them and sometimes even exposing them to trafficking.

When Nepalese migrants go to other countries to work, there is often a syndicate in those countries that will take their passport and their travel documents and then not provide them with the job contracts they were promised. Some are promised that they will be taken to Dubai, and then they are taken to somewhere else like Qatar. They often later find out they have been sold there as domestic slaves or workers. Nepalese migrant women often face sexual exploitation, sexual abuse and physical assault when working in other countries. Nepalese embassies are not that active in protecting the interests of migrant workers. Because of the corruption and political patronage mentioned earlier, a lot of migrant workers don't go through the official channels when they work overseas. They use their own channels, so it becomes very difficult when there are issues that require intervention. This issue has been hidden for a long time. However, at least now it has started to surface and there are some efforts being made to address it. ■

LEE SAN YOUNG

 Lee San Young is the editor-in-chief of *Daily NK*. Founded in 2004, the South Korea-based online newspaper has been frequently cited by international media hungry for news from the reclusive North Korean state. Staffed by a team of dedicated activists, including a number of North Korean defectors, *Daily NK* runs on a shoestring budget while managing a secret network of citizen journalists living in North Korea.

Is one of the aims of your paper to dispel the myth that North Korea is a country full of people who monolithically support Kim Jong-un?

One of the primary aims is to improve access to outside information for all North Koreans, to encourage independent critical thinking and encourage them to form their own opinions and conclusions about what is happening in the world around them. The second, but equally important aim, is to obtain accurate, credible information about North Korea for dissemination to the international community. These two aims enable the international community to get a proper understanding of the facts, and therefore consider more effective approaches to North Korean issues, while strengthening the connections between North Korea's population and the outside world. Based on access to balanced information, the people of North Korea can then determine the future they want for their country on their own terms.

Do you worry that the threatening rhetoric between Kim and President Trump will divert attention away from the North Korean people?

The North Korean regime has achieved its nuclear development goals and now wants to focus on the country's economy to fulfill both tracks of its Byungjin Line policy. To that end, while making attempts to hint at the country's commitment to denuclearization, the regime is trying to spur economic development. For his part, President Trump sees talks with North Korea as a necessary first step toward it becoming a normal nation. These developments are not necessarily bad for the North Korean people. In the process many could realize the truth behind the nuclear component of the Byungjin Line and its role in keeping the regime in power. So, as these events unfold, we must double down on our efforts to send credible, unbiased and accurate information about these developments to the North Korean people.

Donald Trump told the amazing story of Ji Seong-ho in his 2018 State of the Union speech. What was the reaction of the defector community to Trump highlighting Ji's story?

In general, many felt it was encouraging that the President of the United States met with a North Korean defector, and the meeting gave many victims of human rights abuses renewed encouragement in their work as human rights advocates. The message was that the United States would continue to call out North Korea's human rights abuses and support related work, which is surely a pressure point for the North Korean government. Certainly, many share the view that the meeting was used for political purposes, but there continues to be interest and attention toward North Korean human rights issues.

Has the amount of foreign materials getting into North Korea slowed at all because of Kim Jong-un's increased crackdown on outside information and communication with foreigners?

The flow of foreign goods into North Korea has slowed down. The North Korean authorities have launched a spirited campaign to boost domestic manufacturing and encourage North Korean people to focus on domestic consumption. The belief in 'self-reliance and self-development' underpins continued calls to 'fight sanctions from the United States'. However, most North Koreans still prefer South Korean and other foreign-made goods due to the superior quality. Labels on foreign goods are often removed to hide their manufacturing origin and they are sometimes repackaged to look like North Korean products. The North Korean authorities continue to try to crack down on such actions, but many people remain unfazed and continue to find ways to evade the restrictions.

Is there growing dissent against the North Korean regime inside the country?

Using the term 'anti-regime dissent' as commonly understood would be difficult to translate to what we know about life inside North Korea. 'Dissent' and 'opposition forces' as concepts are also ill-defined and difficult to apply to specific contexts. However, through our citizen journalists we know of disparate incidents that continue to occur. Reports of anti-regime graffiti have come to light over the years, including a more recent example in Pyongyang criticizing Kim Jong-un. More research is needed to determine whether this was a rogue actor or is representative of a broader, organized movement, but the fact that it took place in the country's tightly controlled capital means that such an act would have required careful planning, which is significant in its own right.

There are grassroots changes at play too. Residents have demanded that law enforcement present a warrant when conducting domicile searches and elections are taking place at the very lowest level of administration in the country (neighborhood watch leaders). The selection of People's Unit leaders by their constituents represents at least a small step towards raising democratic awareness among North Koreans. In addition, the head of the Ministry of State Security was ousted due to alleged 'human rights abuses'. Whether or not this was the real reason, the mention of a term previously non-existent in the North Korean vernacular is significant. It is increasingly appearing in political lectures and North Korean state media as well, though usually in the State's defense of its own practices. Outside information and international pressure are driving these shifts in perception, and the government finds itself ceding ground, albeit marginally.

Can you talk more about the information revolution? Who is behind outside information getting into North Korea? Is this mostly being done by defectors who are trying to expose citizens to the outside world?

Defectors share information with relatives still in the country (via smuggled Chinese phones), and North Koreans who have traveled to China on visas and returned are sharing their experiences. Traders and merchants share information about the market, which quickly spreads. This is occurring because information is a commodity. Information helps to maximize profits. The introduction of media devices has also contributed to the trend. Radio was once the sole means of connecting with the outside world, but these days people use an array of portable audio and video players, including MP3 players, MP4 players, and portable DVD players referred to by North Koreans as 'notetel'. USBs and SD cards are also pervasive and used to share content. The North Korean authorities continue to crack down and punish those consuming and sharing foreign media, but it does little to impact the demand for such information, and technology is helping to circumvent the State surveillance apparatus.

What percentage of the North Korean people have had to rely for their survival on the market economies that sprang up during the human-made famine of the 1990s? What parts of this economy does the North Korean regime allow, and what parts is it trying to ban?

Technically speaking only women are allowed to participate in the market sphere but in practice almost every North Korean resident, male or female, is involved in the market economy in one way or another. For example, in one family, the husband of a female market vendor may deal with the logistics and transportation side of things rather than clocking in at his state-run enterprise (such workers pay a fee to do so). Meanwhile, the children may help out with odds and ends, and even older generations get involved.

The fallout from the botched currency redenomination in 2009 resulted in a loosening of restrictions in February 2010, and by May of the same year the policies constraining activities at general markets were effectively withdrawn. Market-friendly development has increased under Kim Jong-un, and there has been a subsequent flourishing of the market space. As a result, residents' livelihoods are inextricably linked to the markets, which continue to proliferate. As more individuals leave the State socialist framework to engage in market activities, the societal and economic changes are shifting attitudes further from State ideology. The regime closely monitors such shifts and increases oppressive countermeasures to keep things in check, like harsher punishments for those caught with South Korean media, which is prohibited under North Korean law.

Do you worry that the North Korean regime used the Pyeongchang Olympics as a means of promoting false propaganda?

There is already evidence pointing to the regime's use of the Pyeongchang Olympics for domestic propaganda. The authorities portrayed a theme of international appeasement and joint participation with the South as 'South Korea carrying a white flag' and 'proof of the success of the Byungjin Line'. But residents are finding themselves increasingly at odds with the State narrative, especially due to their exposure to South Korean culture, which in turn engenders more support for unification with the South. The North Korean authorities see this as a threat to their control, which is why efforts to advance the free flow of information throughout North Korea are paramount.

How did North Koreans react to the meetings between the South Korean and North Korean governments where they agreed to pursue a peace treaty and work towards the

denuclearization of the peninsula?

Opinions on the inter-Korean summit among North Koreans are quite varied. Many ordinary North Koreans believe that, as they are told in political lectures, the country's nuclear-weapons program is complete and now the focus will be on economic development to improve people's lives. On the other hand, intellectuals and other elites see it as capitulation, and due to a lack of national power.

But almost every North Korean is supportive of the Panmunjom Declaration, particularly due to the potential for economic exchange and to improve livelihoods. There is less interest in the political details and issues.

Generally speaking, North Koreans are positive about increased inter-Korean exchanges. There is a strong belief that inter-Korean railway and roadways projects will move ahead, as these would be extremely beneficial to the North. Likewise, for the Kaesong Industrial Complex and tourism to the Kumgang Mountain Resort area. ■

Africa

HASSAN AVDULLAHI

 Hassan Avdullahi is a community reporter for the Nigerian organization Connected Development, which aims to help local communities hold their governments accountable for corruption. He is also president of the Borno Literary Society where young people use art, spoken word, poetry, plays, drama and stories as tools for promoting peace.

What are the origins of Boko Haram? Are civilians willing to overlook alleged human rights abuses by the military and support its counter-insurgency efforts because of the barbarism of Boko Haram's war crimes?

Founded by Mohammed Yusuf in 2002, the group Boko Haram has been led by Abubakar Shekau since 2009. From March 2015 to August 2016, the group was aligned with the Islamic State of Iraq and the Levant. Since the current insurgency started in 2009, Boko Haram has killed tens of thousands and displaced 2.3 million from their homes.

Boko Haram was founded upon the principles of the Khawaarij advocating sharia law. It developed into a jihadist group in 2009. The movement is diffuse, and fighters associated with it do not follow the Salafi doctrine. It opposes the Westernization of Nigerian society and the concentration of the wealth of the country among members of a small political elite, mainly in the Christian south of the country.

After its founding in 2002, Boko Haram's increasing radicalization led to a violent uprising in July 2009 in which its leader was summarily executed. Its unexpected resurgence, following a mass prison break in September 2010, was accompanied by increasingly sophisticated attacks, initially against soft targets, but progressing in 2011 to include suicide bombings of police buildings and the United Nations office in Abuja. The government established a state of emergency at the beginning of 2012, which was extended the following year to cover the entire northeast area of Nigeria. This led to an increase in both security force abuses and militant attacks.

The conflict has caused the displacement of millions of people, and hundreds of thousands of people have left Nigeria and fled to Cameroon, Chad or Niger. Boko Haram killed more than 6,600 people in 2014. The group has carried out mass abductions, including the kidnapping of 276 schoolgirls from Chibok in April 2014. Corruption in the security services and human rights abuses committed by them have hampered efforts to counter the unrest.

Most Nigerians support the Nigerian military, considering them a lesser evil than Boko Haram. In the past, the Nigerian Army has never cared about the perceptions of civilians of its activities. They are ironically hailed for their wildness and seemingly institutional arrogance.

What are the origins of the violence between farmers and herders in Nigeria?

They can be traced to a multitude of factors that are intertwined and are based on the operating structures of Nigerian society and the failure of government and policymakers to plan effectively while adapting to the prevailing social and environmental realities. I have identified these factors as follows: overpopulation; global warming; politics and hate speech; and ethnocentrism.

Overpopulation: The population of Nigeria has more than quadrupled in the last 40 years. This astronomical growth has caused significant strain on the land resources in the entire country. The herders are quickly running out of grazing reserves as cities, towns, villages and farms are expanding and encroaching on the established routes of the herders and their cattle. This friction is caused by a rapidly growing population without a corresponding plan to cater for this explosion. This situation is making violence between these two groups very common as they compete for the resources that sustain their livelihoods.

Global warming: Lake Chad, which is situated in northeastern Nigeria, has been shrinking and drying up for the past couple of decades. It now only holds 25 per cent of its original volume of water. This lake supports 45 million people and their livelihoods in four different countries: Nigeria, Niger, Cameroon and Chad. The lake has supported farmers and fisherpeople, pastoralists and herders for hundreds of years. The 45-million estimates is a very conservative figure. With the present reality of a shrinking Lake Chad and a raging insurgency that has taken root in that region, one begins to get a glimpse of why the southward migration of these herders and farmers is creating significant stress on the meager available land and water resources necessary for fishing, farming and animal husbandry.

Politics and hate speech: The conflict is exacerbated by the involvement of politicians looking to make cheap political gains, who take the opportunity to galvanize their bases with populist messages aimed at creating an atmosphere of hate amongst political leaders of farmers and herders. We hear daily on the news how these politicians are taking positions about the conflict and issuing out threats of violence to the other side, so their base will perceive them as being tough on their supposed 'enemies'. These careless statements have led to attacks and counter-attacks. The government doesn't seem to take prompt action to tame this dangerous debacle, probably because it sees an opportunity in the conflict to further the ruling party's political goals. As such, we are now seeing a deterioration in the conflict, with many directly involved in the conflict espousing conspiracy theories not rooted in reality. This does nothing but heighten the tension and suspicion among the herding and farming communities. This has led to a situation where politicians buy arms and ammunitions in secret, and illegally arm militias who go about perpetrating violence on innocent people.

Ethnocentrism: It is well known that when people in a society are experiencing some form of economic or social threat in a multicultural, heterogeneous society like Nigeria, the tendency to revert to ethnic and tribal bias is immediately high. This ugly trait leads to stereotypes, prejudice and discrimination against people based on their ethnicity. This is now a widespread phenomenon in Nigeria. In a nutshell, it seems the problem Nigeria is facing with this farmer-herder violence is that ethnocentrism clouds judgment and prevents people from seeing the situation clearly – and this robs us of the ability to easily rectify a daunting predicament.

We must find solutions to all these problems. ∎

CHIDINMA PERPETUA CHIKWELU

 Chidinma Perpetua Chikwelu co-ordinates the Nigerian Hub of the Afrika Youth Movement, a pan-African, action-oriented, youth-led movement that strives for the participation, development and leadership of young Africans.

Can you talk about the strategies of feminist groups in Nigeria who are working to oppose female genital mutilation, gender-based violence and domestic violence?

Most women in Nigeria, and I believe in the rest of Africa as well, are still not open to accepting the 'feminist' tag due to culture, religion and certain negative attributes it has been attached to. For most men and women, feminism means man-hating. And there have been some man-hating hashtags trended by people who identified as feminists which puts feminism in a bad light, such as #MenAreScum and #MenAreTrash. This made it difficult for many women to understand what feminism means, or to accept it not just as a tag but a way of life. Gender discrimination in Nigeria has been encouraged and reinforced by certain cultural and religious factors militating against women's status and their participation in various sectors of the society. In several traditional Nigerian societies, the status of a woman has been considered as that of a wife, mother and housekeeper. A wife is regarded as the husband's property because the man paid a certain amount as bride price. Challenging this makes you an 'outcast' in society. Despite the inclusion of women's rights in our 1999 constitution, many women do not enjoy the same freedom as men, particularly in the fields of education, economic empowerment and political participation. There still exists inequality between men and women in attaining certain positions in Nigeria. The discrimination against women has pervaded through the Civil Service and Military, with women neglected in the background or retired at a certain level so they won't get to the positions that seem to be 'reserved for men only'. This injustice is being challenged by many women's groups through online and offline campaigns.

Can you discuss some of the work your organization has been doing in Nigeria? What key issues are you focusing on?

Afrika Youth Movement (AYM) is a pan-African, action-oriented, youth-led movement that strives for the participation, development and leadership of African youth, aimed at transforming Africa and achieving their rights to peace, equality and social justice. We are creating a continent that respects the rights of all its citizens. Through our works we promote values that bind our continent together: *ubuntu*, unity, self-determination, integrity and accountability.

AYM is launching hubs across the continent and, so far, we have hubs in eight different countries. The Nigeria Hub was launched on 9 November 2017. This was when I became the co-ordinator. Our key focus is on grooming the next generation of African leaders and achieving outlined goals. Currently, we have about 200 members in Nigeria.

We marked World Menstrual Hygiene Day on 28 May 2018 in the Makoko community. It is a riverine area and a slum where many women and girls have no access to sanitary pads and the people have no access to clean water. Activities for the day were a girls' health education program on personal hygiene during menstruation, and the distribution of sanitary pads. AYM will subsequently visit the community occasionally to donate sanitary pads with the purpose of changing their mindset from using pieces of cloth during menstruation. In addition, girls should also be free to talk about their menstruation. We also identified other projects we can do for the community in line with the UN Sustainable Development Goals, such as renovation of the dilapidated school buildings and provision of instructional materials for effective teaching and learning. We are also working on sensitizing voters in preparation for the upcoming presidential election in 2019. This will be a two-month program that will take place across the country, especially in rural communities where there is high level of illiteracy. The aim is to teach them how to vote and the qualities to look for when electing their new leaders. We are not going to campaign for any candidate or tell the people who to vote for. As a youth movement, we encourage open-mindedness and global inclusion, and we seek collaboration and partnerships within and beyond our local region to carry out projects. ■

SODFA DAAJI

 Sodfa Daaji is a Tunisian who is the North Africa co-ordinator for the Afrika Youth Movement (AYF) and chairs its gender equality committee. The organization promotes the values of *ubuntu*, unity, self-determination, integrity and accountability.

What are some of the major initiatives you are working on at the Afrika Youth Movement?

We are a youth-led movement with more than 10,000 members that is divided into committees. I'm in the gender equality committee, but we also have committees on education, health, peace and security, and agriculture. The gender equality committee works every year on human trafficking. We organized protests in Libya and Nigeria on this issue in 2018. We focus on cases like that of Noura Hussein Hammad in South Sudan, who was initially sentenced to be hanged for killing her husband after he tried to rape her. [Noura was raped by her husband after she was forced to marry him against her will; after an international outcry, the death sentence was commuted to five years' imprisonment.]

Are there any barriers your committee faces when you promote gender equality? Is the idea of gender equality more accepted in some African countries than others?

Every tribe or country tries to justify violence against women by invoking tradition. It isn't easy because when you talk to people who are defending violence against women as tradition, they think that they are right. It's hard to create a line between good tradition and bad tradition. We have workshops that teach women to challenge traditions that perpetrate violence against them.

Since you have become an Italian citizen, do you often get accused of trying to promote so-called Western values in Africa?

When I tell people that tradition and culture are used to oppress women, supporters of the status quo always reply that I'm trying to westernize Africa. I always try to explain to them that my right as a woman to be free is not solely a Western right, it is a universal right. There are some issues that are difficult to discuss in Africa. For example, sex is not talked about because it is seen as an intimate act. I can't go to women and talk about safe sex. But I'm Tunisian and I know how hard it is to discuss these subjects. I come from a very Muslim family and it was very hard for me to challenge their minds and create my own personal freedom and space and to reveal to them that I wasn't a Muslim. What I have seen in Africa is not so much about religion, but about traditional culture.

Do the African women you work with often try to challenge the interpretations of their traditions and cultures in ways that incorporate gender equality?

It varies from country to country. I have perceived that in Ghana, for example, it is not so much about good and bad tradition, it's about interpretation. Our traditions and cultures have been interpreted for so many years by men. This is the problem. Women are part of the tradition, but they included us just to give us rules. So many African women are aware of this. Local African women will say their tradition promotes gender equality, it's just that men interpret these traditions to oppress women. They don't want to challenge the tradition, they want to challenge men to understand or clearly elaborate tradition.

I find this troubling because genital mutilation is justified as part of tradition. This is a harmful practice, so how can it be part of gender equality? I think it's important to challenge the tradition instead of just challenging the men.

This male-dominated interpretation doesn't just happen with tradition, but also with religion. It is time to re-elaborate tradition and religion and really understand what is good, what is bad, and what can be used to empower women and gender equality.

Can you talk about how this reinterpretation can be accomplished by Muslim women, given your upbringing in a Muslim family?

Islam has always been interpreted by men. The Qur'an is different from the way it is often interpreted by men, and this has worsened in the past several years. If you go to Tunisia and speak to older women, they are shocked to see so many veiled young girls. You can be Muslim without the hijab. But religion is too often being used to oppress women.

Do you feel the younger generation is more amenable to gender equality than the older generation?

There are a few young men who agree with us and believe we should challenge tradition and religion. I've been working with men who describe themselves as advocates for gender equality, but they avoid conversations that criticize religion and tradition. They see blasphemy in what we say. This is a problem because what I have perceived in Africa is how faith is a part of daily life. When it comes to religion and tradition, young men think tradition puts limits between what is a good woman and what is a good man. But I still always try to understand their way of thinking, and our group never tries to exclude them. We include them by leading workshops and training to teach them that people like myself are not trying to westernize Africa, we are trying to promote equality for everyone. We still have a lot of work to do because this isn't just a challenge we face with men; some young women also disagree with our beliefs.

Do you think there is too much focus in Africa over whether a person's politics is considered pro-Western or anti-Western?

Most countries in Africa are obsessed with what the West is doing. They still feel the consequences of colonization. I don't think civil wars in Africa can be blamed only on colonization. There are dictators throughout Africa draining the continent of oil and other resources. For example, the president of Cameroon, Paul Biya, is 90 and doesn't even work anymore, yet he is still the president. We need to focus more on preparing for the future than on looking at the past.

Does the Afrika Youth Movement adopt the position of being critical of Western governments while also being critical of internal problems in African countries?

Our position is we need to tell the truth. The reality is that Africa can't survive now without Western help. We disagree when Western leaders address Africans with a sense of superiority, and we also disagree with Western governments offering military assistance to different warring groups and authoritarian governments. This is causing a lot of bloodshed and civilian deaths. For example, in Cameroon (a recipient of US military aid), soldiers are going into homes and raping women on a daily basis.

Do you see a rise in feminist movements calling for gender equality in different African nations?

Yes. Women's organizations are receiving a lot more money than they had previously received. This has allowed them to be able carry out work that used to be unaffordable. The power of the internet has also been helpful. When young girls are thinking about women's equality, they can now go online and learn how to become involved with different women's organizations. Women are also becoming more knowledgeable about their rights, and the importance of fighting for their rights. ■

FARID ESACK

 Farid Esack is a veteran of the struggle against the South African apartheid government. After liberation, he was appointed by President Nelson Mandela as a gender commissioner for the South African government. He is a liberation theologian who has written several books, including *Qur'an, Liberation and Pluralism, On Being a Muslim* and *Whose Qur'an: A Concise Guide to Progressive Islam.*

What do you see as some of the failures and successes of South African politics in the post-apartheid era?

Post-apartheid South Africa, in a liberal sense, is one of the most amazing countries in the world, with a free press, an independent judiciary, a vibrant civil society, a serious commitment to gender and sexual equality and a relatively independent foreign policy. As a Muslim with a not inconsequential bit of international experience, it is arguably the free-est country in the world in which to practice your faith. The same goes for all the other minority religious communities. South Africa does not only protect diversity, it celebrates it. On the negative side, the growing economic inequality and the resultant poverty are the biggest failures of the post-apartheid state. Connected to this is the inability to manage and reduce the crime rate.

What are some of the key areas where you would like to see improvement in South Africa?

The implementation of the socio-economic rights provisions in the Constitution, serious land reform, tackling corruption – both in the private and state sectors – and more attention to crime prevention.

How popular is progressive Islamic theology in the Muslim community?

Broadly speaking, there are two approaches to viewing 'progressive Islam'. The first one is basically a liberal interpretation of the faith which is big on issues of personal freedoms, gender and sexual identity questions and religious pluralism but is indifferent or tokenistic towards issues of class, economic exploitation, caste-ism and imperialism. This is a project uncritically embraced by the Global North. The other approach – now largely decimated in the US in the wake of 9/11 – also embraces, in fact prioritizes, the issues that the liberals are indifferent towards. While I eschew the self-description 'progressive Muslim', I fall in the latter category and prefer to describe myself as a liberation theologian.

As for its popularity, it depends on which approach one invokes, which social classes and what area of the world we are speaking about. In general, it remains seriously undertheorized and liberal Islam is very alive among the upper middle classes. As for the vast majority of Muslims, traditional religion still holds sway. Yet, here too, we need to be careful and not assume that this inevitably translates into 'backwards'. The weaponization of issues such as gender equality and religious freedom by the US in its 'war on terror' has not really helped in the struggle to make Muslim societies more open to change. As for an Islamic theology of liberation, it is still in its nascent stages and really exists on the margins of Muslim society – although the current scholarly and activist interest in 'decoloniality' may be breathing new energy into it.

A lot of talk in the West focuses on good Muslims versus bad Muslims. Do you think this reductionist approach has failed to factor in the historical and political histories of Muslim majority countries along with their historical relationships with the US?

Absolutely. Not only did it fail to factor in the historical relationship of Muslim countries with the US but it also ignored the ongoing role of the US in bolstering, reproducing and multiplying the supposedly bad Muslims through their responses of indefinite detention without trial, rendition, and the legalization of torture. Second, like the meaning of 'terrorist' – and here I speak as someone from a country whose non-racial and non-sexist democracy was attained by a terrorist movement led by someone embraced by the world as everyone's favorite grandfather [Nelson Mandela], the definitions of Good Muslim and Bad Muslim were entirely arbitrary. The Good Muslim was or is one who supports the US – regardless of whether he or she was a democrat or a military dictator, a Wahhabi or Sufi, a feminist or a misogynist.

While there persists a much older idea of Islam and the Muslim being irredeemable enemies of Western civilization with a newly articulated Judeo-Christian basis, immediately after 9/11, Islamophobes found it more politically expedient to abandon the blanket demonization of Muslims and instead to separate the 'Good Muslims' from the 'Bad Muslims' and speak of an intra-Muslim civil war for the soul of Islam. While the Good Muslim versus Bad Muslim thesis was widespread, the badness of the Bad Muslim was assumed; not so the goodness of the Good Muslim. The latter was never to be liberated from the obligation to, first, tirelessly prove his or her goodness by interminable denunciations whenever any 'Bad Muslim' struck anywhere in the Western world and, second, to offer ceaseless declarations of loyalty to Western interests and values.

The US is a curious place. From Washington DC and New York, nations are destroyed and rebuilt – often the same ones simultaneously – and extensive policy documents are produced about 'religion-building', i.e., how to eliminate some tendencies in a religion one day and promote another the next day in one area of the world while doing the reverse in another. So, 'democracy' is pushed for Iran because the current rulers don't like 'us' but not in the totalitarian monarchy of Saudi Arabia because their rulers do. Wahhabism is acceptable for Saudi Arabia and Qatar because they are our friends but its nemesis, Sufism, must be cultivated in the US itself and abroad because it's a good antidote to militant Wahhabism. *Jihad-i-asghar* (the lesser Jihad, or armed combat) was a requirement for the Afghan people when they fought the Soviet invasion and *jihad-i-akar* (personal and spiritual self-transformation) when they fought the US invasion.

What do you think is the proper way to engage in inter-religious dialogue?

Well, I certainly won't speak about the proper way – perhaps, my preferred way. The kind of interfaith dialogue that has come to dominate liberal understandings today is essentially about the open-ended sharing of religious perspectives in the belief that such sharing will contribute to a climate for peaceful coexistence among various religious traditions. The vast majority of those engaged in the organization of such dialogue initiatives come from the 'modernist-liberal' streams within those religious traditions, although attempts are very often made to involve those from the more traditional or orthodox streams in such dialogue. Those who are truly committed to political action are in rather short supply in the interfaith movement. Furthermore, when international organizations put a large premium on securing the support or participation of the grandees of formal religious institutions – I call them the men with the funny hats – then this is often done at the cost of eschewing grassroots engagement and action that could be construed as politically insensitive or controversial.

Those committed to more liberatory expressions of religions who are also committed to the struggle against injustice tend to avoid the time-consuming butterfly dances of inter-religious politeness for more concrete local action for justice and peace. Quite frankly, I am far more committed to inter-religious solidarity against injustice than inter-religious dialogue. ■

TESFAGABIR GHEBRE-EGZIABIHER

Tesfagabir Ghebre-egziabiher is an Eritrean activist for human rights, democracy and gender equality who is currently living in South Africa.

What would you like the international community to know about the situation in Eritrea?

There is nothing that is secret about the situation in Eritrea. We have a military dictatorship that came to power through a struggle for independence that was fully backed by the people. Two years after we won our independence, the people voted for a referendum: the historic vote that sealed our struggle for independence and gave our beautiful nation international recognition. A few years later the elite military leaders whom we respected as liberators turned against their own people. They blocked all roads to democracy and turned the government into a full-blown dictatorship. The regime held the entire citizenry hostage economically and politically. The international community is well aware of the situation in Eritrea, as it has often been described as the North Korea of Africa.

The commission of inquiry established by the International Commission for Human Rights has confirmed that the regime in Eritrea has committed crimes against humanity. However, nothing concrete has been done by the international community. We know the international community does not act if it is not in the interests of the few that control it. To me, the international community only reacts when a certain group is affected.

Unfortunately, the tens of thousands of Eritreans rotting in jails, the innocent people dying in Syria, Iraq, Yemen and Libya do not belong to that specific group. We have all seen the reaction of the world when there were attacks in France, Belgium and so on. I wish people would react the same way to the attacks and sufferings experienced by people everywhere. For this and other reasons, I rely on our own people.

Can you talk about the national-service law in Eritrea, and how it has caused many people to flee the country?

When it was first declared, the duration of national service was 18 months. Eritrea was born after 30 years of struggle – it has had many struggles – so the entire nation initially embraced this law. However, the lack of an adequate facility at Sawa [an Eritrean military camp near the Sudanese border], and the ill treatment of the national recruits by the trainers was a clear indication that the whole national-service law was not something that was studied very well, and it wasn't yielding positive results. It was just a means of getting rid of the youth that was suffering from unemployment at that time. Perhaps the regime was planning the war with neighboring Ethiopia from the early stages after the referendum. The national-service law should have been implemented with proper planning to make an impact on the economy and the participants. At a later stage, national service turned into national slavery. The government forced the conscripts to stay in the military indefinitely with no pay whatsoever. It ruined the lives of two generations of people, forcing the workforce to risk their lives fleeing the country. It has been the darkest part of our country's history since its inception in 1993.

What do you think is the government's reasoning behind denying the citizenry religious freedom, freedom of press and the formation of civil-society organizations?

A well-informed and organized society is a threat to the dictatorship and an asset to democratic governance. Hence the dictatorial regime declared war against religion, the press and civil organizations. As a result, we have a society that is ill-informed, divided and terrorized. Through its terror tactics, the regime instilled fear and mistrust among people, making us its perfect prey.

Could you speak about some of the people inside and outside Eritrea who are working to advocate for positive change in the country?

In a country where there is no freedom of speech and association it is difficult to find advocates fighting from within. However, right-minded Eritreans from all corners of the world are advocating for positive change in the country. I must say sometimes we are too cautious of the type of struggle we are engaged in, and it is dragging us down. No-one wants see Eritrea become another Syria, Libya or Yemen. But it is hard to imagine change only using the tactics of advocacy and nonviolent struggle. We need to mobilize people from within and hit the regime from without while avoiding any unforeseen catastrophes.

What needs to take place to create an atmosphere that supports more gender equality in Eritrea?

A lot needs to be done to create an environment where women are treated equally and with dignity. Women have carried the burden of dictatorship and societal stereotyping for so long. Only removal of the regime and building democratic institutions will guarantee women their deserved place in society.

If the current regime falls, and Eritrea blossoms into a democracy, what institutions and civil-society organizations would have to be formed to prevent the return of oppressive rule?

Post-regime Eritrea will have to have a constitution, free press, sound democratic institutions to safeguard the rights of citizens, trade unions and other community-based organizations. Its job won't be just to prevent the re-occurrence of an oppressive regime, but to protect the rights of the citizens and safeguard hard-won democracy. I am optimistic that there will never be dictatorship in Eritrea again. The current regime managed to exploit the country's historical predicament as an excuse for oppression. It has created enemies to serve as an excuse for its failure. I don't think any government that follows the regime will enjoy such privilege to deceive and manipulate the public. We have learned lessons the hard way. We will never allow anyone to dictate to us again.

Have Eritrean refugees who have fled to European countries been welcomed, or has their treatment varied from country to country? How can people can help Eritreans resettle in new countries?

I don't have much knowledge of the refugee screening criteria and policies of individual nations. There are some countries that are champions of safeguarding refugee rights, and I can only appreciate and be thankful that my fellow citizens and myself have been provided with a home away from home. We remain totally indebted to all those who showed us true humanity. In contrast, I condemn countries and segments of societies that have rejected Eritreans' right to refugee status. Eritrean refugees in Israel, South Africa and others have suffered tremendously due to lack of proper refugee-status determination procedures. The latest move by EU countries to block all refugees crossing the Mediterranean has left thousands of Eritreans stranded in Libya. Human traffickers and warlords are abusing and harassing them every day. The situation is dire. If only they had a place they could call home, they would be willing to go back. Thanks to the regime in Eritrea, home is not the safest place for them to be. It is a pity how some Europeans think Eritreans are economic refugees. No Eritrean youth leaves the country looking for bread, but for peace of mind and personal freedom. I am sure civil societies can play a role in voicing the plight of Eritreans stranded in Libya, and those who remain stateless throughout the world. ■

LEO IGWE

 Leo Igwe is a native Nigerian and a former representative for West and Southern Africa to IHEU, the International Humanist and Ethical Union. He has worked to end a wide variety of human rights violations, including anti-gay hate, ritual killing, caste discrimination and anti-blasphemy laws.

How did you end up becoming a humanist in a country as religious as Nigeria?

Humanism means basing your knowledge on evidence, logic, knowledge and observation. I think the humanist sentiment beats in the heart of everybody and it all depends on if you let the beating manifest.

I say this because I used to teach in a Christian school and one morning during an assembly a teacher came out and asked the students 'do you know Jesus?' Most of them said, 'Yes, yes, I know Jesus, I know Jesus', but one eight-year-old girl raised her hand and said, 'I don't know Jesus'. The teacher was shocked. He said, 'Why do you say that?' She answered, 'Because I've never seen him before.' That struck me – that kind of brutal honesty. This girl hadn't seen Jesus before and she couldn't claim she knew Jesus. Of course, some people would disagree with this child for whom seeing was knowing!

Why isn't humanism more prevalent in Nigeria?

There are many reasons for that. But how Nigerians are educated is one of them. There is always this idea that if you don't accept religious beliefs you can't get a formal education, climb the social ladder and grow in society. So, if you want to grow socially, you have to genuflect before religious models and embrace religious dogmas. For me at some point I just said: 'No, let me explore a life that is close to my ideals.'

I felt like I had to become an adult and be able to stand up on my own two feet before I could slowly peel away at the religious nonsense. When I left the seminary, I made contact with the humanist and skeptics movement. Compared to the Christian and Islamic faiths, ours is a very small movement. And by the time I started the Nigerian Humanist Movement, organized humanists were mainly interested in their own countries and their own part of the world. So, there wasn't much international solidarity.

Things started to change in the late 1990s and I started to get some international support. I started getting literature from people and organizations that shared the same values as me and I started to get encouraged. Slowly, I found out I had many friends and people of like mind out there in Nigeria and beyond. That was kind of a moral boost for me. Today, I'm just happy I was able to sustain the effort and have been able to get to this point.

Does being a humanist in Nigeria come with any risk from the government or from religious extremists within your society?

Yes, it does, because the government mirrors the society. Even though the Constitution states that everyone has a right to practice any religion or belief, that is the Constitution in principle, not in practice. Humanists have no guarantees of their rights, safety or security because the people who are supposed to enforce the Constitution instead try to impose their own religion on people. Their own beliefs trump the Constitution. The risks are most serious in northern Nigeria, where Muslim-majority states implement sharia law.

How prevalent are ritual killings and human sacrifices in Nigeria? Do you see a broader rejection of these traditions in the future?

You always make a security assessment of your movements because you could be killed by a ritualist or a person who is looking for body parts. There is a very strong belief that you can do something with human body parts that has spiritual significance.

There are some very poor people in Nigeria. They start businesses with little experience and little capital and when the business collapses there is no state to provide them with support to take care of their families. Sometimes these people will go to witch doctors, who tell them they need to make a sacrifice. Sometimes they are told to bring human heads and human body parts by their witch doctors. Since these people feel consumed by their needs, they end up killing people or cutting up people's body parts to use them for a sacrifice. The fear that one could be used for ritual sacrifice is very prevalent.

Ritual killing is very pervasive, particularly in rural areas, but it also happens in urban areas. It all depends on where the ritualists feel they can get away with these crimes. Most of the time it is the vulnerable members of the population – people from poor homes or people who are living with albinism – who are targeted for ritual killings. The belief that drives these killings is that a sacrifice will bring good luck and fortune.

We need to challenge this belief, because it is the belief that drives the action. This belief is not just about the traditional African voodoo religion – you see some of the same narratives in Christianity and Islam and all the so-called world religions that reinforce these beliefs. I'm not trying to say every religion is the same, but supernatural, religious and spiritual beliefs really motivate people to commit these atrocities. And these narratives are not going to go away until counter-narratives are provided. When you challenge religious beliefs – be they African, Christian or Islamic – people think you are doing something that should not be done. We have to do away with these notions because unless we do away with them, people will still find a way to justify practices like human sacrifice and ritual killings.

Would a secular education counterbalance the prevalence of superstitions that lead to violence?
Yes, but it has to go with something such as basic medical services. When people get to the state where they take action

against people suspected to be witches it's because they have linked them to some kind of misfortune. People first need to be told that you can't cause sickness through magical means. But we need hospitals to provide basic medical services to people when they are sick. When people are sick, and they go to traditional healers who have little or no effective medicine to take care of the sickness, they look to the supernatural for the source of their misfortunes. This is where the witchcraft narratives thrive.

When so-called healing and medicinal experts tie an incurable illness to witchcraft and point their finger at somebody, people think that person must have been behind the illness. When this happens, people have little inhibition about taking action against that person. This is why there has to be an infrastructural response to these situations in many communities. If there are hospitals, people will not go to charlatans and quacks that have no medicinal knowledge to take care of them. So, education is important, but communities also need the proper health infrastructure to provide them with the appropriate medical therapies when they get sick. ■

LEKAN LATUBOSUN

 Lekan Latubosun is a Nigerian engineer and entrepreneur with a particular interest in political economics.

Has the Nigerian government been able to make reforms to reduce the corruption that has historically been a problem in Nigerian politics?

The straightforward answer is a clear No. The Nigerian government uses anti-corruption language, but it is largely just lip service. There are steps to fighting corruption. The first step is resolve. That requires some minimum morality in which people perceived to be corrupt are avoided. We have seen several situations where people with corruption cases or serious accusations against them remain in office or hang on for a long time while the government vacillates on making clear decisions.

The second step is to set up systems that discourage corruption. Structures, systems and processes are the most effective means of preventing corruption within public space. This should start with a wholesale reform of procurement processes, to drive transparency and inclusive involvement of many more stakeholders, so that all procurement processes include open bidding, crowd costing, and firm and autonomous audit processes.

The clear measurement of output or productivity and setting benchmarks is an important tool for checking corruption, and that is absent at present. Productivity and corruption are inversely related; one increases at the expense of the other. If productivity increases, the space for corruption reduces, and conversely, when corruption increases, the space for productivity reduces. Such productivity benchmarks should be set from the best practices around the world.

Another important reform not being sought is private prosecution. If I have evidence that someone stole money from the government, I could privately approach a law office that would present the evidence to a competent court, which would then determine if prosecution could follow. This would be a step beyond the whistleblower policy, which itself has been messed up by shoddy handling.

It's impossible to detail all of the mechanisms to prevent corruption in one single discussion, but the government effort at fighting corruption has been worse than half-hearted.

Are the Nigerian people seeing the benefits of oil production?

No, they are not. This is made clear when, according to the UN Human Development Index (HDI), Nigeria ranked 152 out of 188 countries surveyed in 2016. Nigeria had more than 10 million children out of school, with an increasing poverty rate at well beyond 60 per cent, the largest population of poor people in the world, and less than six per cent of its people were covered by healthcare. Nigerians are not necessarily supposed to see the benefits of just oil production, but the benefits of a properly engineered wholesome economy.

First and foremost, the revenues from oil are inadequate to deliver profit to the large Nigerian population. The Norwegian population is less than two per cent of the Nigerian population, but its oil receipts are comparable to Nigeria. The Qatari economy has more oil receipts, but it has less than a fiftieth of the Nigerian population. Nigeria's oil receipts are very small compared to its population, so oil production can never deliver goods to the Nigerian economy all by itself like the Saudi or Qatari economy.

To have a wholesome economy, fiscal policy must de-emphasize oil. We continue to benchmark budgets with oil prices, whereas we ought to benchmark budgets with tax rates so as to have a full overview of the entire economy and grow it wholesomely in order to be able to improve HDI, which will in turn affect school enrollment, education, healthcare, skill development, human capital and employment.

What kind of economic development would you like to see in Nigeria? What do you think would be some effective ways civil-society groups and the government could lessen poverty in your country?

To reduce poverty, we need to increase per-capita income and that can only happen through the ingenuity and energy of the people involved in entrepreneurial endeavors. That said, it means that the credit architecture must change. Currently, the credit architecture is a lockdown on the economy. We need an expansionary credit architecture.

We need to bring down interest rates. Interest rates and employment rates have an inverse relationship. That is a law. I do know that the monetary policy is seemingly struggling to hold down inflation, but Nigeria's inflation is due to structural factors or cost-push factors rather than monetary factors or consumption factors or demand-pull factors.

Government must reduce recurrent expenditures and reduce all areas of fiscal burdens which are merely wasteful. Then we need to get private-sector funds into the healthcare sector through comprehensive healthcare insurance coverage. We need to rework education systems at local levels to start in each locality and have local management so that neighborhood schools can have the right level of quality and output. We need to rework our curriculum to be fit for purpose so that secondary-school graduates can be employable and trainable for other high-skilled jobs without needing a degree, but rather work-specific learning and training. This will generally improve HDI. ■

MAHMOOD MAMDANI

 Mahmood Mamdani is a Ugandan who is currently professor of government, international affairs and anthropology at Columbia University in the US. He is a specialist on African issues, including the legacy of colonialism, indirect rule, civil war and genocide. Among his books are: *Saviors and Survivors: Darfur, politics, and the War on Terror*; *Good Muslim, Bad Muslim*; and *Define and Rule: Native as political*.

Can you talk about the US and the idea of a settler democracy?

Unlike all previous exclusions – ethnicity, race and gender – the native question would provide a far more fundamental challenge to the celebration of citizenship in America. Engaging with the native question would require questioning the ethics and politics of the very Constitution of the United States of America. It would require rethinking and reconsidering the very political project called the US. Indeed, it would call into question the self-proclaimed anti-colonial identity of the US. Highlighting the colonial nature of the American political project would require a paradigmatic shift in the understanding of America, one necessary to think through both America's place in the world and the task of political reform of future generations.

Can you talk about the idea of American exceptionalism from the viewpoint of the Native American?

From a Native American standpoint, the American Revolution in 1770 ushered in the independence of the white settler population. Rather than a revolution, it was better understood as a rebellion. It was akin to the independence of Liberia in 1847, white South Africa in 1910, Israel in 1948, and, last but not least, the Unilateral Declaration of Independence (UDI) of the

Ian Smith-led white state of Rhodesia in 1974. Indeed, what is celebrated as the American Revolution today was called the War of Independence for the first 150 years after the event.

Just as the native question in South Africa, Liberia, Israel and Rhodesia forms part of the history of colonial governance in the modern world, so does the history of the relationship between the federal government and Native Americans. If there is American exceptionalism, it is this: treated by organs of the government as a perpetually colonized population, the fate of Native Americans is testimony that the US, the world's first settler-colonial state, continues to function as one.

The uncritical embrace of settler experience explains the blind spot in the American imagination: an inability to coexist with difference, indeed a preoccupation with civilizing natives. American cosmopolitanism has been crafted through a settler lens. The American sensibility remains a settler sensibility in important ways.

What strategies were employed by Western powers to impose colonial indirect rule on African countries?

If direct rule aimed to assimilate elite groups in a civilizing mission, the ambition of indirect rule was to remake the subjectivities of entire populations. It endeavored to shape the past, present and future of the colonized by casting each in a nativist mold: the present through a set of identities in the census; the past through the driving force of a new historiography; and the future through a legal and administrative project. Through this triple endeavor, the colonial state created a state-enforced internal discrimination – for which it claimed a mantle of tradition – thereby effectively fragmenting the colonized majority into so many administratively driven political minorities.

Could you explain how European colonizers used the words 'race' and 'tribe' to divide the people living in the countries they colonized?

First, the census divided the population into two kinds of groups: some were tagged as races and others as tribes. What determined whether you belonged to a race or a tribe? The distinction was not between the colonizer and the colonized, but between the native and the non-native. Non-natives were tagged as races, whereas natives were said to belong to tribes. Races were said to comprise all those officially categorized as not indigenous to Africa, whether they were indisputably foreign (Europeans, Asians) or whether their foreignness was the result of an official designation (Arabs, Colored, Tutsi). Tribes, in contrast, were all those defined as indigenous in origin. Rather than highlight the distinction between colonizers and the colonized, the race-tribe distinction cut through the single category – colonized – by politically distinguishing those indigenous from those foreign. When the state officially distinguished non-indigenous races from indigenous tribes it paid heed to one single characteristic, origin, and totally disregarded all subsequent developments, including residence. By obscuring an entire history of migrations, the state portrayed the native as the product of geography rather than history.

Second, the race-tribe distinction had a direct legal significance. Whether a person was defined as belonging to a race or a tribe determined the law under which that person would live. All races were governed under one single law: civil law. This, however, was not true of tribes, with each tribe governed by a law reflecting its own tradition. Yet most would agree that the cultural difference between races – such as whites and Asians – was greater than that between tribes. To begin with, different races spoke different languages, mutually unintelligible. Often, they practiced different religions. They also came from different parts of the world, each with its own historical archive. No matter how different they were, tribes were neighbors and usually spoke languages that were mutually intelligible; they also claimed histories that were at times shared, at other times overlapping.

Did tribe exist before colonialism? If we understand by 'tribe' an ethnic group with a common language, it did. But tribe as an administrative entity that distinguishes between natives and non-natives and systematically discriminates in favor of the former against the latter – defining access to land and participation in local governance and rules for settling disputes according to tribal identity – certainly did not exist before colonialism.

One may ask: did race exist before colonialism? As differences in pigmentation, or in phenotype, it did. But as a fulcrum for group discrimination based on 'race' difference, it did not. The consensus among scholars of race is that while race does not exist, racism – a system of discrimination, legal or social, based on the perception or conviction that race is real – does exist. Like tribe, race became a single, exclusive and total identity only with colonialism.

As a totalizing identity, tribe was a subset of race. Each represented a language of privilege and discrimination. The colonial state was based on double discrimination, racial and tribal. Racial discrimination was institutionalized in the central state, and tribal discrimination in the local substate. Race was said to be about a hierarchy of civilization whereas tribe was said to reflect cultural (ethnic) diversity within a race. If the central state justified discrimination against the native race on civilizational grounds, the local state justified discrimination in favor of the native tribe on the grounds of origin and difference. ■

NYUON SUSAN SEBIT

 Nyuon Susan Sebit is the executive director of the National Alliance for Women Lawyers (NAWL), an NGO set up in 2015 in the Republic of South Sudan, which had gained its independence in 2011.

Can you describe the mission of the National Alliance for Women Lawyers?

NAWL envisions a South Sudan where the rights of women, girls, children and other vulnerable groups are protected and respected, and the rule of law upheld as the basis of good governance, democracy, access to justice and peaceful co-existence. The main mission is to legally and professionally engage the stakeholders in peacebuilding, dialogue, access to the transitional justice system and rule of law. It is also to get women, girls and children to recognize their various rights through effective and positive engagement with dignity by eliminating gender inequality.

Our aim is to provide access to justice for women, children and other vulnerable people through provisions of *pro bono* legal services. The organization spreads awareness about women's and girls' rights as well as juvenile justice. We provide legal training to communities on basic legal principles and human rights to give them basic knowledge and information about the law and their rights. We also try to narrow and harmonize the gaps between the national law and traditional laws, especially on gender-sensitive issues, as well as engage in the reviews of some national legislations.

Have women been targets of abuse in the civil war in your country?

When there is a war, women are always victims. It has happened in South Sudan just like it has been happening in other countries. Sexual abuse as well as other criminal activities against women have been spearheaded by men in uniform. The majority of those who flock to neighboring countries are women and children. Families are broken, and women become the first-class victims of war. Women have lost their husbands and their children. Having responsibility over the family in a poor environment has become another burden for them. Women are more affected than any other group of people in the country.

Have many of the perpetrators of sexual violence in South Sudan been held accountable?

We are trying to create an avenue and environment where people are held accountable for their crimes. It's challenging because most of the crimes happen in areas that are not accessible. It's very hard to reach out to the victims and for the victims to reach out to us. We also have challenges with the victims themselves, because of cultural stereotypes. The rape cases are perceived by some women as something they cannot talk about openly. They worry that reporting the rape will bring shame to their family. Culture is one of the biggest obstacles.

Another problem is that some people don't trust the justice system. Many believe they will be turned away by the police. What we do is continue to create awareness by talking in different communities to males, females and the police about how victims of sexual violence should be treated to instill the principle of confidentiality and to ensure them of the safety of their information.

Can you talk about your goal of having 25 per cent of governmental and institutional jobs filled by women?

In Article 16 of the Constitution, it says women shall be given equal pay for equal work with men. It also says women shall have the right to participate fully in public life. The Article states: 'All levels of government shall promote women's participation in public life and their representation in the legislative and executive organs of at least 25 per cent as an affirmative action to redress imbalances created by history, customs and traditions.' It also orders all levels of government to 'enact laws to combat harmful customs and traditions which undermine the dignity and status of women'. The 25-per-cent target is to encourage women not to be shy about looking for jobs. The practicality of this article of the Constitution is being challenged. The government and other institutions are not really implementing it, as many of us understand it. Hence NAWL is more effectively working to advance the idea of affirmative action to rural women and their administrators, engage all the stakeholders to understand women's participation at all levels of leadership: traditional leadership authority or another leadership position. Women shouldn't shy away from heading institutions.

Could you discuss your advocacy work for sexual and reproductive rights?

We don't have a Family Law or a Sexual Offense Law. The Constitution is tricky because it says the customs and traditions of a community are to be respected. Article 33 of the Constitution states: 'Ethnic and cultural communities shall have the right to freely enjoy and develop their particular cultures. Members of such communities shall have the right to practice their beliefs, use their languages, observe their religions and raise their children within the context of their respective cultures and customs in accordance with this Constitution and the law.' Some community members believe their customs are protected by the Constitution. We have had discussions with stakeholders and with chiefs of different communities. We are trying to persuade them, and educate them, but it is a challenge.

We wanted to present a policy brief to Parliament about the importance of passing a Sexual Offense Act. They said they were too busy with national-security issues because of the war. We thought it was important because sexual violence was rampant after the war. Women have lost their children, brothers and husbands to war, and they have also lost properties and been subject to sexual violence.

Are women starting to form more groups to deal with the conflict in South Sudan?

There are several women's organizations, but most of them have been affected by the conflict and lack adequate funding. We think it's a good time for women to not just be observers, but to be at the negotiating table. Women are having conversations amongst themselves about how to pursue peace because we believe women shouldn't be divided but should work together for a common agenda. Women's groups from the government, opposition and the grassroots are coming together to fight for the common agenda of peace.

What are the other issues that need to be addressed to create a lasting peace in South Sudan?

The creation of jobs is important and will come when there is security. When there is security, access to humanitarian activities will flow and the farmers will be able to get back to work in their communities. This will reduce the need to have so much food imported from other countries and create everlasting food security in the country. Medical facilities will also then be available. Security is the paramount need.

Some journalists have described the situation in South Sudan as an 'ethnic conflict'. Is that an accurate depiction of what has gone on in your country?

I don't think this is an ethnic war. There are people of different ethnicities who are part of the opposition group and part of the ruling government.

What can the international community do to help bring peace to South Sudan?

We believe it is high time for the international community to support peace in South Sudan. It's important for countries in the Troika [the US, Britain and Norway] to support South Sudan because they played a big role in creating the country. We really need the international community to help us because the situation gets worse every day. I would call for the international community to mediate the peace process. It's time to put pressure on the warring parties to abide by the agreements they have signed. The warring parties must silence their guns because if they do, more humanitarian assistance can reach the people affected by the war. ■

FATOU SOW

Fatou Sow is director of the International Solidarity Network of Women Living Under Muslim Laws. Formerly a professor of social sciences at the University Cheikh Anta Diop of Dakar (Senegal) and the University of Paris-Diderot (France), she is also a member of the Council for the Development of Social Science Research in Africa and the African Feminist Forum. Sow set up GREFELS, a research group on women and law in Senegal. Her research has centered on fundamental rights and the equality of women.

Could you talk about the increase in religious fundamentalism in Senegal?

Fundamentalism is rising in Senegal. More and more Muslim leaders and organizations want to enter politics. Senegal has been a secular state from pre-colonial times, through colonization until today. Since independence, secularism has been inscribed in the Constitution. That simply means separation between religion and politics, separation between the State and the church, and the State and the mosque. People are elected as an individual citizen, not as a religious leader.

Could you discuss the influence of French colonialism on Senegal?

I think that colonization represented a recognizable shift in what Africa was supposed to be if it had not been colonized. I tell my friends that, because of French colonization and the French schooling, some part of us has been 'Westernized'. Some aspects of French culture were absorbed by people in Senegal because of colonialism, but people are deeply rooted in African cultures because they live on the continent. While we have been independent since 1960, we are not yet that economically independent because of neocolonialism, liberalization, global-ization and unequal international trade. I think for the younger generation in Africa, the issue of colonialism isn't whether I am African, or I am not African, it's about the weight of the West in politics, economics and African trade.

What effects do US farm subsidies have on African farmers?

Many people in America, in large firms or state organizations, such as USAID, have advised African countries not to subsidize their crops (peanut, cotton) for trade in Africa. At the same time, farmers in the United States are subsidized at a rate we could never imagine and that would never exist in Senegal. This policy doesn't make African agriculture competitive in markets driven by the subsidy policies carried out in rich countries in the European Union and the US. This is a major challenge for developing countries.

Is there a feeling that African leaders and society should play more of a role in solving local conflicts, rather than outside forces?

We would like to have political issues in Africa solved internally. During the Libyan revolution of February 2011, the opposition forces to Muammar Qadafi and his government started mass protests that turned into an armed rebellion. A very complex situation led to the attack and killing of Qadafi by NATO forces. Although Qadafi was an undemocratic dictator for four decades and a hateful person, the African Union was against the process, as most of the African presidents were reluctant for Western forces to intervene. They promised to negotiate with him and have peacekeeping forces to keep him from his killing his own people. None of the European states that took this fatal initiative listened to the African Union. I can't imagine any African state, or the African Union, going to bomb somewhere in America, South America or somewhere in Europe. They would be stopped. But the more powerful countries, like the United States and Britain, can be involved in a war the United Nations has disapproved of while no African country can do that.

Is there resentment in Africa about Western triumphalism because of the history of colonialism and its dominant role in physically shaping the world?

We should add politically and intellectually shaping the world. Western colonization is resented everywhere. We resent the power of the West that is oppressing us on issues such as colonialism and neocolonialism, unfair world trade, world politics and globalization. Former colonizers have no further need to colonize other countries because globalization does it, with Western firms tapping into oil, water, minerals and whatever resources we have here. We have resentment about the cultural, technical domination by the West over the rest of the world, while we also think that the former colonizers build their wealth on the exploitation of our resources.

Today, we have more and more African migrants traveling by foot and floats to the West – at any cost, including risking their lives – because the West is where there are jobs, educational opportunities and modernity. Europe is complaining that there are hundreds of thousands coming from North and Sub-Saharan Africa, just to cite this continent. Germany itself hosted about one million migrants from countries in crisis. Whatever resentments we have toward the West, we know the West is a place that might afford more opportunities than somewhere else. Africa is one of the richest continents in the world, endowed with enormous natural and mineral wealth. When will its people benefit from its resources? ∎

ALEX DE WAAL

Alex de Waal is executive director of the World Peace Foundation and a research professor at the Fletcher School at Tufts University in the US. He is one of the world's most respected analysts of Sudan and the Horn of Africa. His books include: *Famine Crimes: Politics and the disaster relief agency in Africa; Famine that Kills: Darfur, Sudan;* and *Advocacy In Conflict: Critical perspectives on transnational activism.*

What are your thoughts on the one-sided accounts of US history in Somalia?

The wars of the 1980s, which were the most vicious wars in Somalia, occurred before the collapse of the government. They took place in 1988, 1989 and 1990. Things were better in some regards after the overthrow of the Siad Barre regime. It was the United States, other Western countries and Saudi Arabia that armed Barre to the hilt. The Soviet Union armed the regime in the 1970s, but the Americans began arming Barre after he switched sides in the Cold War. That history is often forgotten but is relevant if you look at the solutions being brought up to deal with the Somali crisis today. They involve the reconstruction of a government that is in many important respects built on the same model as the Somali government that failed in the 1980s and Somalis see it as that same kind of colonial-style dependent relationship, and they treat it that way.

Could you talk about how US aid laws prevented the US government from doing anything to stop a humanitarian disaster in Somalia?

The Patriot Act makes it a criminal offense to provide any kind of assistance to someone on the terrorist list, including al-Shabaab in Somalia. When the United Nations was warning about upcoming famine in Somalia in 2010, the United States cut food aid to Somalia by 80 per cent because of the concern that some of the food would be diverted to al-Shabaab. Despite major efforts by the United Nations, anti-poverty agencies and senior staff in the US's own agency of international development, the aid wasn't restored. This was morally wrong and counterproductive. It took until July 2011, when the United Nations declared there was a famine in Somalia, for the United States to authorize USAID, the UN and international agencies to operate in the country despite the risk of some of the aid falling into the hands of al-Shabaab. This delay cost about 250,000 lives. This huge loss of life was preventable, but the US was more concerned with counter-terror operations in the country. In my view, this was completely unethical. Somalis were understandably unhappy about this.

What narrative can be offered to counter Western stereotypes that Somalia is a hopeless situation?

Part of the narrative is an ironic conservative narrative because the Somalis are exceptionally good at business and handling commerce. You can put government in the hands of the people that know how to run things like the financial sector, the telecom sector and the livestock trade – the sort of things that Donald Trump might approve of – but when you establish a government institution that tries to control and regulate these things in a way that has never worked before, then it's bound to fail. Ironically, I think the narrative that would work is the libertarian story of how Somali businesses function.

Do you feel like advocacy groups in South Sudan painted a simplistic view of the opposition during the Sudanese civil war that glossed over their own human rights abuses?

That is absolutely correct. From the mid-1990s onwards, US advocacy groups correctly said that the South Sudanese were fighting a historically repressive government. But the next step they took was to take the stance that those fighting against evil should be given a free pass on their own wrongdoings. If you look at the writings and speeches by Nelson Mandela, Martin Luther King, Jr, and leaders of other liberation movements in the world, they emphasize that they must hold themselves to a higher standard than their oppressor. But the advocacy groups told the opposition movements that they were going to overlook their human rights abuses, corruption, militarism and rejection of peace agreements because of the oppression they had endured.

What this meant was that, when the South Sudanese People's Liberation Army achieved power when South Sudan became an independent state, it did so with a sense of entitlement and impunity. So, the corruption, lack of democracy and human rights abuses continued to go unchecked. And even when the US government began to criticize the South Sudan government for its corruption and human rights abuses, advocacy groups like the Enough Campaign were not ready to take part in that criticism.

When you look at the public statements of actor George Clooney's Enough Project when the war broke out in December 2013 – with the presidential guard of South Sudanese President Salva Kiir going on an ethnic rampage and killing hundreds, some say thousands, of ethnic Nuer – they played it down. Imagine what their reaction would have been if the presidential guard of a country they were not friendly with went on a rampage and killed hundreds or thousands of members of another ethnic group? They would be screaming genocide. These double standards encouraged disastrous actions in South Sudan.

Do you think the conflicts in Sudan as a whole are more based on power-sharing than ethnicity?

Any ethnic issue in Sudan is very complicated when you drill down into it. All ethnic groups are historically created. When you talk about ethnicity in Sudan, you are not talking about a group of people having very distinct origins, you are talking about political projects for creating an ethnicity. For example, there was a project of Arabization – changing people into Arabs in northern Sudan. There was then a counter-project of Africanization that emphasized people's African roots.

All conflicts in Sudan begin as conflicts over power. The reason they take on an ethnic color is partly because it's very easy to rally people around ethnic labels. This is also the way armed groups mobilize in Sudan. Armed groups don't have the formal, hierarchal command-and-control structures you have in Western armies. What you have is people who fight for a particular commander because they have a personal allegiance to that commander. Rank-and-file soldiers are often unpaid and lack basic training and discipline.

As a result, if you are recruiting people that you want to be loyal to you, you tend to recruit blood relatives and members of your immediate family. People in South Sudan tend to have big families, so you can mobilize a whole company, and possibly a whole battalion, from your immediate relatives. And all these relatives will be ethnically linked because they are all from your extended family. These armed groups don't fight each other because they intrinsically hate each other, or because they have fundamental disputes about the nature of the country, it's just the way political and military power is organized in South Sudan. ■

Middle East and Northern Africa

HAWZHIN AZEEZ

 Hawzhin Azeez is co-founder of the NGO Hevi (meaning 'hope' in Kurdish), which provides humanitarian aid to the people of Rojava (three autonomously run cantons located in northern Syria). She writes passionately about the Rojava Revolution, feminism and Kurdish issues.

Do you see the YPJ [Women Protection Units serving in the Rojava revolutionary armed forces] as serving as role models for women in the Middle East when it comes to promoting gender equality between the sexes?

The YPJ serves as a symbol of resistance and self-protection for all minoritized, racialized, colonized women, not just in the Middle East, but across the globe. They serve just as much as a symbol of resistance for women in the Middle East and Latin America and Asia as Western women, since their resistance is not just against 'Daesh' (ISIS), but against the oppressive political and economic conditions within the capitalist, neoliberal, statist system, as well as obviously the patriarchal system. As a result of the close and interlinked connections between the capitalist system and patriarchy, all women suffer to varying degrees from the unequal conditions and the associated gender and sexual oppressions. In addition, we need to note that the YPJ is not a solitary entity that engages in seismic socio-political and economic changes within the region.

The YPJ is an extension of the Rojava Revolution and the efforts by the people in northern Syria to implement a radical model known as 'democratic confederalism'. This radical model was developed by the imprisoned Kurdish leader Abdullah Öcalan, the founder of the revolutionary liberation movement the PKK (The Kurdistan Workers' Party), who aimed to liberate the Kurds from the oppressions and violent assimilation policies of the Turkish regime. However, when Öcalan was captured through international collaboration with the Turkish deep state, the aims of the PKK and later the liberation psychology and approach of the Kurds changed. The evolution occurred through Öcalan's reading of Murray Bookchin's work, which led to a radical shift in Öcalan's ideology. The entire approach to the liberation of the Kurds and the so-called Kurdish Question changed from a nationalist purely state-centric approach to a radical, stateless, democratic, confederal and multicultural approach – an approach which saw the liberation of women, defined as the first colonized people by Öcalan, as integral and imperative. The formation of the YPJ is therefore an extension of other socio-political, cultural and economic changes which are occurring in northern Syria and not just purely a military one – which often the YPJ is reduced to.

How has the YPJ's role in battling ISIS changed the perceptions of men towards women in your region? Do you hope the YPJ breaks down some of the patriarchal barriers in Kurdish culture?

The YPJ has served to break down many gender barriers not just regionally but also globally, but again we must remember that the YPJ is an extension of the socio-cultural, politico-economic and gender changes being implemented in Rojava and does not stand alone as a movement. The YPJ as a military movement has demonstrated most effectively that women are just as capable of engaging in traditionally masculine work, and the most difficult work of all, defending the community and even succeeding where men may have failed. But, more than that, they have managed to fundamentally reorder and challenge orientalist, Euro-centric views of what Middle Eastern women are capable of. In fact, their resistance was of such significance for gender, socio-political and cultural rights, that it has caused ripple effects across the Western, so-called developed world, which still struggles with entrenching its own women's and gender rights. However, there is still an element of exoticization of Kurdish women fighters, orientalizing them, turning them into some mythical, Amazonian, extraordinary figures of unusual courage and strength in battling Daesh, al-Nusra and other similar organizations. An effort by which the statist, capitalist, imperial international system attempts to water down and dilute the significance of the YPJ. In fact, the YPJ are normal, ordinary women who have been placed in the difficult position of having to defend themselves and the rights of other women in the absence of appropriate alternatives.

How important is it to include people from other races and ethnicities in the YPJ?

It is foundational to the underlying ideology of democratic confederalism, which the YPJ follows. It is important to note that the formation of the YPJ is a reflection of the radical form of co-existence that the Rojava community has accepted. This is multicultural, democratic, promotes ethno-religious diversity and the right for differences to exist. For this reason, the YPJ is open to all women who wish to join and views itself as representing all women rather than just a Kurdish or a Middle Eastern movement.

However, why women choose to join the YPJ is also just as important. The YPJ encourages the notion of women's self-protection in a deeply capitalist, patriarchal, statist world. Hundreds of international volunteers have joined the movement and continue to flow into Rojava to join – though some have been deeply problematic in being clearly rightwing and conservatives whose ideological orientations were contrary to the aspirations of the revolution here. However, some have been clearly ideologically aligned and affiliated with the leftist, socialist, feminist and ecological aspirations of the people here. Ivana Hoffman (code name Avaşîn Tekoşîn Güneş), a South African with German citizenship who joined the YPJ and lost her life fighting against ISIS in early 2015 in Til Timer, represents that international, revolutionary, fiercely ideological and committed group of activists and fighters who have come from all over the world to stand with and in the revolution.

How can people not living in Rojava show solidarity with the revolution?

There is a lot of confusion about what is happening in Rojava due to lack of information, language problems, and the ongoing border issues, which prevent the easy flow of people. However, there is still a fair bit of information emerging from the region and it is essential that those who wish to stand in solidarity with Rojava take the time to inform themselves, to read about the ongoing efforts of the people, both on the military and the civilian side. Just as importantly, it is imperative that solidarity groups and allies read about Abdullah Öcalan's ideology of democratic confederalism and learn who the Kurds are, and what their liberation struggles have involved.

You cannot understand the struggle and the revolution in Rojava if you do not understand who the Kurds are and the historical and political oppressions that they and other minorities have experienced. We also need to remember that this is not a nationalist, Kurdish revolution alone – it is rather a global, humanist revolution that attempts to restructure oppressive societies and produce a bottom-up form of democracy, that empowers citizens and reduces the authority and decision-making capacity of the State, which, as we know, can often be oppressive and exclusionary. ■

JANET BIEHL

 From 1987 to 2000, Janet Biehl, together with her longtime companion Murray Bookchin, published and co-edited *Left Green Perspectives*. She compiled and edited the *Murray Bookchin Reader* (1997). After Bookchin's death in 2006, she wrote his biography: *Ecology or Catastrophe: The Life of Murray Bookchin* (2015). In recent years, she has visited Rojava, in northern Syria, where the revolution has been inspired by Bookchin's ideas.

Having visited Rojava in 2014 and 2015, can you talk about differences between the libertarian municipalism Murray Bookchin advocated and the Rojava ideology of democratic confederalism?

Democratic confederalism is the ideology developed by Abdullah Öcalan while in prison, based in part on Bookchin's libertarian municipalism, a model of bottom-up, face-to-face democracy. Bottom-up democracy made sense for the Kurdish movement because in the absence of an autonomous political system of their own, the Kurds have lived as a minority inside other nation-states, where the authoritarian system in power usually denied and persecuted them. Starting around 2000, the Kurdistan Workers' Party (PKK) discussed and debated it as the basis for a new paradigm. Giving up on the goal of achieving a Kurdish nation state, they adopted Democratic Confederalism around 2005. Kurds in southeastern Turkey and northern Syria thereafter set out to implement it.

Bookchin began developing the program that would become libertarian municipalism as early as the 1950s, when he realized that the next socialist revolutions, post-Marxist ones, would have to be thoroughly democratic in nature, to avoid Marxist tyrannies and to include all citizens. Since the nation-state was bought and paid for by the wealthy and powerful, he rejected the sham 'representative democracy' of legislatures, parliaments and executives. Power, he thought, had to be taken from the hands of the capitalist nation-state and put in the hands of the people. Instead, citizens should govern themselves though face-to-face democratic assemblies. He combed through history, especially but not limited to revolutionary history, looking for instances of such assemblies and found them most notably in the self-governing cities of ancient Athens, in the Parisian sectional assemblies of the French Revolution around 1793, and the town meetings of colonial New England.

Ideas of assembly democracy had long been rejected because of the defects of those systems: the democracy of ancient Athens excluded women, slaves, and non-Athenians; the Parisian assemblies were choked in the blood of guillotines; and the New England town meetings were not only patriarchal but fought savage wars against the local Native Americans. Bookchin's proposal was to bring them up to date, making use of the advances of democratic thinking over the course of centuries. The new citizen democracies would not only exist outside and in opposition to the nation-state, they would include women and ethnic minorities, they would abhor slavery and indeed all hierarchy, they would gain popularity through popular mobilization and empowerment rather than guillotines, and they would distribute wealth among all community members. Bookchin's innovation was to transform the human potentiality for democratic self-government into a concrete program, which was libertarian municipalism.

To manage affairs from the bottom up over broader areas, the citizens' assemblies would form confederations. Bookchin derived this institutional idea from the history of Spanish anarchism, specifically the huge and militant anarcho-syndicalist trade union, the Confederacion Nacional del Trabajo (CNT), which was organized like a confederation. Bookchin proposed that assemblies send mandated delegates to upper levels of the confederal structure, to ensure that power would continue to flow from the bottom up. Over time as the democratic confederations became more popular, with more and more participation, they could constitute a dual power to the nation-state, and the bottom-up power would eventually replace the nation-state.

Murray was known as an anarchist for four decades, from 1960 to 2000, and he long tried to persuade the anarchist movement that democratic self-government of this kind was its natural politics. But he gained little ground and finally concluded that anarchism was individualist at its core. So, he dropped the label in favor of communalism, on the principle that whereas anarchism pits the individual against the state, his project was to pit the community-in-confederation against the State. Bookchin gained fans and loyal readers all over the world, but the broad movement he dreamed of never came into existence. He consoled himself, before his death in 2006, that if anyone was ever interested in the project of creating face-to-face democratic self-government, his program would be there in writing, available for their use.

It turned out that someone was very interested, and much sooner than Murray might have expected. After 1999, when Abdullah Öcalan was sentenced to solitary confinement by the Turkish state, he realized that the PKK needed a new formulation and scoured the works of social theorists East and West looking for sources of renewal. Bookchin's major works had been translated into Turkish, and Öcalan thought his ideas were promising. Around 2004 two organizers in Germany had the idea of facilitating a dialogue between Öcalan and Bookchin through email, but it never really came about, as Bookchin was too sick and weary. But they did have a brief exchange in which Öcalan told Bookchin that he considered himself a good student of his and a social ecologist (another name for Bookchin's ideas). And when Bookchin died in 2006, the PKK wrote a tribute to him, saluting him as a great social scientist of the 20th century and avowing that they would create the first Bookchinite polity on earth.

As I mentioned, Öcalan reworked libertarian municipalism and his own ideas and ideas from other authors into democratic confederalism, and the proposal went to the Kurdish movement. Öcalan recommended to the PKK through his lawyers that they read Bookchin. Once the PKK accepted democratic confederalism in the early 2000s, Kurdish militants set about implementing it in the parts of southeastern Turkey and northern Syria where many Kurds live. In Syria, despite the brutality of the Assad regime, the people began building grassroots democratic institutions, committees and assemblies, illicitly.

In the summer of 2012, in the early stages of the Syrian civil war, the Assad regime essentially abandoned the Kurdish north to concentrate its troops to fight Islamist rebels in the south. The new democratic institutions sprang into the sunlight, proliferated, and became integral to the self-government of three regions or cantons in the north: Jazira, Kobane, and Afrin. This so-called MGRK [West Kurdistan People's Council] system is a system of assemblies and communes and mandated delegates flowing up through various confederal tiers.

Can you talk about your visit to the cantons in northern Syria?

I visited the Jazira canton in December 2014, when the revolution was still very much a work in progress. I was impressed by the enormous importance of public education, especially the institution that Kurds call academies. People of all ages attend academies, dedicated to a wide range of fields including *Jineoloji* [women's studies], language and literature, co-operatives, defense and internal security forces. All the academies, including the military ones, teach democratic confederalism in addition to their specific field.

One of the great changes Öcalan made in democratic confederalism is his emphasis on the liberation of women. Bookchin didn't single out the liberation of women – he was opposed to hierarchy of all kinds, including domination based on race, ethnicity and sexual identity as well as gender, and the domination of man over nature. Öcalan, however, emphasized the importance of liberating women, and gender equality became a pillar of the Kurdish movement. In fact, the three pillars of democratic confederalism are said to be democracy, gender equality and ecology. In Rojava I would add two more: ethnic-religious inclusivity and a co-operative economy.

Did you see many similarities to libertarian municipalism in Rojava?

I found a very strong commitment to the ideas of citizen democracy and to putting them into practice. But it's not a pure bottom-up democracy. In January 2014, the three cantons were in a precarious state. The Turkish state had placed them under a political and economic embargo, in which most of the rest of the world also seemed to participate. Few goods could get in or out. Moreover, the three cantons were seeking international recognition from other states. They were trying to show the world Syria could be a peaceful, inclusive, democratic, humane place. But in vain – the legitimacy of the three cantons or the MGRK system got no takers, no recognition.

So the cantons all adopted a second tier of government, one more like a normal state, in hopes that the international community would take them seriously and recognize Rojava. Each canton created a democratic autonomy administration (DAA), which consists of more traditional executive, legislative and judicial bodies. Unfortunately, international recognition was still not forthcoming – the addition of the DAAs made no difference. But the DAAs co-exist alongside the MGRK system today, dividing up power between them somehow, in ways I'm not competent to talk about. I don't want to give the false impression that this is a pure stateless society – let alone an anarchist society – because the DAAs are more like traditional state institutions.

Their existence may be necessary given the precariousness of the whole experiment, I don't know. On my second visit to Rojava, in October 2015, the people were actively talking about how to keep power flowing from the bottom up. Ideas flow from the bottom, but these ideas are processed, considered and discussed by a legislative council and an executive council in each canton. Everyone seemed aware of the danger that a tiered system of self-government could transform into a conduit for top-down rule, as happened with the Soviets in the Russian Revolution. But people's consciousness seemed to be very strong. They are very educated, and they know their revolutionary history. I found it very inspiring that they were taking this question seriously. I hope one day to return and see how they answered it. ■

SARAH ELTANTAWI

 Sarah Eltantawi is a scholar of Islam who has worked for two Muslim American civil-rights organizations in Los Angeles, Washington DC and New York City. She is the author of *Shariah on Trial: Northern Nigeria's Islamic Revolution* and is working on a book about the rise of the Muslim Brotherhood in Egypt.

Could you explain why hundreds of thousands of Nigerians demanded the re-implementation of sharia law in northern Nigeria in 1999?

The support for amputations and stoning wasn't about regulating the sexuality of peasant women, but rather about bringing accountability to local corrupt officials. One way of putting it is that people marched in the streets in a desperate attempt to try the laws of God where the laws of men had failed. Nigeria was ranked the second most corrupt government in the world in 1999 when people took to the streets. IMF-influenced structural-adjustment programs had exacerbated poverty by removing food and education subsidies, and there was endemic corruption by the government. Nigeria had also elected its first Pentecostal Christian president, and I think this led many northerners – who had become accustomed to Muslim presidents 'in exchange' for so many of the oil resources going to the south – to feel disenfranchised.

The trial of Amina Lawal [she was sentenced by a northern Nigerian court to be stoned for adultery in 2002, though the sentence was eventually overturned] received a lot of attention in the Western media at the same time as the West was planning to invade Iraq. What did you discern from

the level of outrage leveled at the Lawal case compared to debates over Iraq?

The differences in tone on the two subjects caught my attention and piqued my interest. The Iraq War was a triumph of a neoconservative ideology where the ends justified the means. As Madeleine Albright put it during the US/UK-led sanctions on Iraq, 'the price is worth it' even if the price is 500,000 deaths. The same logic applied to the war in Iraq – our objectives were more important than the potential loss of thousands of Iraqi lives.

What struck me about the collision of this discourse with the outrage over the Amina Lawal case was the incongruence between the register of outrage and the scale of the eminent destructions at hand. There was no serious question or debate that hundreds of thousands of Iraqi civilians would be killed in any US-led operation there. The question was simply 'when', not 'if'. For a moment, however – a crucial moment – in the midst of this conversation about Iraq the register of the outrage about Lawal's potential stoning was unmistakably more acute. It is as if the barbarity of what was about to be done to Iraq was collectively displaced on to this African society, with its 'medieval' Islamic system and its hopelessly misogynistic attitudes, and, in doing so, we changed the subject and deflected the civilizational blame, if only temporarily.

Why do you think the Muslim Brotherhood failed in running Egypt after they were democratically elected in 2011-12?

They were never trained to run a country. Specifically, they were not skilled at running a country like Egypt, whose citizens are deeply nationalistic. This is just the reality of Egyptian culture, and there are reasons for it. The Muslim Brotherhood are Pan-Islamists, and most Egyptians are nationalists first and perhaps Pan-Arabists second. Islam is extremely important to Egypt's Muslim citizens, but I think one of the conclusions we must reach is that Egyptians are much more wedded to a traditionalist, culturally infused understanding of Islam than they are to the political and theological abstraction of Islam articulated by the Muslim Brotherhood.

On a more practical level, Egyptians saw what was happening in Libya, and they saw what was happening in Syria, and they didn't want that to happen there. Those circumstances, in addition to years of instability for the average person after the 2011 Revolution, made the average Egyptian acutely security- and stability-minded.

The Muslim Brotherhood, in part because of the history of repression it had endured, had developed into a distinct group that had separated themselves in many ways from the rest of the population. I think that led to statements and alliances that communicated to Egyptians that they didn't have an orientation to run all of Egypt for all Egyptians. The Brotherhood also promised the people involved in the Egyptian revolution that they would not run a candidate for president and then they did. They said they would not contest more than 25 per cent of parliamentary seats and then they did. There is a definite sense that the group betrayed the revolution.

Why were progressives not able to triumph in the elections in Egypt following the overthrow of President Mubarak?

It had to do with the way the elections were set up. There were too many left-of-center groups in the primaries. Votes got split amongst these groups during the run-off elections, and the Muslim Brotherhood ended up winning a clear majority in the run-off elections. It was a structural problem.

Progressives also did not have enough time to organize for the elections. The Muslim Brotherhood had been organizing themselves as a disciplined unit with hierarchy and leadership for several decades. You don't have a similar analogy on the Left in Egypt. The leftwing groups kept saying they needed more time, but the Egyptian army wanted to get the elections done quickly. In addition, there was a referendum in March of 2013 that asked the Egyptian people if they wanted to conduct elections first, or if they wanted to have the Constitution written first. There was a huge debate over this, and the 'let's have elections now' camp prevailed, with the help of strong lobbying from the

Muslim Brotherhood. This strong lobbying was one of the first indications that the Muslim Brotherhood were going to go back on their word not to contest elections after the revolution. This issue also split the Left vote. After they won the presidential election, incidentally, the first thing the Muslim Brotherhood did was rewrite the Constitution.

What did the mainstream and leftwing media get wrong about the popular coup that ousted democratically elected president Mohammed Morsi and the Muslim Brotherhood from power in July 2013?

The Western media should have talked to more local Egyptians on the ground about why they supported the coup. The millions of Egyptians who came to the streets to denounce the Muslim Brotherhood were largely ignored by the Western Left. I was frankly shocked by some of the racism I encountered on this score. One memorable exchange I took part in was about the necessity of consulting 'non-Egyptian sources' to attain an objective understanding of why Egyptians opposed the Muslim Brotherhood. Would anyone consult 'non-French sources' to gain an objective account of why the French... well... do anything? The answer is no. Therefore, there was something rather preposterous about this refusal to understand Egyptians on their own terms at the time. It was as if Egyptians had a duty to conform to stereotypes about Muslim-majority societies finding Islamism to be the most liberating ideology. Many on the Left could not handle the counter-data coming from Egypt during this time. My view on the inability to accept Egyptian actions during that time has always been: 'That's not their problem, it's yours.' ■

YASSIN AL-HAJ SALEH

Yassin al-Haj Saleh is one of the most prominent dissident intellectuals in Syria. He was arrested at the age of 19 for his membership of the Syrian Communist Party and remained in prison for more than 16 years. Among his books are *The Impossible Revolution: making sense of the Syrian tragedy, Walking on One Foot* and *Culture as Politics.*

What are your thoughts on President Trump's foreign-policy approach to Syria?

I don't see any difference in vision between Trump and Obama. Both men prioritize the 'war on terror' over any political or ethical issues related to the Syrian people's political struggle for freedom, change and justice. The Americans are playing an extremely nasty role in the northwestern part of the country. In a way, they are preparing a future of massacres and ethnic struggles in the region. The region is composed of Arabs and Kurds. The US is following the traditional colonial formula of relying on the Syrian Democratic Forces (SDF), which is the Democratic Union Party (PYD), which is the Kurdistan Workers' Party (PKK). The SDF is dealing very disrespectfully with the local population. They are relegating the local population to invisibility and it is the same logic that the people experienced under the Assad regime. The new occupying powers are imposing their rigid, dictatorial one-party system with their personality cult of [militant Kurdish leader Abdullah] Öcalan and completely ignoring the struggle for freedom and change that happened before them. It is as if our history begins now. It is the colonial thing and business as usual.

Trump is submitting Syria to Putin. The fascist regime in Russia will copy itself in Syria with a sectarian element. The

West has a history of colonialism in the Middle East and Russia is no exception. The Russian plan is to rehabilitate Bashar al-Assad and his regime without discussing the real issues like the maybe 200,000 prisoners and the perhaps 75,000 disappeared in Syria.

What do you think would be a smart way for the international community to bring peace and stability to Syria?

The situation is no longer about Syria. We don't need a solution, we need a clear vision of the problem we are in. It's a global thing, it's not just Syria. Our new role may be to invent new tools, new theories and new ways of seeing things. We need a new vision and a new project for the world.

You have talked about the need for a new global movement. Will such a movement need intellectuals and critics that infuse their knowledge and understanding of issues with feeling and deep empathy for the downtrodden?

Addressing the influential powers of the world, my abducted wife Samira al Khalil wrote in some of her papers from Eastern Ghouta after the chemical massacre in August 2013: 'The world is one small village, is not this what you always say? Why are you leaving the population of one neighborhood of this village massacred, sieged and starved?'

A small village it is, indeed. And this is an irreversible universal gain, a very dear one. And God knows that it was very costly. But the global system is bad and worsening. Racism, environmental changes, a global crisis of democracy and a universal hope deficiency are four main aspects of a deteriorating system. World change is more and more of an imperative. There are no ways out of the one world, so we either kill each other in an aggravatingly narrowing world, or find ways for creating new spaces, new worlds, in the one world we share.

But it seems that we lack global movements with new ways of thinking, imagining, communicating and acting. Nation-states and terrorist organizations are not models to imitate. The model for new movements could be that of refugees appropriating the world and those conscientious people welcoming and helping them. I feel that states, the richest and most powerful in particular, consider refugees a far more serious threat than terrorist groups. They are right. States are 'legitimate' monopolies of terrorism, and those terrorist networks are their 'illegitimate' rivals and doubles (they tend to be correlative in a way that you cannot exclude one without excluding the other).

Maybe we have to develop a combination of anti-politics and alter-politics. It is impossible to evade anti-politics vis-à-vis thuggish states like the one we have in Syria, but there is always a need to think of other forms of gathering and organization. Global responsibility is the political and ethical basis for a different world. There is no us and them. We are all them. We are all responsible.

Can you talk about the protests and other nonviolent actions by the peaceful wing of the Syrian Revolution before the Assad regime's ruthless repression made some protesters turn to armed conflict? Is the peaceful wing of the Syrian Revolution still active today?

The uprising was composed solely of a 'peaceful wing' in its first stage that came to an end only after the Assadi state occupied Hama and Deirezzor in August 2011. The two cities witnessed huge demonstrations with hundreds of thousands participating. People thought the regime would be overthrown through occupying central public spaces with their great numbers and expressing their aspiration for freedom and political change. It is noteworthy that the demonstrators were holding the formal Syrian flag while struggling to own politics at that time.

Later on, that flag was replaced by the pre-Baathist flag or 'the independence flag' – this was the country's flag in the years immediately after Syria got independence from the French mandate in in 1946 — that came gradually to be known as the revolution's flag. The replacement symbolized processes of radicalization and militarization among revolutionary environments that found themselves victimized, arrested, tortured and killed in their dozens every day from the beginning. I was in the country at that time, and I was able to monitor the process of militarization: the people were pushed to despair from peaceful demonstrations, and the ones who stopped joining demonstrations took up arms and did not simply stay home. People first relied only on themselves; then they asked for international protection that never came, and only turned to Allah as the last resort. Islamization is a social and political process, and not an essence lurking somewhere only waiting to unfold itself. ■

ANISSA HELIE

Anissa Helie is an Algerian who is now associate professor at John Jay College, New York. She co-edited (with Homa Hoodfar) the book *Sexuality in Muslim Contexts: Restrictions and resistance.*

How important is it for people in the West to understand that issues like homosexuality and abortion are open to diverse interpretations in the Qur'an?

Along with other scholars and activists, I have pointed out that – contrary to claims that Muslim-majority nations' treatment of social issues is primarily informed by their adherence to key Islamic sources such as the Qur'an – the broad cultural and political diversity of Muslim societies, as well as the variation in religious interpretation, cannot be overlooked. As a result of this diversity, and despite references to a 'Muslim world' that is presumed to be homogeneous, legal approaches and national policies can be quite varied on a number of issues. Issues related to sexuality and women's bodily rights (including same-sex behavior and abortion) are no different: they are legislated in different ways in various Muslim-majority countries.

For example, data from 2009 related to 42 Muslim countries highlight the wide scope of legal approaches with regard to voluntary termination of pregnancy, ranging from complete prohibition, to abortion being allowed on a variety of grounds – to preserve the woman's physical or mental health, or on the basis of socio-economic factors, or without any restriction (in other words, on request).

Similarly, more than 15 years ago, when I started writing on same-sex relations in Muslim contexts, 26 Muslim-majority countries condemned homosexuality as a criminal offense, with alleged 'offenders' facing penalties ranging from forced medical procedures (such as anal testing) to imprisonment, or even the death penalty. Aren't such empirical examples making clear enough the fact that 'issues like homosexuality and abortion are open to different interpretations' in the legal arenas of various Muslim-majority societies?

Why, then, does it seem necessary to some commentators to frame this question with such an emphasis on the religious realm? Why is it relevant to focus on the Qur'an in relation to social issues such as sexuality or termination of pregnancy? Why is the religious text seen as so important in this early 21st century? And by whom is the Qur'an (or the Sunnah, or the hadith) cast as paramount in defining citizens' rights? By formulating this question in such a way, aren't 'people in the West' at risk of legitimizing Muslim political actors (whether governments or other entities, including non-state actors) who tend to rely on religious claims when politically expedient, and often to secure their own power?

Drawing a parallel with non-Muslim contexts may help to drive the point home: do people routinely refer to the Bible when envisaging social issues relevant to modern societies with a Christian tradition (European or Latin American nations)? Or, do we systematically assume that the Torah necessarily impacts the life decisions of all or any Jewish New Yorkers? I am afraid that the question itself reinforces an assumption about the primacy of Islam (and of Qur'anic interpretations) as an essential factor in the lives of 'Muslims' – an assumption that most people do not hold with regard to Christians, Jews, Buddhists, and Jains. Hence, I am not sure that the constituency you refer to – 'people in the West' – need to be further encouraged to look at Muslim-majority societies primarily through the prism of a presumed homogeneous 'Islam'.

Do well-intentioned outside groups often make the mistake of taking stances and making demands in countries without first notifying feminists and LGBT activist groups within

those countries of what they plan to do? Does this sometimes undermine the goals the activists inside these countries are working to bringing about?

A range of seemingly 'well-intentioned outside groups' dealing with human rights issues do indeed devise and adopt strategies that are ultimately detrimental to progressive groups – feminist and otherwise – working locally in other contexts. While I (still) recognize that some of these outside groups may simply be mistaken, the fact is that I've witnessed such mistakes being repeated over the span of close to three decades. I am therefore no longer sure that it is truly a matter of 'making mistakes', nor am I convinced that these groups are as well-intentioned as they portray, or imagine, themselves to be.

What motivates these outside groups not only to fail to 'first notify' local progressive groups but also to repeatedly ignore their warnings and consistent feedbacks? Why should outside groups undermine the work undertaken by local human rights defenders who should clearly be seen as their allies – since, in the words of Algerian feminist Louisa Ait-Hamou – they are the ones who 'have fought fundamentalism and terrorism in isolation with our bare hands for a good number of years'?

Sadly, such a situation can only be explained at times by the arrogance displayed by various Left and human rights organizations based in the West. Instead of recognizing the expertise developed over years and decades and at great cost by local human rights defenders, these outside organizations appear convinced, deep down – whether they are aware of their biases or not – that they know better (than their brown little brothers and sisters).

And in the late 1990s, when I confronted a team of Human Rights Watch researchers returning from a fact-finding mission in Algeria regarding their lack of documentation of the widespread violations of human rights perpetrated by non-state actors (in this case, Islamist armed groups such as the GIA – Armed Islamic Group) I was told verbatim: 'This was not part of our mandate.' Really? An estimated 100,000 to 200,000 civilians were murdered, mostly at the hand of armed jihadists, during the bloody decade of the 1990s and it's not the business of prominent human rights organizations to report these massacres? How 'well-intentioned' are these outside groups and how many decades should we believe their biases are just a matter of 'making mistakes'?

Indeed, such outside groups appear at times to simply privilege the strategies that are beneficial to themselves or their nation, at the expense of the broader context and, at times, at the expense of victims of fundamentalist extreme violence. While not-so-well-intentioned groups continue to legitimize Islamists, we, the democrats and feminists from a Muslim background, have been deleted. ▪

MARIEME HELIE LUCAS

Marieme Helie Lucas is an Algerian sociologist and the founder and former international co-ordinator of the international solidarity organization Women Living Under Muslim Laws. She also founded the online resource Secularism is a Women's Issue (siawi.org). She is a harsh critic of all forms of religious fundamentalism.

How has the good Muslim-bad Muslim narrative adopted by many Western leaders played into the hands of the Islamic fundamentalists whom they are fighting? How difficult is it to make the case that Islamic fundamentalism is an extreme rightwing political movement that uses religion as its cover, as opposed to solely a religious movement?

Before I get into your question, let me just explain why it is so important today to use concepts in a very accurate way. Fundamentalists have launched an ideological battle and they have been successfully spreading their ideology through the global adoption of their concepts. Lazy journalists and politicians keep using terms like 'Muslims', 'sharia law', 'fatwa' etc, as if they knew what they were talking about. What is at stake here is the adoption of the vocabulary, hence of the conceptual framework, that the religious Far Right successfully imposes. What is at stake is the promotion of false realities that prevent a free analysis of a situation.

I have been writing for 30 years about the dangers of adopting the language of the enemy, and its categories of analysis, pointing at the fact that it forces us into reasoning within the limits delineated by fundamentalists. For instance, when they impose the terminology 'sharia law', it is meant to make everyone believe that there is such a thing as a universal Islamic body of laws that would be common to all 'Muslim countries'. This is not the case. A quick glance at laws said to be in conformity with Islam across Asia, Africa and the Middle East immediately proves that the 'Muslim world' is not homogeneous. The laws in these countries are not only very varied, but often in total contradiction to each other.

If one looks, for instance, at the rights of women in marriage, one can see that they range from equality of husband and wife in rights and duties to the total submission and absence of rights for the wife. Which of these legal provisions reflects the 'true Islam'? Which one is 'sharia law'? Showing this diversity as well as the contradictions from one country to another reveals the evidently man-made character of the laws, as well as the various sources for these differences. Different interpretations of the Qur'an, selective use of the Hadith, and the incorporation of local traditions into what becomes the official way to practice this religion in a specific location in a specific time, and even colonial laws, when it suits the interests of the powers that be and of patriarchy, are passed off as pertaining to 'sharia' (for instance, the pro-natalist 1920 French law in Algeria, or the Victorian inheritance law in Pakistan).

What would be obvious to all if we were discussing Christianity – that Opus Dei, the Vatican or liberation theology each promote very different types of society, hence very different 'Christian laws' – seems to be difficult to grasp when it comes to Islam. For more than three decades now, we at Women Living Under Muslim Laws have been pointing at the conceptual and political difference between 'Muslims' (believers in Islam) and 'fundamentalists' (a Far Right political movement working under the cover of religion), in order to deflect the lumping together of whole populations on the ground of their presumed religious faith.

This homogeneous, a-historical view of Muslims made its way into the dominant discourse via the Western media and political leaders adopting this fundamental conceptual distinction. However, they managed to twist it and to reintroduce the notion that all of us are 'Muslims'. This is achieved through the 'good

Muslims' versus 'bad Muslims' narrative. The 'good Muslims' are the 'moderate Muslims' – sometimes even labeled in the media 'moderate fundamentalists', a contradiction in terms, as if there could be 'moderate fascists'. This terminology betrays the underlying racist assumption that all Muslims must be fundamentalists and the 'bad Muslims' are the violent ones.

One can understand, under the present circumstances – with the growing presence in the media, and on the ground, of the Taliban, Boko Haram, Daesh, al-Shabaab, al-Qaeda and the like – that believers in Islam attempt to distance themselves from criminal activities by claiming 'they are not good Muslims', 'this is not Islam': this is for them the equivalent of 'not in my name'. But this is no reason for the adoption, globally, at the level of political leadership, of such an apolitical terminology. What it does is create a transnational 'race' of 'Muslims' (good or bad is beyond the question) in which the individual faith of a person is first presumed by his or her geographical origin (or that of his/her ancestors) and later imposed on the individual in the name of preserving his/her identity.

This perfectly suits the Muslim Far Right's political goals which insist a) that no-one can get out of Islam, and b) that they alone, and their repressive follies, represent the true Islam. Labeling 'Muslim' everyone whose family originated, for instance, in the Middle East or Pakistan or Sudan, is the exact equivalent of the way white Europeans or North Americans are labeled 'Christians', or sometimes 'Crusaders', by the Daesh. This does not speak well for the intellectual sophistication of those who use this terminology.

You have been critical of human rights organizations like Amnesty International (AI) and Human Rights Watch (HRW) for their work during the Algerian civil war in the 1990s. Can you explain why?

I had first-hand experience of trying to convince AI during the 1990s that they should report on all the crimes and violations that were committed in Algeria, not just on those committed by the State. If you look at AI's annual reports in this period, you will realize that, during the worst of the Armed Islamic Group (GIA) killings in the mid-1990s, there was a huge discrepancy between the number of pages devoted to violations by the Algerian State versus those devoted to violations committed by armed fundamentalist groups. I spoke repeatedly to AI's representatives in Paris and London about this discrepancy. All I got was that it was for the State to protect citizens against non-state actors. In such a case, this was a blatant misuse of the concept of 'due diligence'. The equivalent would be making De Gaulle accountable in court for the bombs planted by the FLN during the Battle of Algiers, or the Mayor of New York for the planes that destroyed the Twin Towers.

AI was the first human rights organization that was set up in Algeria. The three founding members put so much energy and courage into reporting on all violations, whether committed by the state or by the GIA, Islamic Salvation Army (AIS), Islamic Front for Armed Jihad (FIDA), and all the fundamentalist armed groups. But, in the end, barely anything other than State violations were incorporated into official AI reports. Caught between their headquarters' policy and a totally disappointed population, the three founding members wrote a very moving, private letter to the then Paris-based head of AI. In this letter they reiterated their deep commitment to human rights in general and to AI, while warning about the damage being done to the organization's reputation in Algeria because of its one-sided reporting. They did not get a reply and were expelled from AI without having ever been heard.

Human Rights Watch, which later in the decade also sent inquiry missions to Algeria, followed the same policy as AI, and produced similarly biased reports. I was requested on three occasions to help prepare the HRW visits to Algiers by establishing relevant contacts. I can testify to the fact that, among the persons targeted by the GIA that I suggested as interesting sources of information, no-one was ever met by the successive investigating teams.

I remember the 1990s as a period of 'madness'. We were confronted with a situation in which what people saw with their own eyes, lived through and knew for certain was turned upside down and reinterpreted by organizations that had the power to shape public opinion. For instance, at a time when our friends and colleagues were slaughtered by fundamentalist armed groups, we were told that it was the government slaughtering them. And when progressive people were decimated, they were called 'eradicators' by the human rights organizations and Left media in Europe. This is what the human rights groups did to the Algerian people.

Do you think there is an underlying racism in the notion that women's rights, freedom of religion and freedom of speech are Western values as opposed to universal values?

The underlying assumption is that progressive people and secularists in Muslim-majority countries are not representative of their people; that they are illegitimate. This is a denial of historical facts. Some years ago, we collectively gathered material on 'Our Great Ancestors' – feminists in Muslim contexts – and we found many examples of great feminist figures. The research showed how similar the demands have been across the centuries: education for girls comes first, then economic independence, the right to manage one's own assets, properties and finances, freedom of movement, the right to marry someone of one's choice, the right not to marry and to embrace celibacy. Marriage contracts were negotiated in ways that most Western women today could not even imagine were available to women in Muslim societies (restriction on polygamy, right to initiate the divorce, to have guardianship of children upon divorce, and so on). We can really prove that feminist struggles are indigenous to Muslim contexts.

I believe that, should we undertake similar research on agnostics, freethinkers and atheists throughout the centuries in Muslim contexts, we will come up with another equally well-hidden and extremely interesting piece of our history. Reclaiming this history is a very important strategy for feminists and for secularists, especially because it is something Muslim fundamentalists want to disappear at all costs. Unfortunately, it seems that progressive people in the West also believe that this history does not exist. It is as if the general belief was that 'Muslims' had to be backwards to be authentic. And, yes, of course, this is racism. ■

GIDEON LEVY

 Gideon Levy is a veteran Israeli journalist – a *Haaretz* columnist and a member of the newspaper's editorial board. He is an ardent critic of the Israeli occupation of Gaza and the West Bank; he also supports the Palestinian Boycott, Divestment, Sanctions movement. His latest book is *The Punishment of Gaza*.

What are your thoughts on US President Trump's decision to recognize Jerusalem as the capital of Israel?

Trump's decision puts an end to the masquerade. The US declared itself officially as an unfair mediator and as a one-sided supporter of the Israeli occupation. If Jerusalem is the capital only of Israel, this also means the final end of the Two-State Solution.

How important is it for progressives to condemn the Israeli government's actions while simultaneously criticizing anyone who mixes their criticisms of the government with antisemitism?

The world has the right, and even the moral duty, to criticize Israel. This has nothing to do with antisemitism. This has to do with moral values and respecting international law. The attempt of Israel and its lobbies to present any criticism as antisemitism should be ignored. It is a manipulation.

Do you think Israel is singled out for human rights abuses compared with other human rights-abusing regimes?

It's very clear that Israel is violating international law in so many areas and articles that there has to be some accountability. The fact that there are worse regimes in the world doesn't make any difference. Israel claims to be part of the Western world, part of the free world, part of the liberal world and it's unacceptable that a country that claims to be the only democracy in the Middle East would continue to violate international law in such a brutal way for so many years.

How much support is there on the secular and religious Left in Israel for a peace agreement that recognizes the mutual rights of both Israelis and Palestinians?
Most Israelis don't believe in the possibility of a peace agreement. Most Israelis don't believe there is a Palestinian partner and therefore it's hardly discussed.

How has prime minister Benjamin Netanyahu gained so much popularity in Israel given that he supports a policy that is further to the Right than the country has historically practiced?
It's not based on one factor, but it's mostly based on nationalism, spreading hatred toward the Palestinians and creating this image that Israel needs a strong leader to stop Palestinian terrorism. The main tool Netanyahu uses is to spread fears, and when you spread fears you can then present yourself as the person who can protect and guard people from those fears.

Can you talk about how your views on the Israeli-Palestinian conflict were transformed when you went into the Israeli-occupied territories and talked to the Palestinian people and observed their living situation?
It's not so much about meeting the people; it's more about realizing the brutality and criminality of the occupation. I've been covering the Israel-occupied territories for more than 30 years and the more I've seen the more radical I've become against it.

Do you think the main reasons for the Israeli occupation are nationalism and a sense of insecurity because of Palestinian terrorist attacks?
I think there is a combination of factors. One of the factors is to

have more territory for both security and for religious reasons as well. I think there also is the notion that we are the chosen people and we have the right to do these things. There is also the feeling that we can and, if we can, why not?

Do you worry about the affect the BDS (Boycott, Divestment, Sanctions) movement will have on Israelis who oppose Netanyahu's policies and may be hurt by a boycott in the same manner regular Iranians suffered because of US sanctions on Iran?

I don't know any better tool than the BDS to shake the Israeli society. I opposed the BDS for many years, but when I see there is no hope within Israeli society, the BDS is the only effective tool. At least it isn't a violent tool. It has nothing to do with bloodshed. I truly believe this might have an influence, like it had in apartheid South Africa.

What is your response to critics who argue it would make more sense to boycott people doing business in the occupied territories than to boycott the entire country?

It's impossible to separate Israel from its occupation.

How much does Hamas use antisemitic propaganda to stoke anger against Israel?

Very little, if at all. They don't need it because their struggle is against the occupier and not against the Jewish people. You don't need much to incite against the occupier because every Palestinian witnesses the occupation on a daily basis in Gaza and in the West Bank. And behind this occupation is the occupier and it's very easy to hate the occupier. It's almost impossible not to do so.

What role could the US play in helping create a more balanced peace agreement between Israel and Palestine?

The US could have brought the Israeli occupation to an end within months. If the United States had used Israel's dependence on America to push Israel out of the occupied territories, Israel would have had no choice but to obey. But the US had no intention of doing so and I don't see any intention right now.

Why do you think this is the case?

I have no answer to this question. Why does the US support so blindly and automatically not only Netanyahu, but any Israeli government? The United States is spending too much money on Israel, and I don't see how it is serving American interests. I don't understand why this doesn't become more of an issue in the United States.

What needs to happen in the Israeli and US political cultures to change the way Palestinians are perceived by each government and by its citizens?

They need to be perceived as equal human beings: almost no-one in Israel perceives them as such. People in the United States should ask themselves if military occupation, tyranny and an apartheid situation is something that is acceptable in the 21st century. And, if not, is it OK to finance and support it, and to continue to do nothing to put an end to it?

Given the social-democratic aspirations of some of the founders of Israel, how hard has it been to see what the Israeli occupation has done to Israeli society?

It's painful on almost a daily basis. It's getting worse and worse. It's not status quo. Things are deteriorating from day to day and week to week. ■

HOUZAN MAHMOUD

 Houzan Mahmoud is a Kurdish feminist, women's rights activist and co-founder of Culture Project. She has a Master of Arts degree in gender studies from SOAS University of London. She was born in Iraqi Kurdistan in 1973 and currently resides and works in London.

How important is gender equality to transforming the economies of the Middle East?

Gender awareness and equality are important for any society, not only at an economic level, but for the sake of human relations. We are living in a world where women are still treated as less than equal. This may vary from one country to another. In the Middle East, due to wars and dictatorships, gender equality is still a long way away. Women's liberation movements with a feminist consciousness and vision hardly exist. What we have instead are NGOs funded by the US and the European Union, and through these NGOs certain women are turned into 'divas' who are above ordinary women (the victims of everyday violence).

In the best-case scenarios, women who rule these NGOs, instead of being principled feminists and activists, act and behave as corporate directors, leaders, and presidents. In return, few ordinary women who suffer violence every day get help from these NGOs. These bureaucratic, hierarchical and inaccessible structures of women's NGOs are such that the NGOs receive millions of dollars of foreign and local funding, yet the services they provide are very minimal. There is a lack of solidarity and sisterhood, and there is nasty competition over funding and who gets recognition. A large number of women in these NGOs work for wages; they don't work for freedom. They don't even know what 'gender' or 'feminism' mean. If their NGO's funding is cut, I doubt that they would work one day without wages since to them it's a job, not a cause.

What is the state of women's rights in Kurdish-dominated areas? Does it vary depending on the area and country (Iraq, Iran, Turkey or Syria)?

Kurdish societies are not homogeneous, especially as we are divided between four oppressive and dictatorial regimes. Hostility towards Kurdish women has always existed, and they have been doubly oppressed. Despite all the pressure and persecution, however, Kurdish women continue to fight for their rights: they are secular. They try to negotiate their rights within a secular framework, unlike most of the other women's groups in the Middle East which try to work within something called 'Islamic feminism'. Today, the Kurdish parts of Syria and Turkey seem more progressive and militant in terms of their political and social presence. They don't follow the 'NGOization'; instead, they believe in social and political mobilization.

There is a strong sense of feminism and gender awareness in the wider political movements in Kurdish Syria and Turkey. Women so far have managed to claim their place and are visible everywhere. This is less so, unfortunately, in southern Kurdistan or Iraqi Kurdistan where the NGOization on one hand, and the domination by political parties in power over women's groups on the other hand, have led to the stagnation of the women's cause. I can say that in both Iraq and Kurdistan, the problem of NGOization is a major obstacle to the progress of women's rights and mobilization as a movement.

What impact has the involvement and success of the YPJ (Women's Protection Units) in the Rojava Kurds' battle against ISIS had on other women in the Middle East?

The extraordinary and legendary role of revolutionary Kurdish women, in my opinion, has stunned people all over the world. For the first time in contemporary history, we have witnessed women in arms fighting and leading in high ranks in such a fierce fight against a monstrous Islamist force that is armed with the latest weaponry. Another aspect of the fight is that it is not merely nationalistic or rhetorical, but ideological. These women have made it clear that they are fighting for the rights and freedoms of women at the same time as they are fighting the enemy. To them, the fight for women's liberation is no less important than the liberation of their homeland.

Are you in favor of an autonomous Kurdistan, given the horrific persecution the Kurds have faced in Middle Eastern countries over the years? If there ever is an autonomous Kurdistan, would the nationalists have to be defeated to have a democratic and non-patriarchal country?

As a Kurdish woman who suffered under and witnessed Saddam's fascism and tyranny, of course I want an independent Kurdish state. Kurds, like any other people in the Middle East, have been there from the beginning of time. We have not migrated there or colonized the place. We have been colonized and invaded and ruled by force of terror and arms. One very distinct feature of the Kurds is that they have never ceased to fight for a better life and better living conditions; or for their rights and freedoms. On the question of whether we should defeat nationalists to have democracy, I think nationalism and patriarchy are everywhere. Nevertheless, the Kurdish people have continually struggled for freedom and rights no matter who has ruled them, whether it be an Arab fascist regime or a Kurdish nationalist state. ■

YANAR MOHAMMED

Yanar Mohammed is president of the Organization of Women's Freedom in Iraq (OWFI), a women's rights group that runs women's shelters in Iraq for survivors of gender-based violence. The organization also actively protests gender inequality, discriminatory laws on rape, human trafficking and honor killings.

How does OWFI help female victims of violence in Iraq?

We try to provide a model for sanctioning women's dignity while protecting their safety on a direct level by providing non-discriminatory sheltering access to them. We also work to create awareness at a social level about the vulnerability of women and girls in the current Iraqi political landscape. Because of the corruption and chaos created by the US-led occupation, tribal and Islamic patriarchal forces have become greatly empowered. These are the issues that Iraqi society has to work against to create a more egalitarian and human rights-based society. We campaign against governmental attacks on the rights of women and human rights in general. We did much of that on our radio station Al Musawat Radio before the government closed it in June 2014. They didn't like the tone of our campaigns and how we were challenging the legislation they brought forward that compromised women's rights.

How hard is it for women's rights groups like OWFI to flourish in Iraq?

It is not easy because the majority of the Iraqi Parliament is from religious political parties. These are the people who legislated for the marriage of a nine-year-old female in Iraq within the Jaafari Personal Status Law. These are people from Islamic groups who have discredited OWFI very badly online after our demonstration against the law. We have to be very careful. I used to have a lot of media exposure between 2003 and 2005, but after 2005 my TV interviews were censored on Iraqi television, most of which are government-affiliated. Islamist officials would give very clear instructions that I should not be allowed to speak on the airwaves. It has been better the last couple of years and the censorship has become more relaxed because they have been too busy stealing the resources of the country and building a state of corruption for themselves.

What are the underlying reasons for the high level of violence against women in Iraq?

After the invasion, Iraq was left with no sound governance-building. Security deteriorated and wasn't addressed, so eventually people began to rely on their tribes to get some protection and security. The tribes in Iraq, which had dwindled in influence over the past few decades, are now some of the strongest forces ruling on the ground. The tribal structure in Iraq holds a fully-fledged patriarchal view regarding women. Women are viewed as dependants who should be supportive of the family and shouldn't be thinking of their own life decisions as priorities. I would say the biggest blowback we had in Iraq that hit the wellbeing of women was the rising influence of the tribal social systems. This culture promotes women being treated in brutal ways. Tribalism and religious fundamentalism collaborate to make Iraqi woman live in situations that are different from what Iraqi women experienced in the near past. We have lost so many of the women's rights we had previously gained.

Can you talk about the women who fled ISIS but were unwilling to return to their families because of the shame associated with being a survivor of atrocities committed?

We need to be aware that the people we shelter are not all being sheltered for the same reasons. Some of the women in our shelter have escaped ISIS and their husbands and sons have been killed in front of them. They are traumatized, and they wouldn't be wanted for an honor killing because their tribe no longer exists. There are other women who are escaping honor killings, which may or may not be connected with ISIS. And there are some women who are escaping prostitution, which they were forced into for many reasons, including the dire economic factors. They were detained while being prostituted, and now they want to step out of prison, but their tribes want to kill them because they have 'dishonored' the tribe and the family.

The women who stay in our shelters are a collection of women who have gone through all these difficulties. It's very important to address a tribal and religious society and make them aware that the political and sectarian problems in Iraq shouldn't be something that women should be blamed, punished or shamed for.

Are there differing opinions within tribes as to whether honor killings are appropriate for women who were forced to have sex (by ISIS or another violent Islamist group) without their consent?

Yes, actually there are. I wouldn't give credit generously to any tribes, but there are some individuals in the tribes who feel differently about the honor-killing issue, and they feel it needs to be addressed in another way. We in Iraq are trying to take the opportunity to use what happened to the Yazidi community in northern Iraq to change the mentality of the tribes and society at large. Because thousands of Yazidi women were enslaved by ISIS against their will, the Yazidi religious institution issued a fatwa that those who had been captured by ISIS and survived their violence should be considered as pure. When they say 'pure', they mean they have not been tainted by the violence, specifically the sexual violence; and that their tribes and families should be protecting them and respecting them when they escape from ISIS. It's a humane way of looking at women who have been raped.

For women's rights activists in Iraq, the example provided by the Yazidi community gives us the opportunity to address the rest of Iraqi society, including the Islamist and tribal groups; to tell them that there has been a precedent of a goodwill procedure by the Yazidi community and to say why not try to replicate it? OWFI has put the idea forward in three meetings we had in Baghdad, where we invited NGOs along with people in Iraq. We presented this position to them and we asked them to ask their tribal leaders to issue similar fatwas that speak about the dignity and protection that should be given to ISIS survivors.

Has the situation improved for women since the overthrow of Saddam Hussein, or has it worsened?

The women's situation has regressed dramatically over the past eight years when we compare it to the previous era. It's correct that Saddam was a dictator, but there was a strong government with strong security institutions and individuals would not feel free to hurt women without being punished. The current situation is one where the governmental institutions have become weaker than the Iraqi militias and tribes that are ruling in their own areas and their own cities. In addition, the Islamists who have the upper hand in the government are bringing policies and procedures to deal with women that are taking us back at least 60 or 70 years. Whatever modernity there was in the lives of Iraqi women has mostly been lost because of the US occupation of Iraq. The sound building of a new government in Iraq has failed: instead of good governance, it is the Islamists and tribes that are filling the vacuum because the new government was not built correctly. It was not based on a constitution that gives human rights to everybody and equality to all people.

What were the underlying factors that led to the formation of ISIS in Iraq?

The US plan to empower the Shi'a fundamentalists in Iraq and give them power over the Sunni population was a policy that led to support for ISIS. In addition, al-Qaeda was already in Iraq training future leaders of ISIS who became a second generation of al-Qaeda fighters. There are all these factors, but I think the major factor was US empowerment of the sectarian Iraqi government to oppress the Sunni population in the western half of the country, thereby turning them into supporters of any kind of political opposition. So, when ISIS went into Mosul and occupied it, there wasn't one single bullet fired in opposition. The people were desperate for a political solution and they weren't expecting ISIS to be as heinous and inhumane as they turned out to be.

ISIS is a virus that needs to be eradicated altogether. There is no possibility of speaking any sense to any of the leaders. Of course, it's different when we talk about the people living under ISIS. I have talked to women activists living in areas controlled by ISIS who are doing their very best to try to preserve some humane values in the closed communities around them. I have met these women, whether they come from Arab or Kurdish backgrounds, and the secular egalitarian ones are my favorites. The nationalist activists suffer from the same pitfalls as the Islamists. They continue to be rightwing groups despite some of their practices, which may look egalitarian – like putting the women in the front lines during battles with ISIS. When these women defeat ISIS using force, many feminists and leftists around the world like that, but the reality is that nationalist Kurdish groups will still practice racist discrimination against other ethnicities and will continue to discriminate against women once the dust from the battlefields settles. ∎

MOUIN RABBANI

 Mouin Rabbani is a senior fellow for the Institute for Palestine Studies. He specializes in Palestinian affairs and the Arab-Israeli conflict. He was also a senior analyst with the International Crisis Group and is a contributing editor of *Middle East Report*.

What do you think is the reason for the deep US attachment to Israel as opposed to its other allies?

I don't think there is any single explanation, but I think much of it has to do with how horribly skewed and distorted discussion in the US has been over the years about Arabs, Palestinians and, most recently, Muslims. Muslims have been constantly vilified in American popular culture, media, Hollywood and all the rest on the one hand, while on the other hand you have a highly organized, well-resourced, very effectively functioning pro-Israel movement in the United States, whether it be the Israel lobby, neocons or liberal Democrats who have managed to thoroughly delegitimize anything but the most unconditional and uncritical support for any Israeli policy or depredation over the years. So, in that sense, US support for Israel is not very surprising.

When people talk about US relations with Europe, South Africa, Russia or whoever, the discussion at least at one level is about the United States: is this particular policy, initiative or treaty in the interests of the United States no matter how one defines those interests? When it comes to Israel, the discussion within the US is primarily about whether a particular American policy is good or bad for Israel compared to whether or not the policy is good or bad for the United States.

Have you seen a change in the support Western populations give for Israel's policies?

Certainly, there has been a real groundswell of support for the Palestinian cause, not only in traditional places in what was formerly called the Third World, but also in Western countries, particularly in Europe. In the 1970s and 1980s, you had European governments that took fairly reasonable official positions on this issue, but then you had public opinion that was lagging far behind and was much more pro-Israeli in its instincts than officialdom. Now it's very much the other way around. You have governments that are lagging increasingly far behind public opinion. This offers a real opportunity for Palestinians but, because of fragmentation, disintegration, internal rivalries and so on, it's become increasingly difficult for Palestinians to exploit such opportunities.

Which Palestinian party (Fatah or Hamas) is more progressive in terms of economic policies?

I think you have to begin by pointing out that this is a national liberation movement whose primary reason for existence and primary goal is achieving Palestinian national self-determination. Second, I think your question is relevant in the case of Hamas and Fatah because they also play a role in governance (Hamas in the Gaza Strip and Fatah in the West Bank).

Having said that, both parties' room to make and implement socio-economic choices is very constricted. This is the case for Fatah because of the Israeli occupation and donor dependency. For Hamas, it's because of the donor boycott in the Gaza Strip.

It's important to make distinctions between the socio-economic policies of the Palestinian Authority in the West Bank on the one hand and Fatah on the other because they are not necessarily coterminous. The Palestinian Authority has been seeking a basic neoliberal policy framework, but Fatah has always been akin to an ideological supermarket that has accommodated and sought to co-opt everything from the radical Left to the most retrograde Islamists. Therefore, I think it's fair to say there are different socio-economic platforms within that movement.

The incentive among the rank-and-file members of Fatah – but not the leadership – in recent years has been that Fatah should transform itself from a national liberation movement to a social-democratic party. Given the circumstances, I think that is going to be an aspiration that is going to be very difficult to implement.

In the Gaza Strip, Hamas is pursuing a fairly standard socio-economic policy that has traditionally been associated with the Muslim Brotherhood. These policies consist on the one hand of giving very substantial room and leeway to the private sector, while at the same time implementing social programs for the poor and disenfranchised. Both of these projects are political in nature. In both cases, we see that crony capitalism plays an important part in socio-economic policies. Favorite status is given to businesses seen as political supporters while corruption investigations are opened up against businesses that have fallen out of favor with Hamas.

Do you think suicide bombings and terrorist attacks have been unhelpful tactics in achieving independence from Israeli occupation? Are nonviolent tactics more helpful when it comes to ending the illegal Israeli occupation in the West Bank and Gaza?

I think you are asking two questions. The first is whether armed resistance weakens the Palestinian struggle for self-determination and the second is about whether a specific tactic of armed resistance (suicide bombings) strengthens or weakens the Palestinian struggle for self-determination. I would frame the questions a little differently. Let's start with your first question. Until the late 1960s, the idea of a Palestinian guerilla struggle to achieve Palestinian liberation was not a majority opinion among Palestinians. This was the era of Arab Nationalism and Pan-Arabism and most Palestinians thought of the issue as a broader Arab-Israeli issue rather than on solely Israeli-Palestinian terms. In other words, this was a conflict that pitted Israel against the entire Arab world instead of just the Palestinian people. It was a responsibility that the Arabs at a popular level and increasingly at an official level accepted – that it was the role and responsibility of the regular Arab armies to defeat Israel and liberate Palestine.

This all changed dramatically with the 1967 Arab-Israeli War and the total defeat and discrediting of the regular Arab armies and by extension the so-called progressive Arab regimes. It was in that vacuum that we saw the emergence of the Palestine national movement, particularly the Palestinian guerrilla organizations: first and foremost Fatah, but also Marxist/leftist organizations like the Popular Front and the Democratic Front. These were movements that pursued armed struggle not just as a tactic, but as a strategy, until at least 1982. This Palestinian liberation struggle, pursued independently from an Israeli-Arab confrontation with Israel, proved itself to be capable of placing the Palestinian question on the international agenda. This compelled the international community to give consideration to this issue as perhaps the primary root of instability and insecurity in the Middle East. However, it proved itself to be unsuccessful in actually liberating territories.

Second, popular mass mobilization, particularly within the occupied territories, has proven to be a more effective tactic in confronting Israel in recent years. I do think, at a certain level, there is a relationship between armed struggle and mass mobilization. I question the extent to which mass popular mobilization could have been effective without the basis that had been laid for the prominence of the Palestine question in the 1960s, 1970s and 1980s by the armed struggle. Nevertheless, I think it's fair to say we have witnessed clear limitations to armed struggle and existing opportunities for popular mass mobilization.

You raised the question of suicide bombings, which I think raises several issues. To me, there is a fundamental difference between a Palestinian militant blowing himself up in the middle of a number of soldiers as opposed to a café in Tel Aviv, which is filled with civilians. I think the more appropriate question is: do you think Palestinian attacks on non-civilian combatants have helped or hindered the Palestine struggle, as opposed to isolating a particular tactic that can be deployed on legitimate and illegitimate targets? I also understand that, since 9/11, these kinds of tactics (suicide bombings), irrespective of whether they are used against legitimate or illegitimate targets, have been used to delegitimize those deploying such tactics.

Do you believe there is a moral obligation to distinguish suicide attacks against Israeli soldiers from those against noncombatants?

Are you asking if there should be a moral distinction between legitimate and illegitimate targets? My answer is: of course. I think Palestinians are seeking global recognition and application of international law as a basis for the resolution of the Palestine question. More importantly, Palestinians are asking for recognition and application of international human rights norms in its dealings with Israel. To me, in such a struggle you have to take the moral high ground and be the first to acknowledge and accept and respect and implement the laws of war. ■

FAWWAZ TRABOULSI

 Fawwaz Traboulsi is associate professor of political science and history at the Lebanese American University and the American University of Beirut. He is editor-in-chief of the pan-Arab quarterly *Bidayat* and the author of *A History of Modern Lebanon*.

Can you discuss the military and political aims of Hizbullah?

Hizbullah emerged as a resistance Islamist party affiliated to Ayatollah Ruhollah Khomeini in Iran. This is not something they deny; in fact, they boast about being theologically affiliated with Iran. Hizbullah started the resistance in the movement against the Israeli occupation of Lebanon in June 1982, but they didn't declare themselves as a resistance movement until 1985. It was actually three Marxist groups that initially launched the resistance against Israel in September 1982. For years, you had two formations of the Lebanese anti-occupation resistance: a leftwing resistance which also incorporated the Syrian Socialist Nationalist Party, while on the other hand you had Hizbullah under the denomination of the Islamic resistance.

Since 2000 when Israel withdrew under the impact of the resistance movements, Hizbullah was left as the only resistance party because the Syrian regime forbade the other formations of the resistance and adopted Hizbullah as the sole resistance party. Lebanon has basically been free of the Israeli occupation since the year 2000, except for few dozen square kilometers in the South and the Shebaa Farms. Hizbullah has not been active in any operations inside Israeli territory, with the exception of its defensive wars against Israel in 1996 and 2006. As far as I'm concerned, Hizbullah is a force of national defense for the Lebanese territories. They are resisting occupation on their own territory

The other part of Hizbullah is a political party that is part of the ruling class in Lebanon. It has participated in all the major ministries, it has a sizeable parliamentary group and many neoliberal decisions that have been made in Lebanon have been met with silence from Hizbullah.

Things get complicated when Hizbullah intervenes in Syria to support a dictatorial regime and it moves a concentration of its troops from south Lebanon to fighting the Syrian opposition on behalf of the Syrian regime. These actions have been opposed by not only the 14 March group, but also by people who were defenders of Hizbullah's right to bear arms. These same people won't accept that these same arms should be used in what started out as a peaceful revolution by the Syrian people.

How do you distinguish between national liberation movements and terrorist groups?

National liberation movements act against foreign occupations that use violence to maintain their power. Throughout the period after World War Two, national liberation movements began as groups opposed to the occupying powers. Hizbullah emerged as an anti-Israeli organization that opposed the Israeli occupation.

Opposition groups, including Islamists, that fight against the regime of Bashar al-Assad in Syria cannot be considered terrorist groups. Once you start talking about terrorism, you should think of terrorist states. Israel ranks high on the list of terrorist states.

But couldn't national liberation movements that oppose occupations also be guilty of terrorism if they kill civilians that don't identify with their cause? For example, ISIS has opposed the Syrian regime while also committing horrific atrocities against Syrian civilians...

I'm differentiating between ISIS and the rest of the Islamist militias fighting Assad. This whole region has been kidnapped by one major vision and one major idea called the universal 'war against terror'. The internal problems and interests of the people in the region have been put aside in this 'war against terror', including supporting terrorist regimes and the most reactionary regimes, such as the oil monarchies and dictatorships.

In addition, demonizing ISIS will not help in defeating it. The proof is that ISIS is the product of unemployment, the collapse of agriculture and the American-Iraqi war. During the war all tribes were militarized and turned into militias. Rather than include them in the army, the two Shi'a parties that dominated Iraq didn't include the elements that would eventually form ISIS. You cannot understand ISIS without understanding the American occupation of Iraq and you cannot understand the Syrian ISIS without understanding the Iraqi ISIS. You cannot defeat ISIS if you do not deal with the huge problems that ISIS is exploiting: communal problems related to the Sunnis of north Syria in Iraq and the marginalization of the countryside and the collapse of agriculture under the neoliberalism promoted by Bashar al-Assad's regime. Some leftists in Europe and the States still think Assad is a socialist.

ISIS does kill civilians, but I don't know the number of civilians they have killed in comparison to the number of civilians that have been killed by Bashar al-Assad's explosive barrel bombs. Some leftists see Assad as defending himself against American imperialism at a time when it's obvious that President Obama took no actions to get rid of Assad. It's so obvious that Mr Obama delivered the task of solving the problem of Syria to Mr Putin.

Has Hizbullah's support in Lebanon decreased because of its support for Bashar al-Assad's regime?

Yes. The Hizbullah of the 1980s and 1990s was a Shia party – in fact, it's more of a Shi'a party today than it was then – but it had the support of many people throughout the country. It was a force of resistance to the occupation of 10 per cent of Lebanese territory by Israel. But Hizbullah in power has lost a lot of the support it initially had because it covered up all the exploitation and corruption of the neoliberal regime that was imposed on Lebanon from the end of the Israeli-Lebanon war led by the late Mr Hariri, who supposedly could have been killed by Hizbullah. In economic and social terms, Hizbullah cannot boast of having represented the interests of the marginalized, the poor, the workers and the peasants who constitute a good part of the party's partisans. Hizbullah has veered more and more towards the middle classes and the rich Shi'as who provide them with money and donations. Hizbullah will continue to lose popularity as it becomes more of a traditional part of Lebanese politics. Hizbullah does this all in the name of having to fight one battle, which was once the battle against Israel, but is now against the Syrian rebels. ■

ROBIN YASSIN-KASSAB

 Robin Yassin-Kassab is a journalist who also co-edits pulsemedia.org. He is the author of *The Road from Damascus* and co-author (with Leila al-Shami) of the Rathbone-Folio prize-shortlisted book *Burning Country: Syrians in revolution and war*.

What do you think is the best political solution for Syria?

What should happen is that all foreign forces should leave the country – and that includes Sunni terrorists and extremists who come from elsewhere to join Sunni extremist organizations. It also includes the more than 100,000 Shi'a militias, who have been organized by Iran, that are occupying Syria. The Russians and Americans should also leave, and the situation should be left to Syrians. I think the Syrians should have been allowed to get rid of Bashar al-Assad. He would have fallen if it hadn't been for massive foreign intervention on his side. I don't imagine there would have been immediate peace and prosperity after the war ended, but the process towards building a more representative and decentralized government could have been ongoing amongst Syrians. Now we have no hope of this happening because the war has become regionalized and internationalized. So much of what is going to happen is in the hands of Russia, Iran, Turkey and the United States. Democratic nationalist fighters and the democratic local councils where people have been elected in liberated areas have to be brought into the political process for a real peace process to work.

How long did the peaceful demonstrations last in Syria before people finally took up arms in response to brutal repression by the Syrian government?

There are still people who go out on Friday and protest unarmed for the same things: social justice, freedom, and opposition to all forms of authoritarianism. They went out and protested in 2011. The Syrian revolution really didn't start to look like a war until the summer of 2012, although there were still enormous peaceful demonstrations going on at that time.

Can you talk about Russia's role in the Syrian civil war?

When the Russians came in, they concentrated their fire not on ISIS, but on the democratic nationalists and the FSA militias. There was a concerted effort to take the urban areas held by revolutionary forces. These urban areas were the basic support network for the FSA, local councils and democratic alternatives to the State. The FSA does still exist: it has always existed as an umbrella term referring to thousands of fighters who just want to end Assad's misrule over Syria. However, the FSA is split up, under siege and dominated in some areas by transnational groups like Jabhat al-Nusra.

Do you feel like more aid from the Obama administration to the Free Syrian Army would have toppled Assad even with the Iranians and Russians backing the Assad regime?

When the Russians intervened militarily in September 2015, the Assad regime was in control of about one-fifth of the national territory. This was the case despite the huge number of Iranian proxies in the country at the time. What spurred the Russians to intervene was that the Iranians flew to Moscow and said, 'you have to come rescue Assad, or he's going to fall'. There was a group of Islamists and jihadist groups called Jabhat Fateh al-Sham [previously known as the al-Qaeda-linked Jabhat al-Nusra] in the northwest, which was supported by the FSA, that had taken Idlib and were coming up through the coastal areas, which is supposedly the regime's heartland. It was very problematic that one of the leading groups in the coalition of fighters taking these territories from the Assad regime was al-Nusra. Still, Assad was falling. I don't think it would have taken that much to change the situation.

What Syrians really needed from the Obama administration was anti-aircraft weaponry. I don't think it was necessary for the Americans or any other country to give Syrians weaponry to fight their way into Assad's palace or home town. I think they should have given them the weaponry to defend themselves and their community. If civilian communities are being bombed in a way that deliberately targets civilian infrastructure (schools, hospitals, homes) and there is no diplomatic way of stopping this, then the civilians have a right to defend themselves. There were times when the Obama administration gave the Turks, Saudis and Qataris the green light to send the Syrian fighters anti-tank missiles, but not anti-aircraft weaponry.

Do you think the US would have been justified in arming the FSA if a fraction of the weapons were getting into the hands of jihadist groups?

If we found out that two per cent of the weapons given to the FSA got into the hands of al-Nusra, I don't think this would have been an enormous problem. Most of the weaponry used by the rebels was captured from the Syrian regime. As for ISIS, most of its weapons were captured when the Iraqi army fled Mosul. These are the weapons the US showered on the government in Iraq.

What would you say to critics who ideologically sided with the Free Syrian Army, but who were concerned about the prospect of a showdown between the United States and Russia if the US government were to support a no-fly zone or take some other action that could lead to armed conflict between the two nuclear-armed states?

I don't think Putin is insane. I think it's absolutely impossible that he would risk a nuclear standoff with the United States over his grandstanding in Syria. Russia is weaker than the United States in military terms (nuclear-wise and militarily) and the Russian government understands this. I don't think the United States wanted to have a confrontation with Russia either.

Obama said chemical weapons were a red line, then the Assad regime used chemical weapons in 2013 that killed 1,500 people in a few hours, and the red line disappeared. The United States handed the Russian government and Russian prime minister Sergei Lavrov control over pressuring the Syrian regime to dispose of their stockpile of chemical weapons. Relinquishing an area to another savage power is still horrible imperialism.

Is there hope for an alliance between the FSA and Kurdish Syrian Democratic Forces?

One would hope. The Syrian democratic forces are controlled by the Kurdish Democratic Union Party (PYD). Some Arab refugees are returning to areas under PYD control, but others are not returning because they worry the PYD will give these areas back to Assad. Both sides share some blame for the conflict between them. The mainstream revolutionaries on the Arab side should have been very clear in 2011 that they accepted Kurdish autonomy and self-determination in areas where the Kurds were in the majority.

On the other hand, the PYD both is and isn't a revolutionary force. To most people in Syria, the PYD looks more like a Kurdish nationalist force than a revolutionary force. This goes back to the relationship between the Assad regime and the PYD, and its parent organization the Kurdistan Workers' Party (PKK). PKK nationalist leader Abdullah Öcalan was protected and allowed to live in Syria by President Hafez al-Assad. Hafez, and later his son Bashar, allowed the PYD to flourish in Syria because the PYD tended to focus on the Kurdish struggle in Turkey, not the struggle for civil rights for Kurds within Syria. When the regime withdrew from a lot of areas in northern Syria in 2012, it withdrew from the Kurdish majority areas without a fight and handed these areas over to the PYD. By capturing the Castello Road, the PYD helped the regime and Iran to impose the siege on Aleppo city, which later led to the city's fall. Some months before, the PYD had occupied Tel Rifaat and other Arab-majority towns in the Aleppo province. The PYD said they were taking these regions from jihadists, but they were taking them from FSA militias. These were towns that had local democratic councils, and people fled by the thousands when the PYD arrived. ∎

Europe

NADEZDHA AZHGIKHINA

Nadezdha Azhgikhina is a Russian journalist and writer. She is vice-president of the European Federation of Journalists and a board member of Free Word Association. She is also a member of Rights in Russia, which was founded in 2010 to mark the first anniversary of the killings of Moscow human rights lawyer Stanislav Markelov and journalist Anastasia Baburova.

What do you think are Vladimir Putin's motives for trying to influence the US elections?

Honestly, I do not think that the Russian government (or Collective Putin) had plans or intentions to interfere in the US elections any more than China, Iran, the Arab states or any other actors. Like many other Russian liberals, I can't believe that Russian trolls and hackers, even the best in the world, could destroy the oldest and strongest democracy in the world and its elections.

Would it be accurate to say Putin was trying to damage Hillary Clinton, but that he still expected her to win?

Nobody expected Trump to win, even Trump himself. It's clear Russian leaders were preparing to deal with Clinton, despite her strong anti-Russian statements.

What do ordinary Russians think about Robert Mueller's investigation of any links between Donald Trump and the Kremlin?

Many intellectuals in Russia think American Democrats don't want to accept the fact that Americans voted for showman Trump and, instead of analyzing their own mistakes, decided to find an 'external enemy'. The demonization of all of Russia as a 'place of trolls and a threat to the democratic universe' in the American media reminds Russian liberals of Soviet propaganda and makes them frustrated and unhappy.

Russian liberals looked to the United States as a role model, an ideal state and an ideal democracy for decades. 'Russiagate' ruined this ideal. Its simplification and Hollywood-style exaggeration of the 'Russian threat' is a terrible disappointment to Russian liberals. We all lost our dream, and our ideal.

How popular is Putin in Russia right now? What do you think are the reasons for his popularity?

Putin has the strong support of most Russians. Even if his popularity, according to the latest polls, went down after the announcement of 'pension reform', he has the stable support of the majority. Recent elections showed that many people who never voted for Putin before voted for him in 2018. People voted for stability and didn't see any other leader. The opposition is weak and puzzled. Many people would like to see a strongman as a leader. Anti-Russian sanctions also created a basis for more support for Putin. The everyday lives of ordinary people are getting tougher and state propaganda talks about 'Russia being under siege'. Sanctions, I should say, had the opposite effect from that intended – Russians did not protest, but united around the leader, and let authorities restrict free press and civil society.

How strong is anti-Americanism in Russia today?

Anti-Americanism is stronger than at any time in my lifetime. During the Soviet era, many had real interest in and sympathy with the United States, despite the propaganda. Russiagate has challenged these feelings. Many Russians today, as sociologists say, believe that America is the enemy of Russia. It will take a long time to change this view. Of course, there are many people that still have positive feelings about America, and recent polls show that the anti-American position is down from last year. It is a sign of hope. It means that propaganda is not that efficient, and people have begun to think on their own.

Have Russian dissenters been critical over their government's role in Syria propping up Assad?

I do not think we could define critical voices as 'dissenters' today, like in the Soviet era. Today, a number or groups and even parties (Yabloko, for example), make strong critiques of Russian foreign policy and the Russian role in Syria. Many Russians do not like the Syrian campaign, but some do believe that it could be an instrument against terrorists on the global scale, and in Russia as well. At the same time a strong anti-war movement, like the anti-Chechen war movement in the mid-1990s, does not exist.

Do any links exist between Russian liberals and the American Left?

Links between Russian liberals and American leftwing activists are not very strong. Left ideas are not popular because of the post-Soviet syndrome. Ideas of social justice are close to the program of Grigory Yavlinsky [Azhgikhina was an authorized representative of Yavlinksy in the 2018 Russian elections] and his party Yabloko, but very few in Russia really read this program, and he had no chance to promote it on the national stage. I do believe this plan will, at some point, be a fruitful strategy for Russia. Yavlinsky has links with leftwing Democrats in the US. Maybe those links could help to develop new networks in the future. ■

PREDRAG KOJOVIC

 Predrag Kojovic is the president of Nasa Stranka (Our Party) in Bosnia Herzegovina. Nasa Stranka is a multi-ethnic political party of a socially liberal orientation that stands for solidarity, social justice and broad civil liberties.

How difficult was it to develop a multi-ethnic party in Bosnia Herzegovina after the brutal wars in Bosnia and Serbia?

As you can imagine, it was very, very hard. Nationalism scars the social tissue of society in such a way that its recovery, apart from intense nourishment, requires additional time, courage and luck. It is particularly difficult if the conflict ended without a military winner and the perpetrators of crimes are not held responsible and are walking freely among their victims – or are even glorified by their side. Then you add to all that a monumental failure of the international community to apply its own principles to the case of Bosnia Herzegovina. We are a social-liberal party, which, by definition, means we're not nationalists. It's hard to convert people who still have strong nationalist feelings. I'm counting mostly on the younger generation. Some people are too wounded by the war in the 1990s to recover and move forward.

What institutions can be set up to dissuade people from being influenced by ethnic exclusivism and nationalism?

The most important state institution for prevention of that kind of evil is our schools – for the curriculum not to be written by nationalists or extremists. Unfortunately, now we have schools that teach exactly that – nationalism. You need a bigger percentage of good people with a good education system. Good education teaches you to question everything. I think education is our best chance. Fortunately, schools are not the only sources of information kids have today. They roam the internet and it counters the influence of educational propaganda and their parents.

What do you think were the key factors that made people, particularly the Serb militias (but, to a lesser extent, Bosniaks and Croats as well), capable of perpetuating such horrific violence in the Balkan wars?

Well, that's the question that has been haunting me for a long time. What turns your neighbor – you used to leave your kids with them when you were busy – into a killer? I do not know the answer, but it's been done over and over again – and not just in this part of the world. Or maybe the struggle between good and evil is in fact a struggle between modern and primitive. It's very possible to make killers out of very ordinary people. It's amazing how the public is brought into that psychological state.

What factors undergirded the Bosnian Serbs' violence during the Bosnian War from 1992 to 1995?

About 90 per cent of the Serbs were mobilized in the 1990s to defend Yugoslavia. Franco Tuðjman was the elected president in Croatia and he was very militant. Everything in that country looked like 1941 when the Nazi-backed Ustase government remorselessly persecuted Jews, Serbs, Gypsies and Croat anti-fascists. Now the Serbs saw themselves as fighting to defend Yugoslavia against the Croatian Nazi state of 1941. When the Serbs got around to Bosnia they no longer knew what they were fighting for.

Does the atmosphere that allowed the Balkans to explode into violence in the 1990s still exist today, or have there been positive steps made to mitigate tensions between the Bosniaks, Croats and Serbs?

Violence, to be 'successful', requires political mobilization but also resources: arms and military organization capable of performing killing in an organized way. The resources part is missing today but the rhetoric for political mobilization is still around. However, I do not believe that many people would volunteer, especially those who did before. Steps that would permanently take us away from that possibility require political courage that our current leaders do not have.

What is Nasa Stranka doing to push back against the widespread discrimination the Roma are facing in Bosnia Herzegovina?

It is part of a struggle for equality for all citizens of Bosnia Herzegovina also known as 'Sejdic-Finci'. Sejdic-Finci relates to a court case brought to the European Court of Human Rights by Roma activist Dervo Sejdic and by Jakob Finci, who is Jewish. They argued that the Bosnian Constitution – negotiated as part of the Dayton Peace Accords that ended the Bosnian War – discriminated against Roma, Jews and other minority parties because certain electoral posts like the tripartite presidency could only be held by Serbs, Croats and Muslims. The court decided in favor of Sejdic and Finci and Bosnia's leaders said they would fix the problem, but they have yet to do so. However, we do recognize that the Roma ethnic group is particularly vulnerable and representatives in legislative bodies often bring up Roma issues and demand action from the government regarding their position, or, more precisely, the lack of their presence in the educational and government system.

Is Nasa Stranka satisfied with how Bosnia's court system has tried people suspected of committing atrocities during the wars in the Balkans?

In such a widely corrupted state, the court system cannot be an exception. National parties infiltrated the judicial system with party soldiers who then made political decisions in legal cases. As a matter of fact, the judicial system became one of, if not the biggest, obstacle to both justice and reforms. It is unfortunate that the judicial system has been built and is still controlled by the international community and their inadequate representatives. ∎

SONJA LICHT

 Sonja Licht led the Fund for an Open Society in Yugoslavia (later Serbia) from 1991 to 2003. She established the Belgrade Fund for Political Excellence in 2003, which is a member of the Council of Europe's network of schools of Political Studies devoted to democratic capacity-building.

Do you worry about the rise of nationalism in many countries today?

Far Right nationalism is spreading in Europe – and not just in Europe, but all over the world. Just look at President Trump in America. This is not just about economic hardship; it is also about the negative sides of globalization. The danger in Serbia is not the return of a Milošević-type of nationalism, but a globalized version of nationalism. This is how it has to be understood. There is huge Euroskepticism within the European countries themselves. In addition, the migration crisis was generated by, among other causes, very wrong policies in the Middle East by the United States, Britain, France, Turkey and Russia. All of this is making the picture much more complex in the Balkans. The Far Right in Serbia is less influential than the Far Right in many of our immediate surrounding regions. The Far Right in other parts of the region (including Austria, Germany, France) has been on a serious rise. The major issue for Serbia and the whole of the Balkans is the European perspective, because this perspective strengthens anti-nationalist feelings and anti-nationalist policies. I hope Serbia will eventually normalize relations with Kosovo as well.

What reforms need to be made to revive the Serbian economy?

As in all the post-socialist countries, a modified, but still neoliberal, economic model was accepted in Serbia. There was no other alternative because everybody from the European Union to the World Bank to the International Monetary Fund have been insisting on the same model of fiscal consolidation and tough monetary policy. Privatization in Serbia meant a huge stealing of assets and we didn't learn the lessons from other nations who tried privatization earlier. We do have a very, very serious problem.

Do you think there is a middle ground to what has been called the politics of austerity that is pushed by the IMF and other institutions?

I'm convinced that there should be a middle ground. I'm also very sorry there was a huge lack of ideas and efforts to create an alternative model of transition by social democrats, especially in Western Europe. They were not ready to offer a different model for the post-socialist world, so even they themselves accepted neoliberalism, as did President Clinton in America. I'm deeply convinced that this is one of the main issues that made all these countries so vulnerable. I'm not advocating a state-owned economy because it proved to be inefficient as well, but I'm sure we needed a much more gradual approach. The slogan was 'first you privatize and then comes everything else'. I must say sometimes it reminded me of the slogan in the first years of the Soviet Union: 'Industrialization and electrification and then we can build democracy.'

You can follow it from Russia to Albania: most of those privatized companies went into the hands of former party officials, secret-service officials and people who had insider information. They became the new tycoons.

For me, one of the most paradoxical examples of this kind of hasty privatization was the privatization of the Serbian media. It didn't bring economic challenges as was the case with privatization of corporations and industry, but the private media is so extremely commercialized that you don't have serious objective critical journalism any more. This is not just a problem in Serbia, it is a global problem. We are all victims of reality-show culture.

Why is it important for Serbia to become part of the European Union?

It is important for all the countries of this region. It's important because a number of bilateral tensions and potential low-level conflicts can be solved within a broader integration into the European Union. At one point several years ago, Hungary and Slovakia were on the verge of open conflict and the fact that both these countries were in the European Union transformed this conflict into a political process. The European Union still has an integrative power in this part of Europe. Serbian citizens can feel emotional ties with Russia, but they are aware that being part of the European Union brings you a level of stability and security. It will also bring Serbia a feeling of belonging to a broader 'family'. If it remains on the periphery, or on the periphery of the periphery, especially during times of global disorder, this leaves the country with many more immediate and longer-term dangers. This is obvious any time you look at the globe.

Do you think it's important in Europe to increase civil discussions about the importance of democratic inclusivism, specifically in terms of the migration crisis that has led many refugees and immigrants to flee to European countries?

I don't really see another way for Europe. Of course, there is always an alternative. They could build a Fortress Europe. I'm not a historian but I don't really buy that argument because I don't know of any fortress that was strong enough to resist huge ongoing pressure coming from the outside. I don't believe this is feasible. Also, I don't believe the European understanding of identity would remain the same – in fact it would become the opposite – if Europe builds a fortress and embraces an isolationist-style politics. I had a conversation with a western European diplomat and he was trying to explain to me that what he thinks should be done is to have immigration policies like those that are in place in the United States, where Europe could pick and choose who to let into the country. This strategy is not even successful in the United States, which has a much better model of integration than Europe. What this gentleman and others like him have forgotten when they promote this policy is that Europe is not surrounded by two oceans. Europe simply cannot isolate itself without building huge walls and I don't think those walls can protect Europe from the outside world. We would isolate ourselves for a while, but we would destroy our values and that wonderful and precious European slogan 'Unity in diversity'.

What reforms do you think need to be made to make the European Union more beneficial for all its citizens and countries?

The European Union has a chance to be an organization that can overcome the most serious downsides of globalization, but this can only be achieved if it starts paying attention to social needs and social rights. The EU needs to stop being a model that is helping the rich become richer. I fully agree with German Chancellor Angela Merkel's policy towards refugees, but I was very critical of her policy towards Greece because Germany supported the banks and gave up on Greece. I'm not advocating that Greece has to be relieved of its own responsibility, but I do think there were smarter ways that could have helped get Greece out of its economic quagmire. There is this attitude among many that Greece was not good enough for the EU – let's get rid of them. This attitude would drive the EU to repeat the mistakes of Yugoslavia. Yugoslavia disintegrated into a bloody war and the only two [former Yugoslav states who are] members of the EU – Slovenia and Croatia – are not any better off in the EU than they were in the former Yugoslavia. In the former Yugoslavia they were the most developed parts of the federation and they benefited from that position; now they are in a much less favorable position. I don't want to say that they are not better off than if they had stayed outside of the EU after the fall of Yugoslavia, I simply mean that if the entirety of Yugoslavia had entered the EU, the two most developed parts would be in a much more prosperous position now.

As someone who has lived during the horrors of the Balkan wars, how do you think this level of ethnic hatred develops? What countervailing narratives and programs can be developed to stop that kind of indescribable cruelty from breaking out?

I was asked this question in different countries in the 1990s from Italy to the United States and usually my response would be the following: give me your media for a year and you will have the Balkan wars on your territory. It is very easy to instigate hatred. You instigate it by raising the level of fear and insecurity first, and then everything else comes later. Look at how many people, including young people, are still ecstatically supporting President Trump. Would you have thought, with that kind of rhetoric, he would become the president of the United States? No, you wouldn't. Why is that any more an enigma? It was very clear what he was doing from day one. He was appealing to the very lowest common denominator. He was stoking feelings of anxiety and insecurity in people who are basically looking for someone who will tell them he will fix it all. I don't think anybody should be surprised about what happened in my part of the world. You are living with the same phenomenon despite having a more developed media, and more developed democratic institutions. This still wasn't enough to prevent Trump from being elected president.

We had camps, we had Srebrenica and we had rape based on ethnic hatred. Unfortunately, we went through atrocities that no-one thought could happen after World War Two; at least not in Europe. What people in Serbia ignored or were not aware of was that many people, especially Serbs, who went through the atrocities of World War Two – not so much in Serbia but in Croatia and Bosnia – had the feeling the atrocities never ended. People were exterminated by the Ustasha regime during World War Two only because of their religion and nationality and many people still feared that this history could repeat itself. It is almost impossible for citizens to prevent these kinds of wars because the political class is the one that creates the climate. We dissidents didn't have the mechanisms for preventing the developments that led to the outbreak of wars in the 1980s and 1990s in Yugoslavia.

It is much easier to fight a political battle. I'm talking about my experience fighting the Milošević regime. We managed to create small islands of freedom and resistance in Serbia. We also had a few weak, but important, independent media outlets that would not have survived without foreign donors. Political battles depend on how eager people are to get organized to fight for their basic rights and the basic rights of society. The resistance built into a bigger movement by the end of the 1990s that was able to get rid of Milošević and his regime.

Do you think Milošević would have fallen without the NATO bombing of Yugoslavia?

Yes, he would have fallen more quickly. I will give you two examples that prove my statement. He was so weak in 1997-98 that he made two totalitarian laws: one was a law against the universities, and the second was a law against the media. Both laws were so hostile against anything independent in those two fields that it created huge resistance in society. You could see that Milošević was transforming an autocratic state into a totalitarian state, which simply wasn't going to be accepted without huge resistance. ■

ROGER LIPPMAN

Roger Lippman edits Balkan Witness, a progressive website that covers the history of the wars in Kosovo and Bosnia and expresses solidarity with the people in those countries who were victimized by Serbian aggression. Lippman was a prominent US anti-war activist during the Vietnam War and a member of Students for a Democratic Society.

What motivated you to create Balkan Witness?

I had been tuned in to what had been happening in Yugoslavia for quite a few years, having been there as early as 1982. I was in the San Francisco area when the war started, and I was listening to Pacifica Radio. At 6pm they had the news program, which gave a factual version of what was going on. But at 5pm there was an opinion show that was completely aligned with the Milošević position. I was astonished that this progressive radio station, KPFA in Berkeley, was expressing sympathy with Serbian aggression, with a lot of leading Left intellectuals endorsing this position. So I started collecting articles that better represented my own understanding of what was going on over there and emailing them to people. I then found that a much easier way to distribute that information was through a website. I started Balkan Witness in April 1999. This was before everyone had a website; it was my first.

What was your position on the Kosovo War?

I don't think the US went in to get control of some outdated lead mine or a notional oil pipeline route. In Kosovo or Bosnia, there really is not a lot there for someone else to want. But I wouldn't say US intervention there was humanitarian in the sense that it represented a government policy based on humanitarianism.

The Kosovo intervention was in response to a situation that was destabilizing in Europe itself, where there was a threat of a war that would involve NATO members on both sides, like Greece versus Turkey. Serbia's atrocities in Kosovo also contributed to a disruption of the ability to do business in that part of Europe. Those atrocities were creating waves of refugees that neighboring countries were not pleased to be receiving. Western powers cared about such matters in Europe, but not in Africa. That helps explain why the US got involved in Kosovo and not Rwanda. Of course, there were complicating factors. It was such an obviously unfortunate situation that nobody intervened in Rwanda, that Western powers felt like they needed to make up for it in some way. There was a little more heightened sensitivity to deal with a situation like the one in Kosovo.

If you read what I have written on NATO's intervention in Kosovo, you will see that I did not outright endorse it; but I did challenge opponents of the intervention to come up with plausible alternatives to intervention. And I myself have been unable to think of an alternative to intervention. The way the intervention was done was not admirable, even though it ultimately succeeded in its purposes. It wasn't necessary to destroy the infrastructure of northern Serbia, far removed geographically from Kosovo. And it was unfortunate, at least tactically, to rule out a ground intervention so early, even though a ground intervention would have been very difficult if you know anything about the physical realities of things like roads in Kosovo. I don't have the expertise to make that evaluation. Yugoslavia had something like the fourth-biggest army in Europe, and Serbia inherited most of that. To invade a country on its own turf, you're at a disadvantage.

Do you believe the NATO invasion escalated the Serbian crimes in Kosovo?

I have dealt with that argument on Balkan Witness to a fair extent, especially in refuting Noam Chomsky. You can't say that the massive destruction and attacks on civilians, which began roughly the same day as the NATO invasion, were spontaneous. They had to be pre-planned both in terms of politics and logistics. It takes so much equipment and machinery and planning to wreak that kind of havoc on a country and population. All the equipment was in place and it was rolled into action in that one day. There is no reason to believe that wasn't going to happen anyway. Furthermore, as is well documented by various international agencies, there had been a very high level of Serbian war crimes in Kosovo over the prior year.

What are your thoughts on Slobodan Milošević's complex relationship with the United States during the Balkan and Kosovo wars?

Treating Slobodan Milošević as a negotiating partner instead of as a madman and a mass murderer was a policy problem from very early on. It's almost a structural problem in American diplomacy to give credence to people like him. That only encouraged him and gave him more power and more strength. He shouldn't have been enabled in that way.

Do you think the victims of past US atrocities (such as in Vietnam, Laos, Guatemala and Iraq) that were as bad as Serb atrocities in Kosovo, Bosnia, and Croatia should have also received international help to prevent crimes against humanity or genocide?

The point being made by Chomsky and others is that the United States treats plenty of populations in the world in an aggressive and exploitative way, and the question is, do they have the right to fight back? Of course, that answer is yes. And you hope that they would do it in a way that serves their cause. I'm against the US victimizing civilians abroad, and I'm against anyone else (or the US government for that matter) victimizing US civilians.

Can you talk about the distinctions you make in terms of the leftists you have criticized for their stances on Bosnia and Kosovo?

There is a whole range of culpabilities. Some are outraged supporters of Milošević and some are on the uninformed, confused end. Most of the people I have critiqued who could be considered part of the Left have done something politically useful in their lives. That is why I am so saddened by their positions on issues regarding Yugoslavia. That said, what I've observed about their work on Yugoslavia has forced me to call into question some of the other work they have done and look a little deeper.

That's especially true with Chomsky. If you look at things within the framework of what he's said about Yugoslavia, I have a lot of problems with his past work. I certainly don't discard all of it. If I've learned anything from this whole experience it's 'think for yourself' and 'think critically' when you read people who are supposed to be leftwing intellectual leaders. Don't just accept them because they are heroes; analyze what they are talking about.

My big problem with Chomsky is that he feels like he has to be an authority on everything, and there is practically no question he won't answer without an authoritative opinion. That doesn't mean he knows anything about it. I think he found himself in a position on Yugoslavia where people were looking to him for answers, and he gave answers that turned out to be flawed, but he will never back down from them.

So, then you go back to his position on the Khmer Rouge war in Cambodia. It seems he was pretty seriously wrong about that, as were a lot of people, but he will not admit that at all. When you look a little deeper you can learn from how he behaved around Kosovo, and that forces you to revisit everything he has ever said, to sort out the value from the sophistry. Some of these war-crimes deniers – and I would include Diane Johnstone, Edward Herman, Michel Chossudovsky and Jared Israel – have a position that is neo-Stalinist, essentially endorsing the Milošević style of operation, and I have no use for any of them.

What do you think are the most important issues the Western Left and the international Left must confront today?
We must evolve beyond binary, Cold War-era think and keep a moral compass. That means siding with the victims and opposing criminal, expansionist wars no matter who initiates them. ∎

GEORGE MONBIOT

DAVID STELFOX

George Monbiot has been a columnist for *The Guardian* since 1996. He writes about myriad subjects including the environment, corruption, inequality and social justice. Among his books are: *Heat: How to Stop the Planet from Burning*; *Age of Consent: Manifesto for a New World Order*; and *Feral: Rewilding the Land, Sea and Human Life*.

There has been a lot of criticism of neoliberalism by the Western Left. Do you think the Left has overlooked the threat of the neofascist movements we are seeing in Europe and the US?

I don't think these two issues can be easily separated. I see neofascism being a response to neoliberalism. Neoliberalism says the State doesn't have a legitimate role in governing, redistributing wealth and improving the position of the people at the bottom of the society. This causes people to turn their backs on politics because politics can't deliver any more. When someone shows up offering a form of anti-politics instead of reasoned debate, they latch on to him because he appears to be the voice of authenticity. It's the closure of effective policy that neoliberalism has engineered that clears the path for neofascism.

Can you talk about how neoliberalism alienates us from one other?

Neoliberalism tells us that society should be conceived as a market. We achieve the greatest good by leaving human relationships to be governed by the invisible hand of the market. The combination of the marketization of society with the escape from taxation and regulation by the rich has allowed the rich to effectively cede from democratic constraint. Neoliberalism creates a society where the common good retreats and is almost conceived to be an alien concept. It's unsurprising we've become alienated from each other, from the living world, from the civic realm, and ultimately from ourselves. So many of the crises of neoliberalism – the financial crisis, the economic crisis, the political crisis and the ecological crisis – come together in the form of psychic rupture with massive impacts on our mental health.

Will honestly confronting climate disruption in the press force people to question the feasibility of our entire political system?

To admit anything is to admit everything. As soon as you accept that there is a flaw in the traditional economic system, you accept that that flaw is going to be fatal not just to the economic program, but to everything that flaw touches. The flaw of climate breakdown alone shows the system cannot be sustained on its current trajectory. When I talk about the system, I'm not only talking about neoliberal economics and neoliberal politics, I'm talking about the system of economic growth. There is a Left-Right consensus that economic growth is good. Keynesian economists and neoliberals both want perpetual economic growth. This would be fine if the planet was also growing, but the planet isn't growing. So, as a result, we are already bursting through planetary boundaries. People have talked for years about the impending environmental crisis, but the environmental crisis is already here. One planetary boundary after another is being breached. You can't continue on this growth trajectory: we have already breached environmental limits with 2017 levels of growth. And we want to double that rate of economic growth by 2041: you just can't do it.

What is an economic alternative to Keynesian economics or neoliberalism?

My favorite approach is Kate Raworth's 'Doughnut Economics', where she reframes economics with new diagrams to set a new economic goal. Presently, a proxy goal of economic growth has been the only goal that everyone aims for. But perpetual economic growth is a goal that will lead to catastrophic consequences. Raworth says our goal should be human wellbeing within environmental limits. When she draws how this would work, it takes the shape of an American doughnut. The inner ring is the level of sufficiency below which we should not fall: we should have our basic needs meet. The outer ring represents our planetary boundaries that we should not breach. The safe and just place where we should be is between those two rings in the doughnut. Just that act of reframing economics in a new light is crucial.

Now we must ask ourselves what shifts we have to make to occupy the safe place between the inner and outer ring of the doughnut. One of the most important shifts we have to make is a shift back towards the commons. Most people don't even know what the commons are because they have been so neglected in economic and political discourse. The commons are a resource controlled by a community, and rules and negotiations are developed by that community to control it. This resource can't be sold or given away. The commons isn't connected to the State or the market, communism or state capitalism: it's something completely different. The commons aren't reliant on economic growth. The idea is the commons (resource) contributes to a steady level of wellbeing for the community that manages it. Because it can't be sold or exchanged for cash or other forms of capital, people have a vested interest in sustaining it to allow for a steady stream of wellbeing rather than one lump of cash followed by destitution, which is the current capitalist model.

It's very interesting that when we have political or economic debates they are all around one axis, with the State at one end and the market on the other. If you are on the Left, you want more State and less market, but if you are on the Right, you want more market and less State. But there are actually four sectors: the State, market, household and the commons. Because we have neglected those last two, we find ourselves having a profoundly distorted debate, which ensures that much of the opportunity to make a just economic transition is denied to us.

Do you worry that, when faced with an issue as serious as climate change, the Left might forget about other important environmental issues like soil loss, overfishing, species extinction and deforestation?

One of the alarming revelations I've had is that climate breakdown is only the third most urgent of our environmental crises. That is not meant in any way to downplay the urgency of addressing climate breakdown – it makes the issue even more urgent – it's just to recognize the two issues that are even more important, which are the ecological cleansing by land and sea of food production. Civilization can rebound from a famine, war or plague, but if you lose the soil, it's curtains. There is no way to come back from that. Even if the soil regenerates in a thousand years' time, we can't start from scratch any more because we have already exhausted the most accessible minerals and sources of fuel. In addition, fish catches are declining by one per cent a year. The catches are down despite bigger fishing boats with bigger engines and bigger nets. This is a sign of the whole system collapsing. ■

MARYAM NAMAZIE

 Maryam Namazie is an Iranian-born writer and activist. She is a spokesperson for Fitnah – Movement for Women's Liberation, One Law for All and the Council of Ex-Muslims of Britain. She hosts a weekly television program in Persian and English called *Bread and Roses*.

Is there a frustration that the needs of progressives, secularists and liberal dissidents within Iran are not being discussed enough by Western progressives?

I think the problem is that many Western progressives have turned their backs on progressives and dissenters from countries like Iran or other countries in the Middle East and North Africa, as well as Muslim communities within Western nations themselves. I think a lot of this goes back to this whole idea of multiculturalism as a social policy. There is this idea that has its origins in identity politics that solidarity has to be given to this imaginary homogeneous community rather than with progressive movements. When there is solidarity from these Western progressives, it is with the Iranian regime because it is seen to be an anti-imperialist regime, even though it's suppressing the progressive and working-class movements in the country itself. Western progressives seeing Islamists rather than dissenters as allies is hugely problematic. We witness people in the West who see themselves as progressives siding with Islamists and Islamist movements rather than with ex-Muslims, or progressive Muslims or freethinkers from that background.

Do you worry that Far Right European movements and Islamists are both using the recent migrant flows into Europe to promote a homogenized version of Islam?

The only difference between migrants and citizens is a piece of paper. Amongst migrants, just like amongst citizens, there are different points of view: there are heroes and reactionaries, and there are women's rights defenders and misogynists. It's important to look at migrants as individuals. Even if there are a few migrants who have committed crimes, it is unfair to place collective blame on a large number of people, most of whom haven't committed a crime and are trying to escape an intolerable situation. It's important to distinguish the actions of individuals in what's considered a group, and the right to political asylum, welfare, healthcare and human rights.

Can today's multiculturalism be replaced by a form of multiculturalism that recognizes universal values and gender equality?

I think multiculturalism as a lived experience is a powerful thing. I think a lot of people when they use the term multiculturalism are talking about this lived experience. They live in societies with lots of different people from different backgrounds living alongside one other. These are all positive things and I think all societies are better because of the contributions of newcomers as well as people who have been there since birth.

The problem occurs when multiculturalism becomes social policy. There is more emphasis on differences then similarities. This leads to communities living separate but unequal lives. For example, in Britain we have faith-based schools and faith-based services, as if we can't go see a doctor who doesn't have the same beliefs as we do. We also have faith-based courts such as Jewish courts or sharia courts where there is discrimination against women. You have citizens in this country who don't have the same access to the same rights, services and education as the rest of the country. You have children of Muslim parents who are going to Islamic schools where they are taught that they need to be veiled, they can't listen to music, they can't take pictures of themselves and they can't mix with boys. This is happening to children from a very young age. These are not prescriptions for a multicultural, plural society as people envision it to be, but a society that is completely segregated, separated and unequal.

Do you think one of the biggest problems with multiculturalism is that cultural preservation is being placed above cultural and religious choice?

It does restrict the space when it's said that there is only one authentic culture and one authentic religion that people must adhere to. And it's those in power that determine what the limits of that culture and religion are. This limits the space for people to live and think as they choose. It can be very repressive and suffocating. It doesn't look at the fact that religion itself is a lived experience for many people. They pick and choose what to believe. They take aspects of religion they like and ignore aspects that they don't like. They don't necessarily follow religions to the letter. Most people are born into a religion because of an accident of birth. They are brought up as Muslims, as I was, because of where they were born but Islam can be very much in the background and not play much of a part in their daily lives.

This idea of homogenized religions also erases the dissenters and the freethinkers. We're disappeared from the public space. We can't be seen any more. We can't be heard. When we try to speak, we're called Islamophobes and inciters of hatred and discrimination. Those are things I've been accused of, merely for saying 'I also exist, and I also have a voice; I don't believe in Islam and I want to be able to criticize it'. Why is the offense to the religious more important than the offense to me? Why can't I also speak up about things I find offensive, while simultaneously defending the right of other people to express themselves? ∎

PRAGNA PATEL

Pragna Patel is a founding member and director of Southall Black Sisters, a London-based women's rights group that helps women escaping all forms of gender-based violence, including domestic violence, rape and forced marriage. She was one of the founders of Women Against Fundamentalism and was named one of the 100 most influential women in the world by *The Guardian*.

What are the goals of Southall Black Sisters?

We have always sought to find another way of dealing with various forms of oppression without creating hierarchies of struggle – without prioritizing one as more important than the other and without compromising key equality and human rights principles for all. For example, as black women, we have always challenged racism in societies, but we have also challenged gender inequality and other inequalities within our own communities. A lot of people on the Left who have been very progressive on the issue of race have always – sometimes crudely and sometimes in a more sophisticated way – argued that gender equality takes second place to racial inequality. We always stood up to that and said 'No', because to be silent against some forms of oppression in order to talk about other forms of oppression is to be complicit in those other forms of oppression.

How do you disentangle Islamism from anti-Muslim bigotry?

Islamism is a fundamentalist religious movement that manipulates religion for political gain. It is a Far Right political movement. Anti-Muslim bigotry, on the other hand, exists as a form of racism. We oppose anti-Muslim racism on the one hand, but at the same time we also oppose the resurgence of religious fundamentalism within our communities, like the manifestation of political Islam (or fundamentalism) because of its profound human rights ramifications for women and other minorities within those so-called religious communities. We can't afford not to talk about those ramifications out of a fear that we would be fueling stereotypes of Muslims as barbaric and backward. That is a charge that is laid on us now even by some progressive leftist elements.

I think the term Islamophobia has done two things. First, it shuts down debate and space for dissent in our communities and in the wider society because anyone who wants to question religion is immediately accused of Islamophobia. Political Islam accuses people of Islamophobia if they question anything, including the role of women and discrimination against women. It's very problematic because it's used to police and suppress dissent, and this ultimately leads to the legitimization of so-called blasphemy laws. At this point, any kind of challenge to political Islam is regarded as offensive and is denounced as blasphemy. And who gets to decide what constitutes blasphemy? The Religious Right?

Second, Islamophobia allows the Religious Right to define what constitutes Muslim identity and allows political Islam to use Islamophobia to demand ever-increasing laws to police dissent and to deal with the so-called threat of blasphemy. It allows for a politics of the 'right to be offended' to develop within all religions even though no such right exists. This helps to stifle and silence dissent and shrinks secular spaces. It prevents political expressions of solidarity and empathy against racism from forming from within and outside many minority communities.

I prefer to use the term anti-Muslim racism when referring to genuine hostility, racism and hatred aimed at Muslims. I think anti-Muslim racism is widespread and is increasing. It's leading to multiple injustices ranging from the way the State has institutionalized it through draconian anti-terrorist laws to the kind of daily lived reality of Muslims who fear attacks and who are threatened and humiliated by anti-Muslim racists. I prefer the term anti-Muslim racism to Islamophobia because it allows space for the recognition of the reality of anti-Muslim racism, but only as one of many forms of racism. This is important because ultimately you need solidarity with all other groups facing other types of racism to successfully challenge all forms of racism and bigotry.

Has multiculturalism mutated into something that could be better described as multifaithism?

Absolutely. I argue that, following 9/11 and following the resurgence of religious fundamentalism in all religions, what we've seen is a shift in state policy: a rejection of multiculturalism, and instead an embrace of multifaithism. It's an interesting shift because, on the one hand it's come because of this backlash against multiculturalism, but at the same time, paradoxically, the State is actually accommodating the growth of religious identities and the framing of minority communities solely along the lines of religious identities. We're seeing a consolidation of communities whose identities are being framed entirely from religious perspectives. So whereas previously, in the era of multiculturalism, you consulted community leaders who may or may not have come from religious backgrounds, now the State feels the need to only consult with religious leaders based on the assumption that they represent the interests of everybody in minority communities. These communities are now being viewed purely through the prism of religion. These are communities that used to be characterized according to ethnicity and race but are now being characterized only by their religion. So, we are no longer black communities, or even South Asian communities, we're now Hindu, Muslim and Sikh communities.

How has this heightened communalism along religious lines hurt the exercise of choice within minority communities?

I think it has massively hurt the exercise of choice and freedom. There are profoundly negative consequences for those who are most powerless within these communities – those who don't wish to be defined solely or at all by religion, who are secular or women for example. Our stance is that religion is inherently discriminatory, especially towards women. Historically, that has been particularly visible in relation to women's sexuality, reproductive rights and marriage and family. That's true with all religions. If you look at where the faultlines are in all religions they are around issues to do with women's reproductive rights, sexuality, child custody and marriage and divorce.

In addition to women, sexual minorities are more or less placed by all religions outside of their communities. With the rise of religious fundamentalism – by which I mean a deliberate political return to a pure form of religious existence that features literal interpretation of religious texts – what we are seeing is a reinforcement of discrimination against women and sexual minorities because of the promotion, encouragement, reproduction and legitimation of very strict gender roles and of very strict responsibilities and duties that go with those roles. What we're seeing is that those who wish to dissent from religion – either because they choose not to respect those aspects of their religion that don't accord with their lived realities or because they wish to reject religion altogether – are all now seen as very threatening. In all religious fundamentalist movements, it's not really those outside their communities that are perceived as the real enemy. The real enemy is deemed to be those that lie within these communities, because internal dissenters are more threatening to the value structures, hierarchies and social values of that community.

In Britain, do the more progressive Muslims, Hindus and Sikhs who support the separation of church and state and believe religion should be a private matter get as much media coverage as the religious fundamentalists?

There are internal dissenting voices and struggles going on within our communities and I'm a part of that struggle, particularly the struggles waged by women within these communities who want to challenge the Religious Right. But there are two problems. One is that the Religious Right is dominant, and it uses threats and intimidation and violence to get its way; but the other major problem is that the State feels that as long as the Religious Right is not impacting on public-order issues, it can be actually encouraged to have public space. The State encourages the Religious Right to be the interlocutors between state and community. That has made it very difficult for other dissenting voices to be heard and to be accepted as authentic and legitimate – especially if they challenge the idea of religion in the State. ∎

GITA SAHGAL

 Gita Sahgal is a writer and director who is also an activist for women's and human rights. She is executive editor of the Centre for Secular Space, which opposes all forms of religious fundamentalism, provides a platform for secular voices and defends universal rights. She was formerly head of the Gender Unit at Amnesty International. Among her documentaries are *Love Snatched*, *The Provoked Wife* and the award-winning *The War Crimes File*.

If multiculturalism is going to be used in a positive sense does it need to be redefined in a way that encourages people to choose which culture to embrace, as opposed to assuming everyone wants to stay within the culture in which they were born?

There was a good side to multiculturalism and it's still there to a point in the arts world, but much is being shut down. Thirty years ago, there were organizations built up by minority groups, including cultural organizations, women's rights organizations and police-monitoring groups. These groups also did work on racism practiced by the State as well as street-based racism. The old multiculturalism consensus was more at ease with itself. It was bad on women's rights, but it was great at putting on plays in other languages and having musicians from various cultures perform.

People like me who criticize multiculturalism as a social policy always support a very diverse cultural policy. To me, one of the biggest answers to extremism is for people to understand their cultures. I don't mean that people need to be stuck in them, or that they need to stay within that culture: they should be able to reject it if they want to. But they should understand the literature of their cultures and understand that there has been a huge intellectual questioning by people within their cultures. Today, they know nothing about that.

How would you explain the Hindu Right's rise to power in India?

The Bharatiya Janata Party won a stunning a victory in India in May 2014, but it was because the Center completely collapsed. There wasn't a good candidate for leadership. Rahul Gandhi was running for merely dynastic reasons. He wasn't impressive. The Congress Party was mad with corruption. And it made the mistake of doing what the Labour Party did in Britain; it didn't fight on the good parts of its record. The Congress Party is neoliberal in many ways, but it did introduce water welfare programs to stave off mass starvation and poverty during hard times. Those programs have done well based on university research of their effectiveness. But Congress didn't run on the good things they did.

The people wanted a change and BJP-affiliated Prime Minister Narendra Modi projected himself not so much as a Hindu nationalist, but as someone who would support development for the people in India, and that's the forum he ran on. Modi is a Far Right fascist, but this atmosphere of terror didn't come from things he immediately said. However, people started doing things and saying things and Modi and the senior ministers kept silent.

Can you talk about the opposition to the Hindu Right in India?

Great scholars are challenging the views of religion that were peddled by the Hindu Right, which has led to several scholars being killed by the Hindu Right. But there has been a huge writers' movement – and my mother Nayantara Sahgal has been one of the people most prominently involved. The writers don't have any weapons except their pens and they have given up the awards they got from the government literary academy. The literary academy has always been an organization of other writers who give out the rewards, so people are proud to receive them. During a meeting, literary academy members said they upheld the right to life and they upheld the principle of freedom of expression. They were sort of forced into that situation. And the reason they were forced into that situation was that, even though they had countervailing pressures from the government and from writers who were pro-government, there was such public anger in India about this that the literary academy couldn't lie down.

Can you talk about your critique of the way your former employer Amnesty International and other human rights organizations portray Islamists?

It's this tendency that if they have a victim they want to see that person as a pure victim. And what the feminists have said – and Marieme Helie Lucas has been the most powerful proponent of this idea – is that the victim can also be the perpetrator. When someone has been hideously treated and tortured, of course they deserve human rights and due process under the law. We have no quarrel with any of the human rights frameworks on these matters, but these same people could have committed gross violations of human rights. There has been loads of talk in Amnesty about making non-state abuses something that Amnesty should research, and they just didn't do it. It was the policy people who kept obstructing the will of the movement by saying 'No, we're just focusing mainly on states'.

Could you talk about the role your award-winning documentary played in the establishment of Bangladesh's International Crimes Tribunal [looking at war crimes during its 1971 war of independence]?

The film *The War Crimes File*, which I made in the 1990s, has been used to mobilize for a tribunal in Bangladesh. The [International Crimes] Tribunal has been very, very problematic because a lot of people think Bangladeshi Prime Minister Sheikh Hasina wanted to attack the Jamaat-e-Islami leaders. But in 1971 these guys were not the leaders; they were former students of the Jamaat who were actively engaged in death squads.

The genocide in Bangladesh that occurred in 1971 is very important because Islamists weren't the only ones that were involved. And whatever the flaws of the Tribunal – and there are many – the people that have been arrested have been the correct ones. What you never hear is that it really took a mass movement of people collecting evidence, making films, being arrested and setting up tribunals to make the Bangladeshi genocide something that will not be forgotten. The massacres that took place during the war were like what later happened in Yugoslavia and Rwanda. Everything that happened in the 20th-century wars that we know about happened before in Bangladesh. ■

INNA SHEVCHENKO

Inna Shevchenko is the leader of FEMEN, the worldwide movement of women that stages its demonstrations against patriarchy – especially dictatorship, religion and the sex industry – through topless protests. She was born in Ukraine but was forced to flee to France after she chopped down a wooden cross in Kiev to protest the prosecution of the band Pussy Riot and Russian President Vladimir Putin's close relations with the Russian Orthodox Church.

Can you explain the origins of FEMEN's protests?

We believe we changed the meaning and definition and concept of a woman's body in general, where it's not used any more for a man, but for women's interests. We decide when our bodies will be sexual, and we decide when these bodies will be political. We transformed our naked bodies into our political tool, into a poster, into our own 'Democracy Wall'. We have used this attention to address women's questions, starting in Ukraine and then becoming international. From 2008 to 2010, we tried to address women's questions in a different form. We tried to work with organizations, with the government and with deputies. We organized demonstrations of 100 to 250 girls wearing pink clothes – because we believed pink clothes could draw attention to social issues – and we were carrying huge banners with statistics and important information. We were totally ignored. We couldn't get a line in the newspaper, and we couldn't get people to stop and read our posters, even though it was a totally pink crowd of women. We were knocking on doors, but whenever these people heard it was about women's issues, the door was closed. That was it.

The only way we could address women's questions was by breaking into the international news to help foster public debates. The international media would force the national media to discuss the issues we were trying to get addressed. No-one was interested in listening to women, but everyone was interested in looking at women because of deeply rooted patriarchal culture that portrays women as sexual objects, where women's bodies are tools for male satisfaction or enrichment. Whenever you try to promote something or sell something you use a women's body and it works. We said: 'OK, we're going to use the instrument that patriarchy is using to oppress us and we're going to use it against them.' We said: 'OK, you can look at us, but you will see something completely different.' It will not be a woman with a passive body, smiling. It will be a woman in the street with a body that expresses political slogans and demands. And she will not be smiling, she will be screaming and shouting out her slogans. She will not be passive, she will be active. She will finally represent herself and her needs, not those of the men's world. We adopted this attitude of a warrior or soldier. We put something that has always been at the center of women's oppression – her body – and made it a symbol of self-liberation.

Do you worry the media will focus on your bodies alone while ignoring the messages written on your bodies?

We knew there was a risk they would focus on this, but at the same time we knew this would attract attention. We also knew that we would completely reshape the image of a naked woman in the mainstream media. You can't find a FEMEN image without a message on our bodies. You can watch our breasts as long as you want, but you can't ignore what's written on those breasts, and what those breasts are saying and screaming. A FEMEN naked body is a body that speaks and fights.

You can observe naked women everywhere. They are in the streets, they are on television, and they're on the cover of magazines. But they are all expressing one sexual meaning, so we decided to show our bodies as rebellious, strong and political. For example, FEMEN protests are not put on the cover of Ukrainian papers that feature naked women. We are not on the cover of *Playboy*; we are on the cover of the *New York Times*. If our enemies were solely focused on our naked bodies and our naked breasts, I doubt they would be arresting and torturing us like we were tortured in Belarus. If people solely focused on our naked breasts, I don't think we would receive death threats. If the media wrote about our protests only because of our naked breasts, we wouldn't be featured in the news on primetime.

Can you expound on how FEMEN grew to become an international organization?

We started in Ukraine as a little group of women volunteers without many resources at our disposal and we turned into an international movement. This happened not because we did something on purpose. It actually happened quite naturally because women all over the world started to contact us and say, 'Well, in my country they are trying to do this'. For instance, in Spain a conservative party that is connected to Catholic institutions like Opus Dei was trying to pass a bill forbidding abortion and we believed a FEMEN tactic would be useful to fight against this bill, so women in Spain started activity against the bill. The same thing happened in other countries. Women's questions are global, international questions; therefore we act at a global, international level. After moving to France in 2012 I actively worked on building FEMEN International together with women in different countries, and today the movement is present on two continents.

You have been a strong defender of freedom of speech and people's right to say the unsayable. Do you believe too many countries have been willing to either ban or discourage speech that is deemed insulting to a religion or culture?

I think the global illness of society is political correctness. We live in a time where discussions should be very open and diverse. We see discussions solely going in a politically correct direction and this is something that gives space for extremism and hate speech to develop. Whenever we talk about religion, governments only want to hear from people who belong to the specific religion being discussed. For example, they wouldn't want to hear a Christian talking about Islam, or a Muslim talking about Christianity and Judaism. Atheists or ex-believers are particularly silenced. Any time you try to address the objective mistakes of one or another religion it will be perceived as intolerance, hate speech and racism. People really believe that religion is a race. For example, whenever you criticize Islam as an ideology, a set of dogmas, and condemn it for violence and discrimination against women and minorities, you get called a racist. There is no such thing as a right to not be offended. There is a right to speak out. There is a right to freedom of speech. I think that today we are not able to enjoy freedom of speech fully because of this global demand for tolerance and political correctness, particularly towards religion. The world praised those who were killed by terrorists at *Charlie Hebdo*. They became national heroes in France, but before they were killed by terrorists my very good friends at the newspaper were described as Islamophobes and racists. When they were killed, they suddenly became the heroes of freedom of speech. This is the hypocrisy of public debates. I believe the restrictions and demands for the respect of religion and religious feelings is one of the biggest obstacles to freedom of speech today. And if we were honest and brave enough to hear opinions we don't agree with, the cartoonists from *Charlie Hebdo*, as well as many others, would still be alive. Our duty is not only to accept people with different opinions, but also to support them. If the marginalized voices sound louder, if public debates are more open and diverse, we will never hear the shots of Kalashnikovs again.

Do you ever worry about generalizing about religions, since every major religion is interpreted by people in a variety of ways that range from progressive to rigid and patriarchal?

One of the mistakes that can be made by those who criticize religious institutions is to be too dogmatic and to generalize. We are careful to try to avoid this, but the mainstream media doesn't understand this. We should be able to intellectually understand the difference between criticizing, mocking or disagreeing with ideas and the people who adhere to them. If you criticize a religious institution, the media will often generalize it and immediately identify you as a racist or an offender, even if you objectively criticize one aspect of a religion for promoting violence and abuses against human rights, including women's rights.

We don't organize protests against Muslims, Jews or Christians. There are many spiritual as well as some confessional people among us too. Many believers are our closest allies. There are a thousand and one ways of being Muslim, Jewish or Christian, and many of the believers work hard to reform their religious institutions and reinterpret the dogma through a humanist and feminist vision. We criticize religious ideas that deny dignity and freedom. What we are screaming about is the bad sides of religious institutions that should be criticized and addressed if we want to move forward as a society. ■

LINO VELJAK

 Lino Veljak is a philosophy professor based in Zagreb, Croatia. He was a founder of the Association for Democratic Alternatives in Yugoslavia. Among his books are: *Marxism and Theory of Reflection, Authoritarianism and Democracy* and *From Ontology to Philosophy of History*.

Do you think most Croatians have confronted and accepted the past crimes committed by former President Tuđjman's regime in their name?

Unfortunately, my answer must be a negative. The confrontation with the black sides of recent history were insufficient, and the result often is that most of the population believes the war crimes committed by the Croatian side were only incidents, and not the results of a systematic policy. The rightwing minority of the population even believes that the crimes against the 'historical enemies (including the civilian population, women, children) must be justified because, in the righteous war, crimes cannot be committed'.

Was a big factor in these wars how organizations and politicians like Milošević portrayed the Serbs as Yugoslavia's great victim, while dehumanizing non-Serbs as the entitled others?

That was an important part of the strategy of ethnical homogenization: the Serbs (but at the same time – in Croatia – the Croats, and other ethnicities) were systematically presented as innocent victims and the Others as enemies, wild beasts or non-human beings.

Many leftists have criticized post-communist countries for

privatizing their economies before the proper democratic structures had been created to prevent widespread corruption and looting of formerly public assets. Was Croatia able to avoid this kind of corruption after the Yugoslav wars?

The privatization in Croatia came during the Yugoslav wars under Tuðjman's regime. Because of this, the corruption was a structural part of the process of the transformation of public property to private property. The people close to Tuðjman's party had the opportunities to become owners of formerly social resources (factories, companies etc). In this sense Tuðjman's legacy is visible in contemporary corruption in Croatia. For example, the destruction of most important Croatian company Agrokor – connected with widespread corruption – can be explained through the fact that the owner of this company, Ivica Todorić, obtained the social resources on which he grew this company because of his support for Tuðjman's party.

Many countries are experiencing a wave of religious or nationalist fundamentalism. What would your advice be to leftists trying to counter the messages being promoted by the purveyors of these ideologies?

Only through the development and progression of critical spirit and a democratic political and social culture is it possible to immunize the individuals and communities against all types of fundamentalism. It's necessary to capacitate the people for differentiation between truth, probability and lie; between reason and unreasonableness! ■

ED VULLIAMY

 Ed Vulliamy is a veteran reporter for the British newspapers *The Guardian* and *The Observer*. He is best known for his work exposing the horrors of the concentration camps run by the Bosnian Serbs. In 1996, he became the first journalist to testify in war-crimes trials at The Hague; in the same year he was named International Reporter of the Year. Among his books are *Seasons in Hell: Understanding Bosnia's war* and *Amexico: War along the borderline*.

What are your thoughts on American exceptionalism?

We in Britain grew up on American culture. There was something exceptional about America. When it came to my work in America, the political side of American exceptionalism became something completely different. It was kind of the flipside of culture that gave us Jefferson Airplane, the blues, Steppenwolf – and Bob Dylan, for Christ's sake: the most exceptional poet of my youth. I'm not an anti-American European. I'm a European who grew up on BB King, Bob Dylan and Jefferson Airplane. However, I was in Golden Square demonstrating against the war in Vietnam and I was in the Chile Solidarity campaign after the CIA coup of 1973. It was when I came to live and work professionally in America that I started to understand American exceptionalism from the inside. It's this extraordinary mixture of hubris, aggression, greed and stupidity.

Iraq was the hallmark of my American sojourn, which was from 1994 to 2003. I was there for 9/11, living 20 blocks north of where the Twin Towers fell. I was there for the exceptional response of the city of New York to that attack: the carpets of flowers, the tributes, the gifts, the peace flags, the peace signs all over Union Square and Washington Square. And I saw how that very dignified response was morphed and manipulated into something very different. It was the politics of vengeance that hallmarked all the things I knew indirectly: the dirty wars in Latin America, the backing of coups in Guatemala and Chile. Now I was faced with this professional nightmare of covering the surge to war after 11 September 2001.

There are people a lot more qualified than me to talk about the consequences of American exceptionalism across Central and Latin America and the Middle East. In Central America, it's grotesque and stupid. The empire of the Eagle has been toppled and thrown out of Latin America and it's been thrown out of the Middle East, except for the stockade of Israel. It's disgraced. American exceptionalism now is the primacy of corporations that behave the same way as the British, French or other corporations in ravaging economies, natural resources and the environment to feed what Steppenwolf once called the monster decades ago.

Can you talk about your coverage of the Iraq War?

I'd been in Iraq in 1991 and I was under no illusions about Saddam Hussein. I saw the ravages of Saddam's counter-attack on the Shi'a uprising, which could have taken Baghdad if George HW Bush had wanted to do it. But he wanted the Baath Party to stay in power in Iraq with Saddam expelled to Kuwait. So I knew a lot about Iraq.

One problem with [American] exceptionalism, [is that] there is this crass stupidity. For example, if you asked most Americans if Saddam Hussein was a fundamentalist they would probably say yes, despite the informed excellence of the best of the US media. And if you asked a lot of officials and journalists if Saddam Hussein was a fundamentalist, they would probably say yes. But he wasn't a fundamentalist, he was a terrifying Stalinist tyrant. But, in the order of things, ghastly as he was, which is worse, that or this? That is the hubris of American exceptionalism.

I remember going horse racing in Saddam Hussein's hometown in Tikrit and it was a wonderful day. It was just cigarettes and fun and I'm half-Irish and if there are people who know horses as well as the Irish it's the Arabs. I don't think people who make policy in America think of Iraq as a country where people went horse racing in Saddam Hussein's hometown and drank beer and smoked cigarettes.

Could you discuss the culture of voyeuristic violence embraced by both Islamic State and the Mexican drug cartels, and how it differs from past perpetrators of genocide and mass atrocities?

I think what we've got in Islamic State is an armed cult that resembles more a narco cartel than a political movement. Yes, they have ideological window dressing for what they do while the Zetas are all about money and the accoutrements that go with being a successful narco. I make no apology for these revolting people; I abhor and would never seek to justify what they think and do. But I do think this is something new and something interesting. I think it comes from the same ghastliness that has always been there in humanity, but also something postmodern, post-political and post-moral about our world: a new way in which a turbo-capitalist, digitalized world alienates people. I think turbo-capitalism alienates the poor woman or man (differently) to the point at which becoming a fundamentalist becomes an attractive prospect. I think we live in a world where reality and fantasy have become completely confused because of the product of digitalization and the internet. There is a sliding scale from gratification to extreme violence on the internet and there is a sliding scale between gratification and extreme violence in the world.

When I grew up, the idea of war photography was that you showed the other side's atrocities. If you were against the war in Vietnam, there was a purpose to that picture of the running girl, bombed by napalm. If you were against the coup in Chile, there was a reason for those pictures from inside the stadium in Santiago. But what ISIS does and what the narcos do is they show their own atrocities. They say: 'Look, we can cut people's heads off; look we can chop up women and it's good fun,' and people respond. Violence becomes not something you can point out in horror, but something that you can put out to increase recruits. It's an appeal to the internet culture. It's the difference between masturbation and real sex. You don't have to just sit there and play war games on your computer – you can do it for real.

Did you see this kind of phenomenon while covering the concentration camps during the Bosnian genocide?

I got a very good look at this phenomenon of people taking pleasure in committing brutal attacks of violence by covering the Bosnian concentration camps. The orgies of violence were recreational. They were connected to alcohol and partying. They were having a good time. If you were working at the Birkenau extermination camp during World War Two there was a lot of work to do. You had to get them off the trains, down the platforms and into the gas chambers. I'm sure there was recreational violence in Auschwitz, but it was quite hard work and you had to get it right. This is different, this is fun and that's why it's frightening, and we don't seem to be talking about this much or talking about how it's all connected to everyday life on the internet in pseudo-porn, misogynistic-porn and violent porn and other forms of violence.

These separations between legal and illegal, between cyber and real, between everyday life and shocking stories on the news are fake boundaries. When we see these poor migrants and refugees from Syria and Africa coming to Europe, this is our world. We created this. When you look on the television and see decapitated bodies in Mexico hanging from the bridges, there is a direct connection between this and your life: your society takes the drugs, your banks welcome and clean the profits – they admit it and are not prosecuted; they are part of this violence, with impunity. The atrocities you see out there are all part of your life, your bank, your participation in the new turbo-capitalism. I call it the lie of legality. The idea that there is some line between licit and illicit is a lie, just as the idea of a line between what is real and unreal becomes blurred, by digitalization and 'virtual reality'.

To be honest, I am not 'progressive' any more, because I don't believe in progress (not least because of what we are doing to nature and the environment). I think we are in an abyss. I know every generation thinks it is witnessing the end of something. but mine may just be on to something. ■

IAN WILLIAMS

Ian Williams is the United Nations correspondent for *Tribune* and a senior analyst for *Foreign Policy in Focus*. He has written for an abundance of newspapers and magazines around the world including *The Australian*, *The Guardian* and *The Village Voice*. He was born in Liverpool, England, but currently lives in New York. Among his books are *UNtold: The real story of the UN in peace and war* and *Political and Cultural Perceptions of George Orwell*.

How should the US government have responded to the terrorist attacks of 11 September 2001?

There was no excuse for attacking Iraq. The attack on Iraq was a completely gratuitous abuse of the political circumstances. As for Afghanistan, it gave the world a wonderful chance to pull together. There should have been a modern national force in Afghanistan. But what the United States did was basically restart their old war. They got the warlords to fight back against the Taliban. One of the things that has made the Taliban attractive to a lot of Afghans is the warlords.

What are your thoughts on American exceptionalism?

In some ways I find it inexplicable, but it's not unique here. Surveys in Britain have found an increasing inability to relate to who we are at war with. It's not as bad as in America, but it's not exactly reassuring. One of the things I noticed when I came here is that there doesn't seem to be any sort of historical oral tradition. When I was a kid growing up in Liverpool, even though I was born after World War Two the grandparents, parents and older siblings told stories about the war. We didn't learn about World War Two and Adolf Hitler from textbooks, although we did get extra details. We got it by almost a process of social osmosis: it was around us, people spoke about it, adults spoke about it. That form of oral tradition is almost gone with the television, I suspect. People don't sit around the house and talk about things anymore and, if they do it, they do it with separate cohorts. The kids will go off and talk about it in one place, while the adults will go off and talk somewhere else. I think that historical background that you get through society as a whole is crucial. If a subject is not taught in school, it doesn't get through at all in the absence of that oral tradition.

Can you talk about the role American exceptionalism has played fostering the lack of knowledge most of the public has about the darker aspects of US foreign policy?

It goes right back to Plymouth Rock. They believed they were building a city upon a hill and the Founding Fathers were essentially descendants of Puritans who came over here to build a whole new society that they thought was purer and better than everywhere else. The fact that they were coming and raping and looting and stealing someone else's land led them to demonize them [Native Americans]. So here you are, you're in a foreign country, you're demonizing the only other people with whom you have had contact and all that has been reinforced over the years. During the time of 9/11 I was amazed at how little concept there was that this was payback. The US had armed and supported the Taliban and rebels against the Soviets who were now doing this to us. It doesn't justify it, but it is a considerable factor to be taken into account.

Are you disturbed by the 'all soldiers are heroes' narrative that is often championed by the mainstream and rightwing media?

The iconic story about this that you might want to look up and use as a text involves Warrant Officer Hugh Thompson. He landed the plane on My Lai [an infamous massacre of Vietnamese civilians by US troops] and threatened to shoot US soldiers for raping and killing in the village. He didn't get a medal and recognition for his efforts until the Clinton administration was in the White House. And this guy was a true hero in the context of American exceptionalism. He landed a plane and threatened to shoot his own troops for violating all the laws of war and humanity. That's no small deal.

How has the assumption that America is always morally in the right limited the spectrum of debate within the country?

If you accept as your basic national premise that the US is almost invariably right, then it's very hard to break out of it. It's very hard to have any rational discussions at all about recent foreign policy because it's always conducted on the bedrock assumption that the US is right. The Vietnam War, for example, was highly controversial at the time; people were elected who opposed it. Yet somehow, by a process of historical momentum, John Kerry was attacked for telling the truth about it. The popular steamroller of historical consciousness is that the people who opposed the Vietnam War were traitors. No apologies are due to the Vietnamese who died.

What are some American interventions that you thought were justified?

I was totally in favor of US troops going to Macedonia. That was one of the most effective and timely interventions in UN history. The US sent peacekeeping troops on the border between Macedonia and Serbia and Milošević didn't dare move. If the US had done the same in Bosnia there wouldn't have been the Balkan wars. In Rwanda, if the United States had sent in troops in the beginning, the massacre probably wouldn't have happened. Bombing Serbian gun sites in Bosnia was perfectly acceptable. I was elated, it should have been done much sooner. In Bosnia, it was the British and French who cleaned it up in the end because Clinton was so mesmerized by the isolationists in the Republican Party that he didn't dare actually commit US ground forces. He actually ruled out an invasion, which was the only thing Milošević feared. The British and NATO decided to go ahead anyway. The US didn't intervene because of isolationism from the Republicans.

I was against the bombing in Kosovo because it was costly and ineffective. Clinton wanted to intervene, but he couldn't commit US ground troops because he couldn't have risked US casualties because Republicans would have made an issue with him. He insisted on bombing and, to ensure no US pilots would be shot down, he insisted they couldn't fly lower than 15,000 feet. So here you are in this cloudy, mountainous region dropping bombs from 15,000 feet. That was just multiplying the possible effects of collateral damage. It destroyed the moral and popular vindication for the campaign. Clinton had the right instincts, but his own inherited political caution led him to disagree with himself effectively. ■

STASA ZAJOVIC

 Stasa Zajovic is the co-founder of the Serbian branch of Women in Black, which is a worldwide network of women committed to peace with justice and actively opposed to injustice, war, militarism and other forms of violence. She has participated in or founded many activist campaigns or coalitions, including the Women's Peace Network, the International Network of Women's Solidarity, and the Network of Conscientious Objectors and Anti-Militarism in Serbia.

Have new cultures of moral integrity blossomed in Serbia that will help prevent militarism, patriarchy, nationalism, ethnocentrism and future wars?

Yes, but this new culture which we promote is unfortunately the culture of the minority. The majority live under the prejudices of militarism, patriarchy, nationalism and ethnocentrism. Fortunately, only a small number of rightwing radicals want to participate in future wars.

You have discussed the need for Serbian citizens to confront their government's past crimes to create a better future. How much of the Serbian population has come to terms with the crimes committed in their name in places like Srebrenica, Omarska, Sarajevo and elsewhere?

Thanks to the mainstream media, our population doesn't want to recognize the crimes committed in our name in different Balkan countries (Bosnia Herzegovina, Croatia, Kosovo) and in Serbia (against non-Serbian citizens). Without substantial changes in the general social, political and cultural climate the people cannot come to terms with these crimes against humanity. But a better future is impossible without critical confrontation with the past.

How difficult was it for Women in Black to protest militarism during the Balkan wars, given the tendency of people to rally around the flag during wartime?

It was very hard. But after 1999, most of the population didn't want to participate in these wars; or to serve militaristic warlords like Slobodan Milošević. This change had its prehistory in our resistance to war. Between 1991 and 1999, there were more than 300,000 people, mostly young men, who left their country to avoid regular military service or mobilization of reservists. And from October 1991 to the spring of 1992 there were around 50 protests of reservists in Serbia with 55,000 participants. They refused to participate in war crimes and killings. ('We refuse to kill our people, friends and brothers who live in other republics of ex-Yugoslavia or belong to other ethnicities or religions.') Women in Black supported all these initiatives, and especially gave help to the deserters.

How would you define patriarchy, and what role does it play in stoking unnecessary wars?

Patriarchy is a system grounded in the idea and personalized as father of the family, or father of the tribe, or father of the nation, and it is the basic model for all historically created types of injustice. This occurs not only in the sense of oppression against women, or oppression against exploited social classes or in the sense of different types of despotism and tyranny, but also in the sense of militarism. Militarism produces the wars, and it is based on the patriarchal mentality.

Do you think cross-country solidarity between groups can help counter the nationalistic feelings that often lead to war?

Cross-country solidarity between anti-war groups could help counter nationalistic feelings, and such solidarity could create new spaces for reconciliation and peacebuilding based on the feminist conception of justice. It is necessary that similar groups in different countries create networks of solidarity and common activity oriented to real peace and real justice.

Can you explain how feminist justice can help make a society come to terms with its past crimes and seek forgiveness for the victims of those crimes?

The feminist approach to justice – especially in the context of post-war societies in former Yugoslavia – does not negate the existing models of transitional justice and constitutional mechanisms of justice, but rather tends to reflect on them while including the gender dimension in the theory and practice of justice and creating new models of justice. This approach is an act of feminist responsibility motivated by insights into the invisibility of women's contributions to the processes of transitional justice (women are marginalized and reduced to objects of violence). The feminist approach represents the act of righting an injustice inflicted on a very considerable number of women who have participated in nonviolent resistance to war, and this is a basis for the processes of trust and reconciliation and peacebuilding in our region and in the world as whole. The victims as witnesses demand criminal sanctions for war criminals, but they also advocate for non-criminal sanctions: restorative justice. This confirms the significance of the joint peace work of victims and other peacemakers, including the front line of the feminist peacemakers. ∎

AFTERWORD
by Andy Heintz

It is all too easy to feel overwhelmed by the range and scale of the world's problems. The election of leaders from the Far Right in many countries is frightening, as is the increasing popularity of extreme rightwing parties that used to be considered on the fringe of society. There are the sadistic, soulless and Realpolitik-driven tragedies in Syria and Yemen, the senseless, heartbreaking state-sanctioned genocide of the Rohingya people in Myanmar, and the civilization-threatening nature of climate change and all the other environmental crises that the international community has yet to seriously confront. The world also faces an immense global refugee crisis that has invoked heartless, barbaric and cruel responses by many governments in wealthier countries, including putting up walls, borders and fences to keep out those fleeing the threat of torture and death in their native countries.

But there are also solidarity movements treating refugees as equal partners and fellow citizens. There are movements opposing both the parties of the Far Right and religious extremism. There are reformers challenging cultural traditions that have been used to justify patriarchy and relegated women to second-class citizens. There are inspiring groups, especially in Latin America, directly opposing neoliberalism and extractivist-based development in favor of more sustainable models that are environmentally friendly, progressive and protect the rights of indigenous people. These international examples are worthy of the support of everybody who considers herself or himself as on the Left – and this book has tried to highlight inspiring activists and thinkers from every continent who form part of this broad and multifaceted resistance movement.

Globalization has failed to meet the basic needs of millions of citizens not because trade between nations is a bad thing, but because globalization has been too influenced by corporations and their lobbyists with very little democratic input from the people negatively affected. This doesn't mean globalization hasn't helped many people escape poverty – there is much evidence to show that it is has helped people working in certain occupations – but it has also left many others feeling disoriented, helpless and without a proper safety net to adjust to job losses that result from technological innovations, automation and unfair trade policies. A more democratic form of globalization where all citizens feel like they have a voice is sorely needed. In addition, any trade agreements or global trade rules must never deprive people of basic healthcare, affordable medicine, freedom to grow their own food, freedom to protect local communities from environmental pollution, respect for the rights of indigenous populations, and basic access to shelter, affordable food and clean water.

While the problems of the world can make one feel overwhelmed, now is not the time to submit to the temptations of apathy, cynicism or empathy fatigue. We must remember that we are not just fighting for a better world and a cleaner planet for ourselves, but also for future generations. As Thomas Paine said, 'I prefer peace. But if trouble must come, let it come in time, so that my children can live in peace.'

Let us create a world where all human beings see each other as equal partners who share certain moral obligations to each other. Let us aspire in principle to Paine's famous quotation (minus the male-centered language): 'The world is my country, all mankind are my brethren, and to do good is my religion.'

The task in front of us is not an easy one, and the problems we face are complex and can't be solved by short-term solutions, but we must confront them because to remain indifferent could have catastrophic consequences for us all. Let us get to work.

INDEX